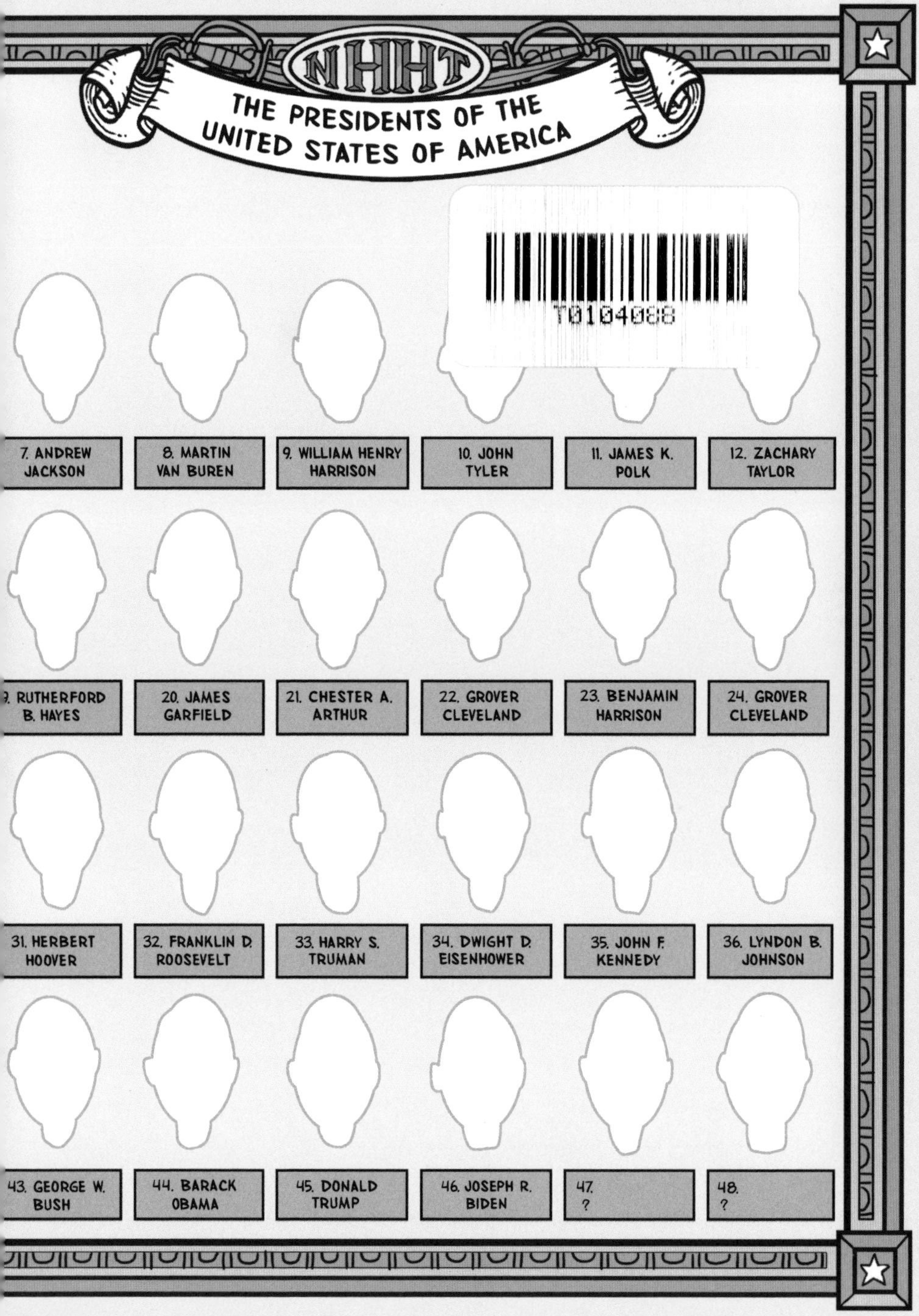
NHHT
THE PRESIDENTS OF THE UNITED STATES OF AMERICA
7. ANDREW JACKSON
8. MARTIN VAN BUREN
9. WILLIAM HENRY HARRISON
10. JOHN TYLER
11. JAMES K. POLK
12. ZACHARY TAYLOR
. RUTHERFORD B. HAYES
20. JAMES GARFIELD
21. CHESTER A. ARTHUR
22. GROVER CLEVELAND
23. BENJAMIN HARRISON
24. GROVER CLEVELAND
31. HERBERT HOOVER
32. FRANKLIN D. ROOSEVELT
33. HARRY S. TRUMAN
34. DWIGHT D. EISENHOWER
35. JOHN F. KENNEDY
36. LYNDON B. JOHNSON
43. GEORGE W. BUSH
44. BARACK OBAMA
45. DONALD TRUMP
46. JOSEPH R. BIDEN
47. ?
48. ?

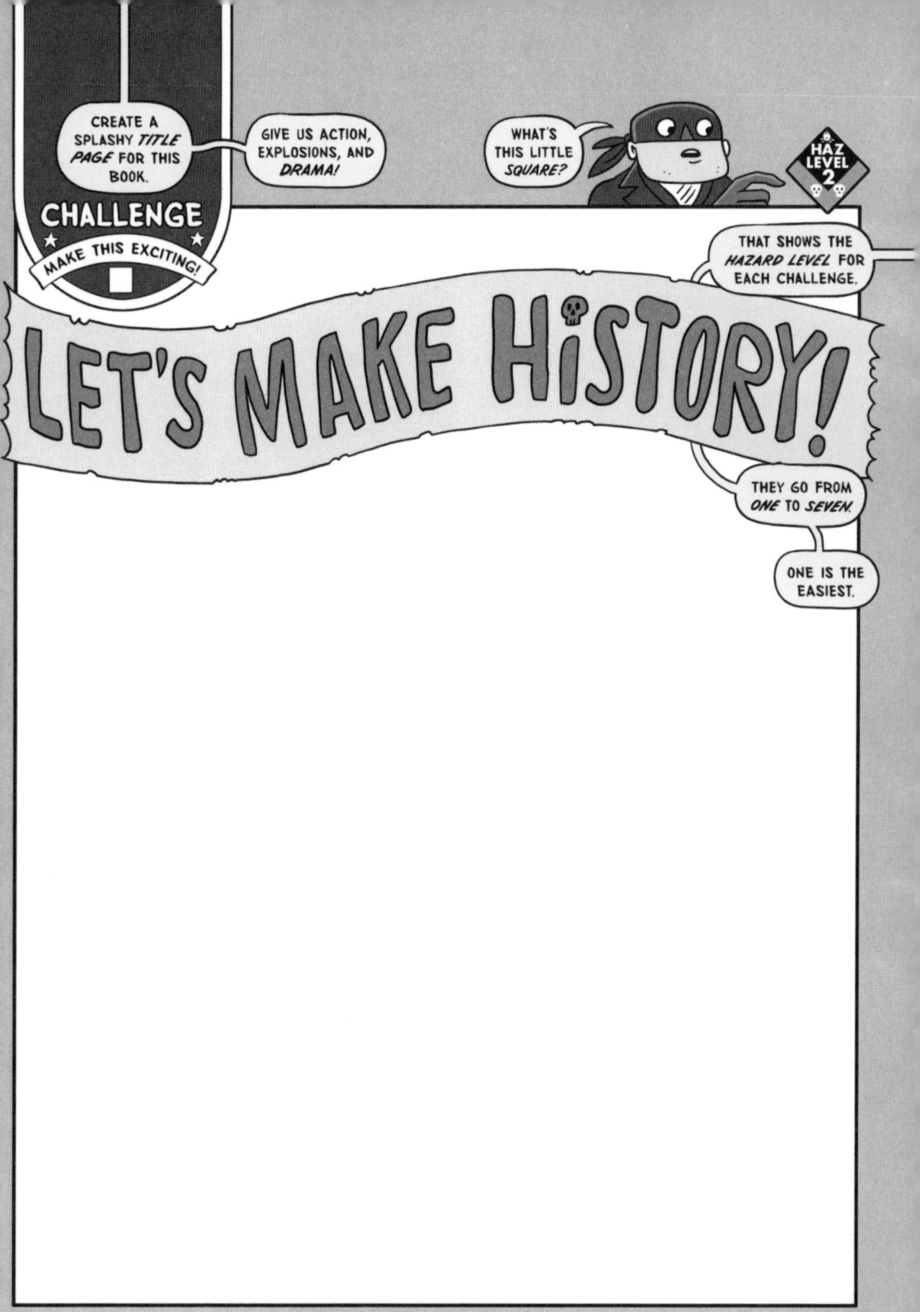
CREATE A SPLASHY *TITLE PAGE* FOR THIS BOOK.
CHALLENGE
MAKE THIS EXCITING!
GIVE US ACTION, EXPLOSIONS, AND *DRAMA!*
WHAT'S THIS LITTLE *SQUARE?*
HAZ LEVEL 2
THAT SHOWS THE *HAZARD LEVEL* FOR EACH CHALLENGE.
LET'S MAKE HISTORY!
THEY GO FROM *ONE* TO *SEVEN.*
ONE IS THE EASIEST.

AMULET BOOKS, NEW YORK

LIBRARY OF CONGRESS CONTROL NUMBER 2022932921

ISBN 978-1-4197-6552-0

TEXT AND ILLUSTRATIONS COPYRIGHT © 2022 NATHAN HALE
BOOK DESIGN BY NATHAN HALE

PRINTED AND BOUND IN CHINA
10 9 8 7 6 5 4 3 2 1

AMULET BOOKS ARE AVAILABLE AT SPECIAL DISCOUNTS WHEN PURCHASED
IN QUANTITY FOR PREMIUMS AND PROMOTIONS AS WELL AS FUNDRAISING
OR EDUCATIONAL USE. SPECIAL EDITIONS CAN ALSO BE CREATED TO
SPECIFICATION. FOR DETAILS, CONTACT SPECIALSALES@ABRAMSBOOKS.COM
OR THE ADDRESS BELOW.

AMULET BOOKS® IS A REGISTERED TRADEMARK OF HARRY N. ABRAMS, INC.

ABRAMS The Art of Books
195 Broadway, New York, NY 10007
abramsbooks.com

FOR CHAD,

WHO GOT ME INTO
THIS MESS

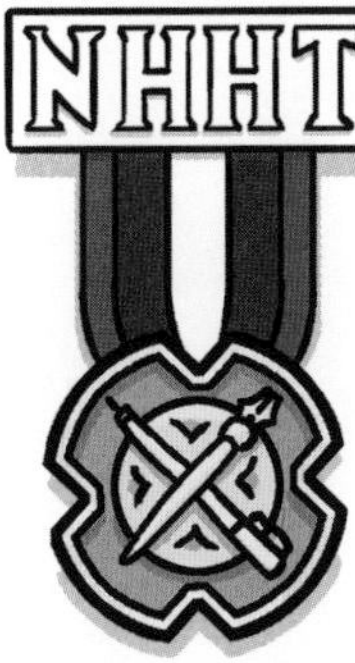
NHHT

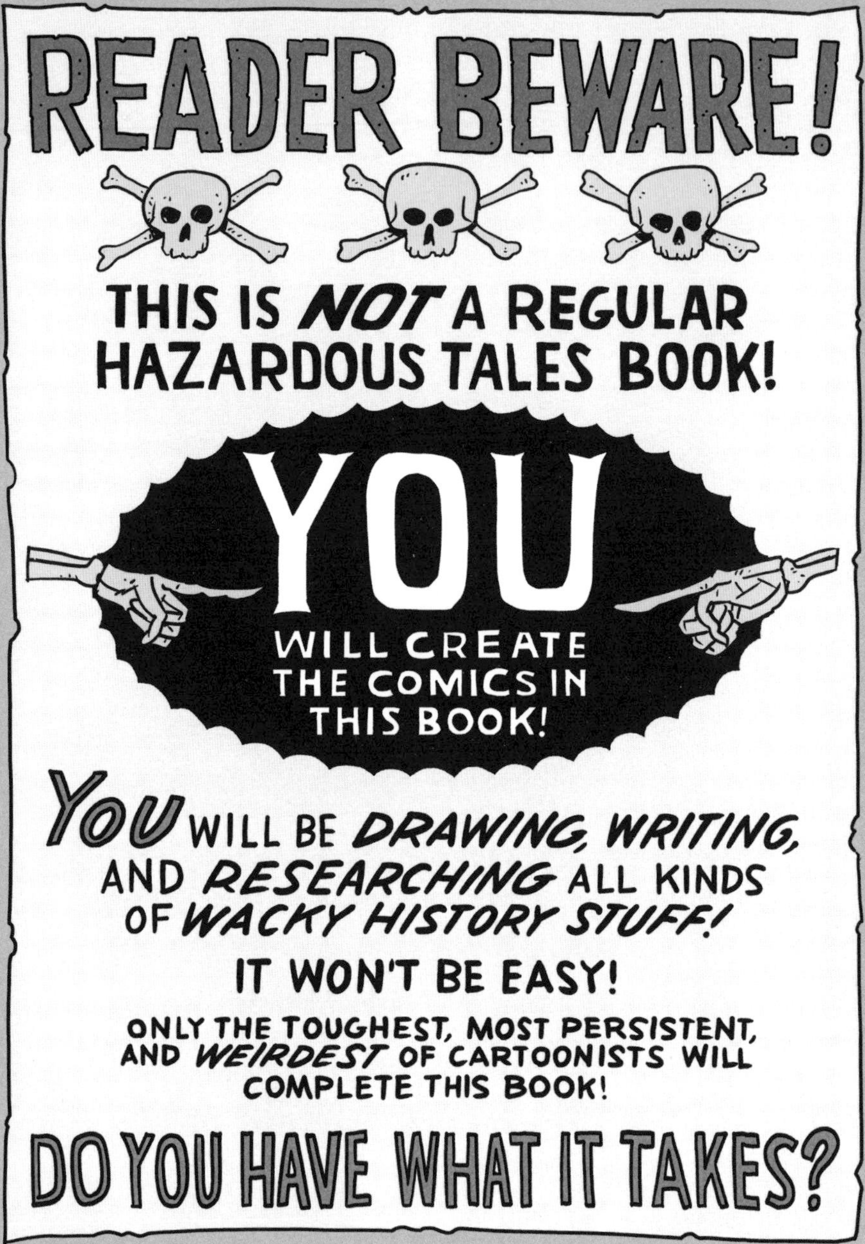
READER BEWARE!
THIS IS NOT A REGULAR HAZARDOUS TALES BOOK!
YOU
WILL CREATE THE COMICS IN THIS BOOK!
YOU WILL BE DRAWING, WRITING, AND RESEARCHING ALL KINDS OF WACKY HISTORY STUFF!
IT WON'T BE EASY!
ONLY THE TOUGHEST, MOST PERSISTENT, AND WEIRDEST OF CARTOONISTS WILL COMPLETE THIS BOOK!
DO YOU HAVE WHAT IT TAKES?

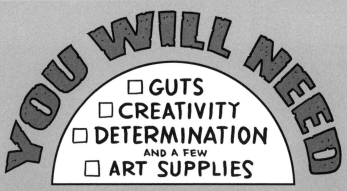

YOU WILL NEED

☐ GUTS
☐ CREATIVITY
☐ DETERMINATION
AND A FEW
☐ ART SUPPLIES

THESE WILL BE *OKAY*

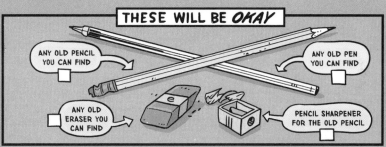

ANY OLD PENCIL YOU CAN FIND ☐

ANY OLD PEN YOU CAN FIND ☐

ANY OLD ERASER YOU CAN FIND ☐

PENCIL SHARPENER FOR THE OLD PENCIL ☐

THESE WILL BE *MUCH BETTER*

A DRAWING PEN FINELINER ☐

NICE PEN 01

A CLICKY NEW MECHANICAL PENCIL ☐

click click

05

THE MOST POPULAR OF THESE IS CALLED A *SAKURA PIGMA MICRON.*

A KNEADED ERASER ☐

THIS IS THE STRETCHY TYPE OF ERASER.

IT'S VERY FUN TO PLAY WITH.

YOU CAN GET THEM IN SETS,

OR ALONE ON A BLISTER PACK.

DO NOT STRETCH IT OVER YOUR HEAD!

SUPPORT YOUR LOCAL **MOM-AND-POP ART SUPPLY SHOP**

JIMBO'S ART HUT

SALE!

FANCY COMIC PENS

FANCY COMIC PEN

GET A SIZE 01.

IT CAN STICK IN YOUR HAIR LIKE GUM!

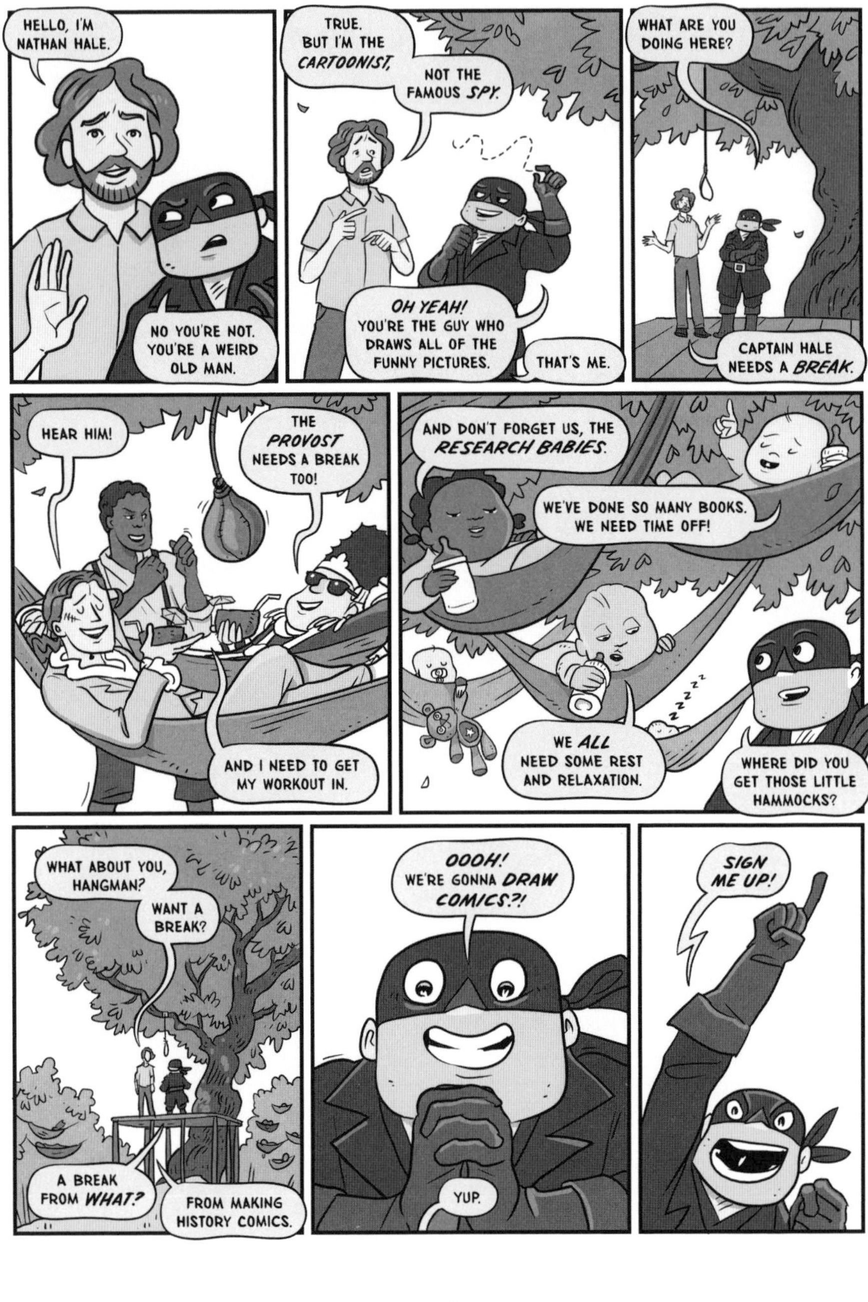
HELLO, I'M NATHAN HALE.
NO YOU'RE NOT. YOU'RE A WEIRD OLD MAN.
TRUE. BUT I'M THE CARTOONIST,
NOT THE FAMOUS SPY.
OH YEAH! YOU'RE THE GUY WHO DRAWS ALL OF THE FUNNY PICTURES.
THAT'S ME.
WHAT ARE YOU DOING HERE?
CAPTAIN HALE NEEDS A BREAK.
HEAR HIM!
THE PROVOST NEEDS A BREAK TOO!
AND I NEED TO GET MY WORKOUT IN.
AND DON'T FORGET US, THE RESEARCH BABIES.
WE'VE DONE SO MANY BOOKS. WE NEED TIME OFF!
WE ALL NEED SOME REST AND RELAXATION.
WHERE DID YOU GET THOSE LITTLE HAMMOCKS?
WHAT ABOUT YOU, HANGMAN?
WANT A BREAK?
A BREAK FROM WHAT?
FROM MAKING HISTORY COMICS.
OOOH! WE'RE GONNA DRAW COMICS?!
YUP.
SIGN ME UP!

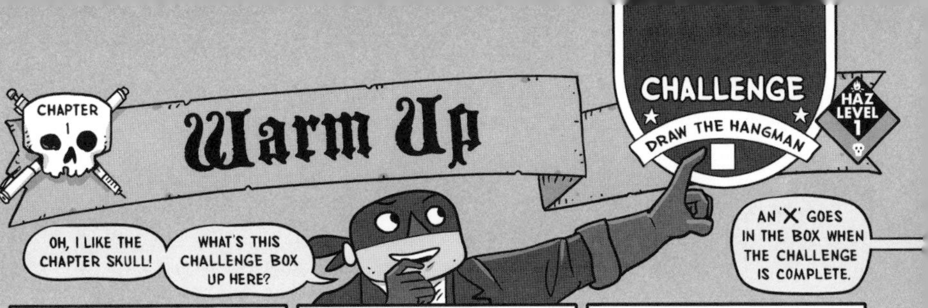
CHAPTER
1
Warm Up
CHALLENGE
DRAW THE HANGMAN
HAZ LEVEL 1
OH, I LIKE THE CHAPTER SKULL!
WHAT'S THIS CHALLENGE BOX UP HERE?
AN 'X' GOES IN THE BOX WHEN THE CHALLENGE IS COMPLETE.

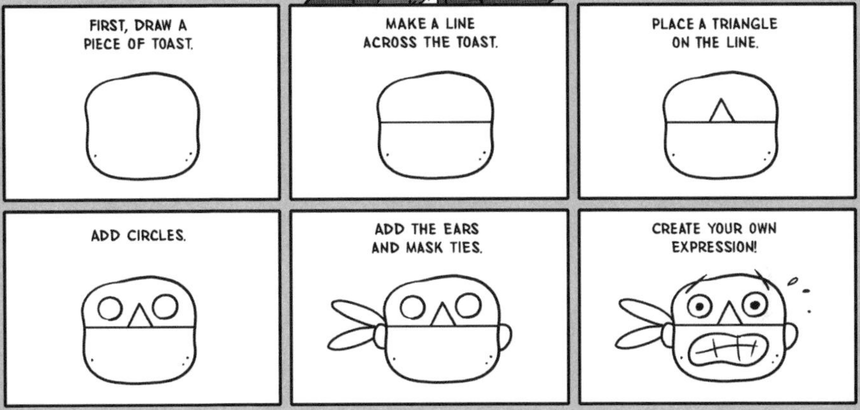
FIRST, DRAW A PIECE OF TOAST.
MAKE A LINE ACROSS THE TOAST.
PLACE A TRIANGLE ON THE LINE.
ADD CIRCLES.
ADD THE EARS AND MASK TIES.
CREATE YOUR OWN EXPRESSION!

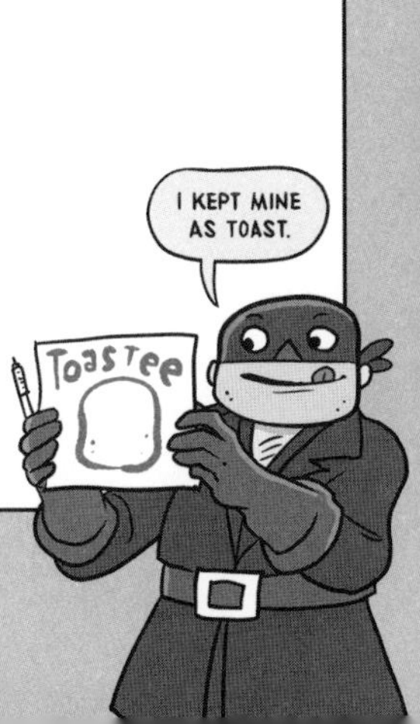
I KEPT MINE AS TOAST.
Toastee

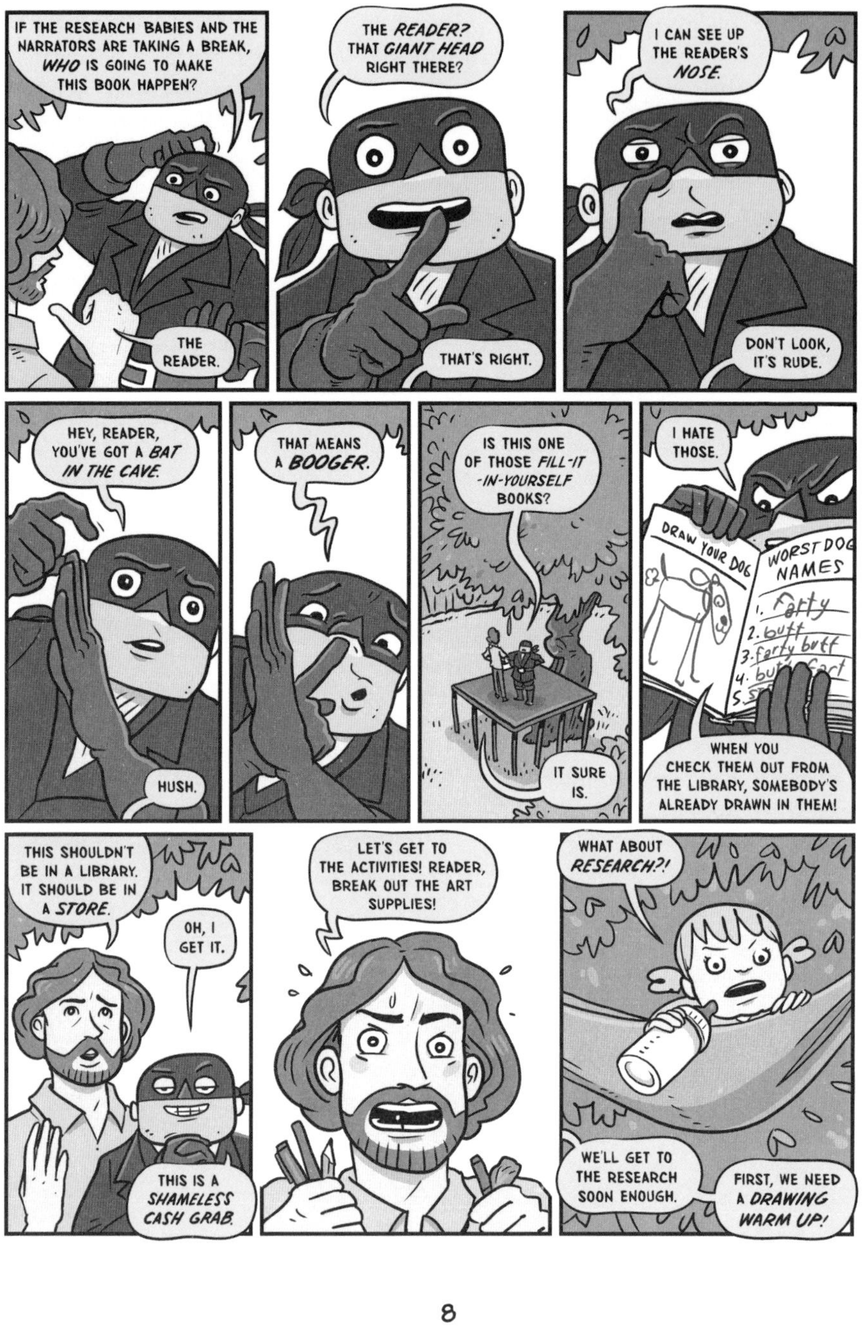
IF THE RESEARCH BABIES AND THE NARRATORS ARE TAKING A BREAK, *WHO* IS GOING TO MAKE THIS BOOK HAPPEN?
THE READER.
THE *READER?* THAT *GIANT HEAD* RIGHT THERE?
THAT'S RIGHT.
I CAN SEE UP THE READER'S *NOSE.*
DON'T LOOK, IT'S RUDE.
HEY, READER, YOU'VE GOT A *BAT IN THE CAVE.*
HUSH.
THAT MEANS A ***BOOGER.***
IS THIS ONE OF THOSE *FILL-IT-IN-YOURSELF* BOOKS?
IT SURE IS.
I HATE THOSE.
DRAW YOUR DOG
WORST DOG NAMES
1. farty
2. butt
3. farty butt
WHEN YOU CHECK THEM OUT FROM THE LIBRARY, SOMEBODY'S ALREADY DRAWN IN THEM!
THIS SHOULDN'T BE IN A LIBRARY. IT SHOULD BE IN A *STORE.*
OH, I GET IT.
THIS IS A *SHAMELESS CASH GRAB.*
LET'S GET TO THE ACTIVITIES! READER, BREAK OUT THE ART SUPPLIES!
WHAT ABOUT *RESEARCH?!*
WE'LL GET TO THE RESEARCH SOON ENOUGH.
FIRST, WE NEED A ***DRAWING WARM UP!***

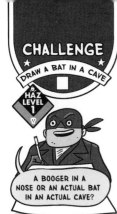

CHALLENGE
DRAW A BAT IN A CAVE
HAZ LEVEL 1
A BOOGER IN A NOSE OR AN ACTUAL BAT IN AN ACTUAL CAVE?
READER, DECIDE AND DRAW! YOU ARE NOW THE *CARTOONIST!*
SKETCH ON!
I *SKIP* THE SKETCH AND GO STRAIGHT TO *INK*.
YOU CAN DO IT THAT WAY IF YOU LIKE *DANGER*.
I LIKE TO USE A PENCIL,
THEN INK IT WHEN I'M HAPPY WITH THE SKETCH.
ARE THEY SUPPOSED TO RESEARCH BATS OR CAVES?
NO. THIS IS A DRAWING FROM YOUR IMAGINATION.

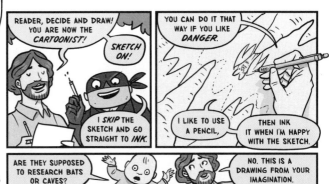

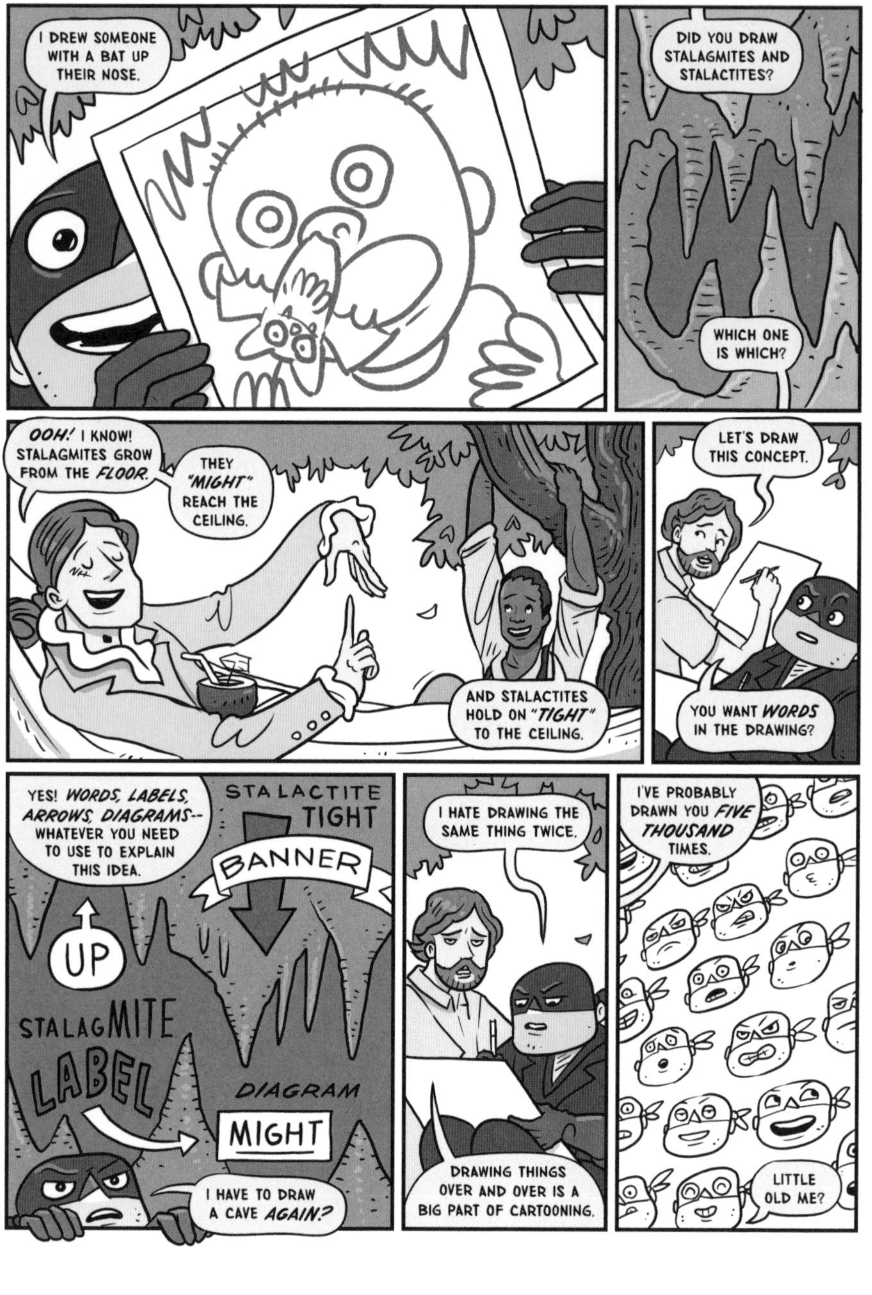
I DREW SOMEONE WITH A BAT UP THEIR NOSE.
DID YOU DRAW STALAGMITES AND STALACTITES?
WHICH ONE IS WHICH?
OOH! I KNOW! STALAGMITES GROW FROM THE FLOOR.
THEY "MIGHT" REACH THE CEILING.
AND STALACTITES HOLD ON "TIGHT" TO THE CEILING.
LET'S DRAW THIS CONCEPT.
YOU WANT WORDS IN THE DRAWING?
YES! WORDS, LABELS, ARROWS, DIAGRAMS-- WHATEVER YOU NEED TO USE TO EXPLAIN THIS IDEA.
STALACTITE
TIGHT
BANNER
UP
STALAGMITE
LABEL
DIAGRAM
MIGHT
I HAVE TO DRAW A CAVE AGAIN?
I HATE DRAWING THE SAME THING TWICE.
DRAWING THINGS OVER AND OVER IS A BIG PART OF CARTOONING.
I'VE PROBABLY DRAWN YOU FIVE THOUSAND TIMES.
LITTLE OLD ME?

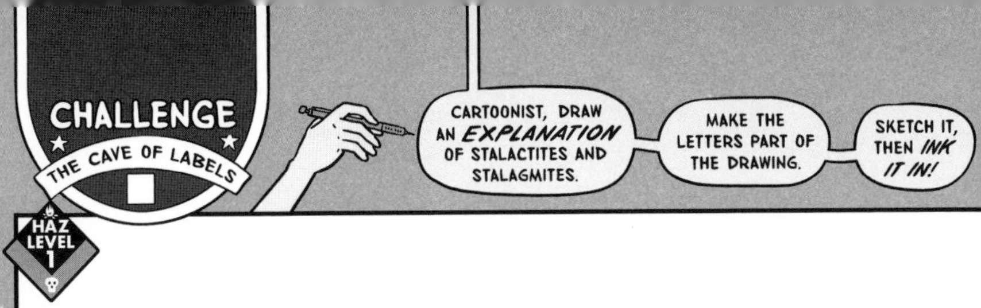
CHALLENGE
THE CAVE OF LABELS
HAZ LEVEL 1
CARTOONIST, DRAW AN *EXPLANATION* OF STALACTITES AND STALAGMITES.
MAKE THE LETTERS PART OF THE DRAWING.
SKETCH IT, THEN *INK IT IN!*

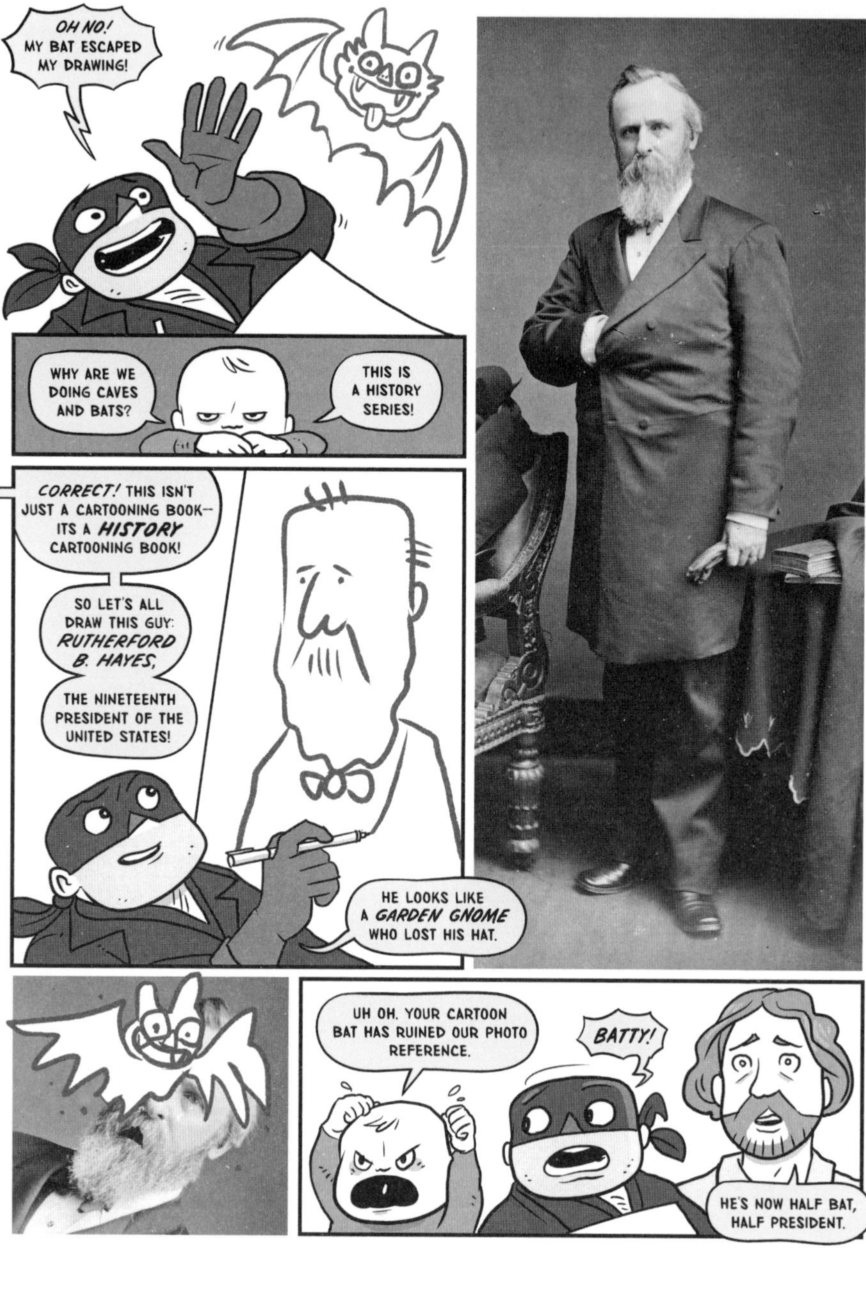
OH NO! MY BAT ESCAPED MY DRAWING!
WHY ARE WE DOING CAVES AND BATS?
THIS IS A HISTORY SERIES!
CORRECT! THIS ISN'T JUST A CARTOONING BOOK-- ITS A HISTORY CARTOONING BOOK!
SO LET'S ALL DRAW THIS GUY: RUTHERFORD B. HAYES,
THE NINETEENTH PRESIDENT OF THE UNITED STATES!
HE LOOKS LIKE A GARDEN GNOME WHO LOST HIS HAT.
UH OH. YOUR CARTOON BAT HAS RUINED OUR PHOTO REFERENCE.
BATTY!
HE'S NOW HALF BAT, HALF PRESIDENT.

Brady-Handy photograph collection, Library of Congress

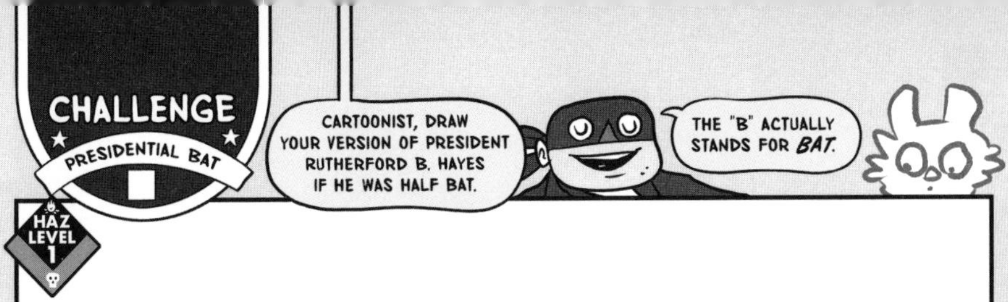
CHALLENGE
PRESIDENTIAL BAT
HAZ LEVEL 1
CARTOONIST, DRAW YOUR VERSION OF PRESIDENT RUTHERFORD B. HAYES IF HE WAS HALF BAT.
THE "B" ACTUALLY STANDS FOR *BAT.*

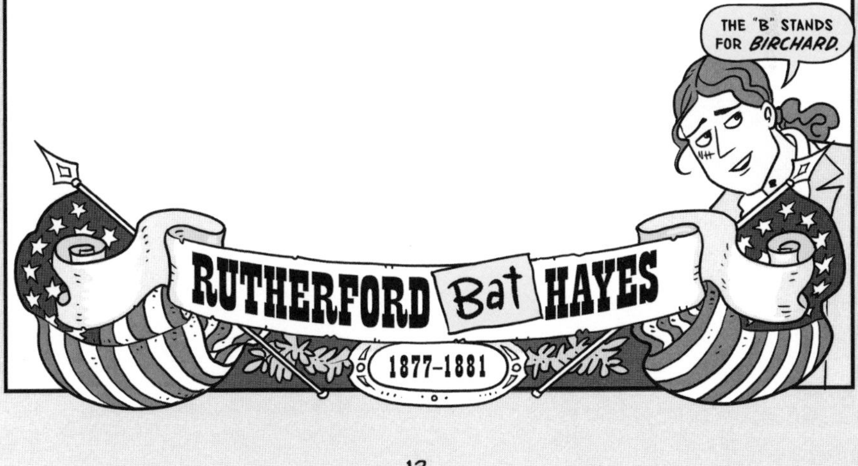
THE "B" STANDS FOR *BIRCHARD.*
RUTHERFORD Bat HAYES
1877–1881

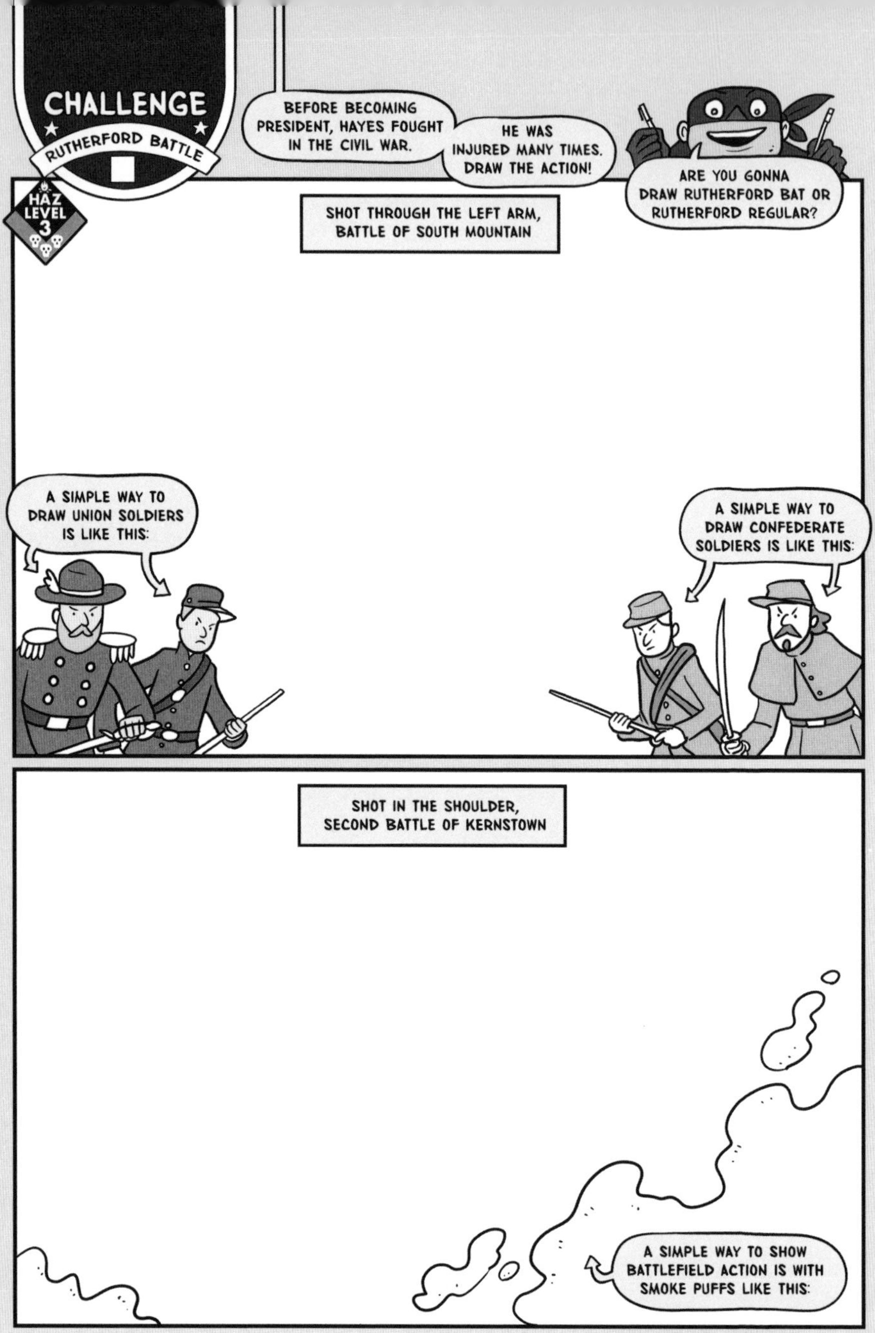
CHALLENGE
RUTHERFORD BATTLE
HAZ LEVEL 3
BEFORE BECOMING PRESIDENT, HAYES FOUGHT IN THE CIVIL WAR.
HE WAS INJURED MANY TIMES. DRAW THE ACTION!
ARE YOU GONNA DRAW RUTHERFORD BAT OR RUTHERFORD REGULAR?
SHOT THROUGH THE LEFT ARM, BATTLE OF SOUTH MOUNTAIN
A SIMPLE WAY TO DRAW UNION SOLDIERS IS LIKE THIS:
A SIMPLE WAY TO DRAW CONFEDERATE SOLDIERS IS LIKE THIS:
SHOT IN THE SHOULDER, SECOND BATTLE OF KERNSTOWN
A SIMPLE WAY TO SHOW BATTLEFIELD ACTION IS WITH SMOKE PUFFS LIKE THIS:

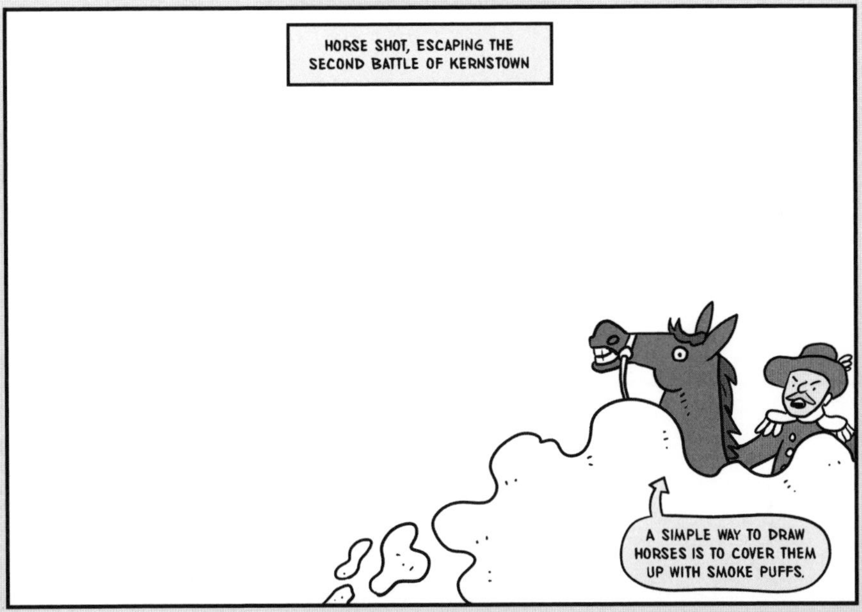
HORSE SHOT, ESCAPING THE SECOND BATTLE OF KERNSTOWN
A SIMPLE WAY TO DRAW HORSES IS TO COVER THEM UP WITH SMOKE PUFFS.

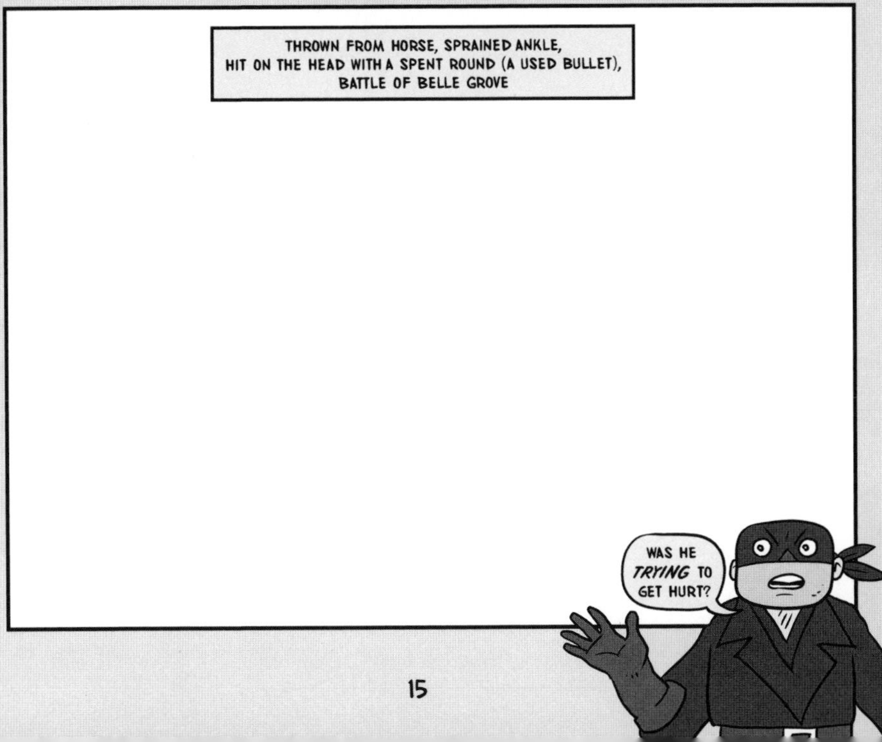
THROWN FROM HORSE, SPRAINED ANKLE, HIT ON THE HEAD WITH A SPENT ROUND (A USED BULLET), BATTLE OF BELLE GROVE
WAS HE *TRYING* TO GET HURT?

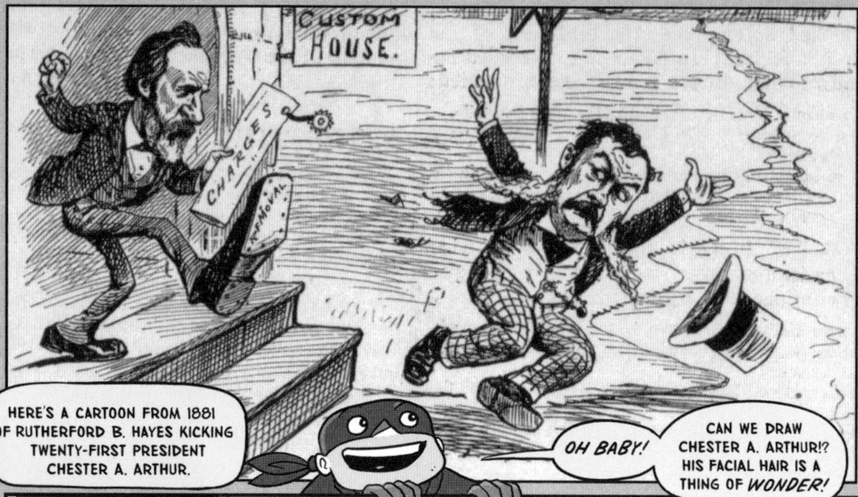
CUSTOM HOUSE.
CHARGES
REMOVAL
HERE'S A CARTOON FROM 1881 OF RUTHERFORD B. HAYES KICKING TWENTY-FIRST PRESIDENT CHESTER A. ARTHUR.
OH BABY!
CAN WE DRAW CHESTER A. ARTHUR!? HIS FACIAL HAIR IS A THING OF *WONDER!*

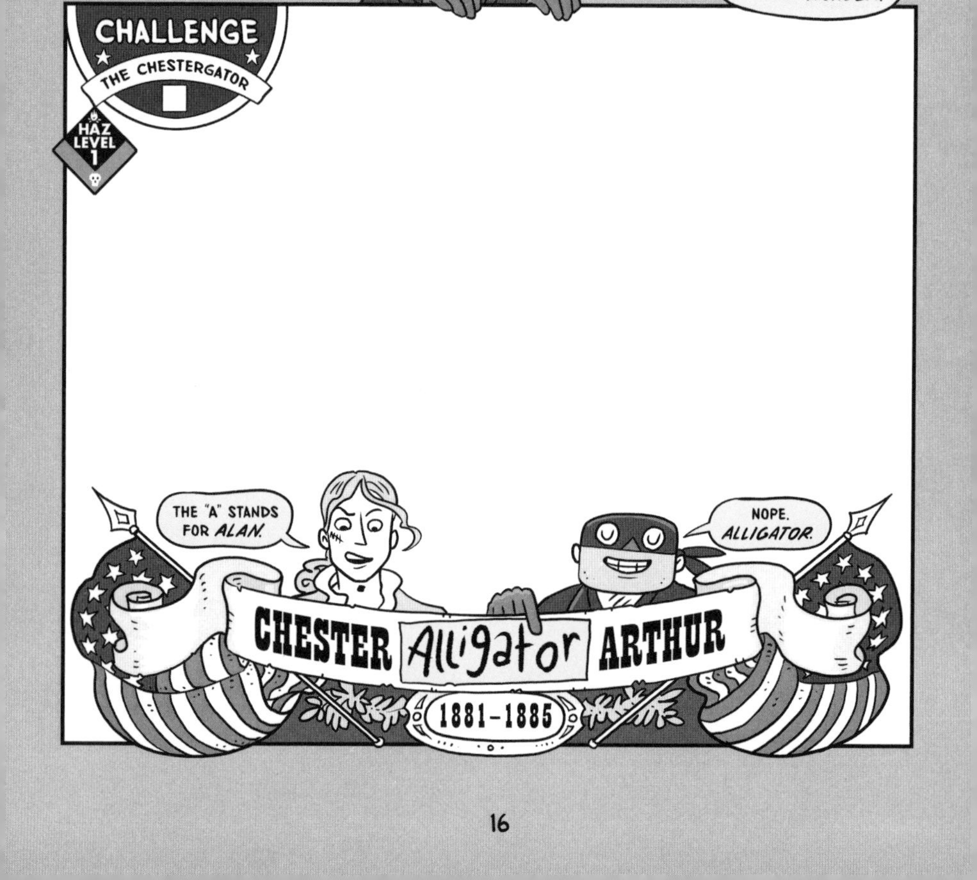
CHALLENGE
THE CHESTERGATOR
HAZ LEVEL 1
THE "A" STANDS FOR *ALAN.*
NOPE. *ALLIGATOR.*
CHESTER Alligator ARTHUR
1881–1885

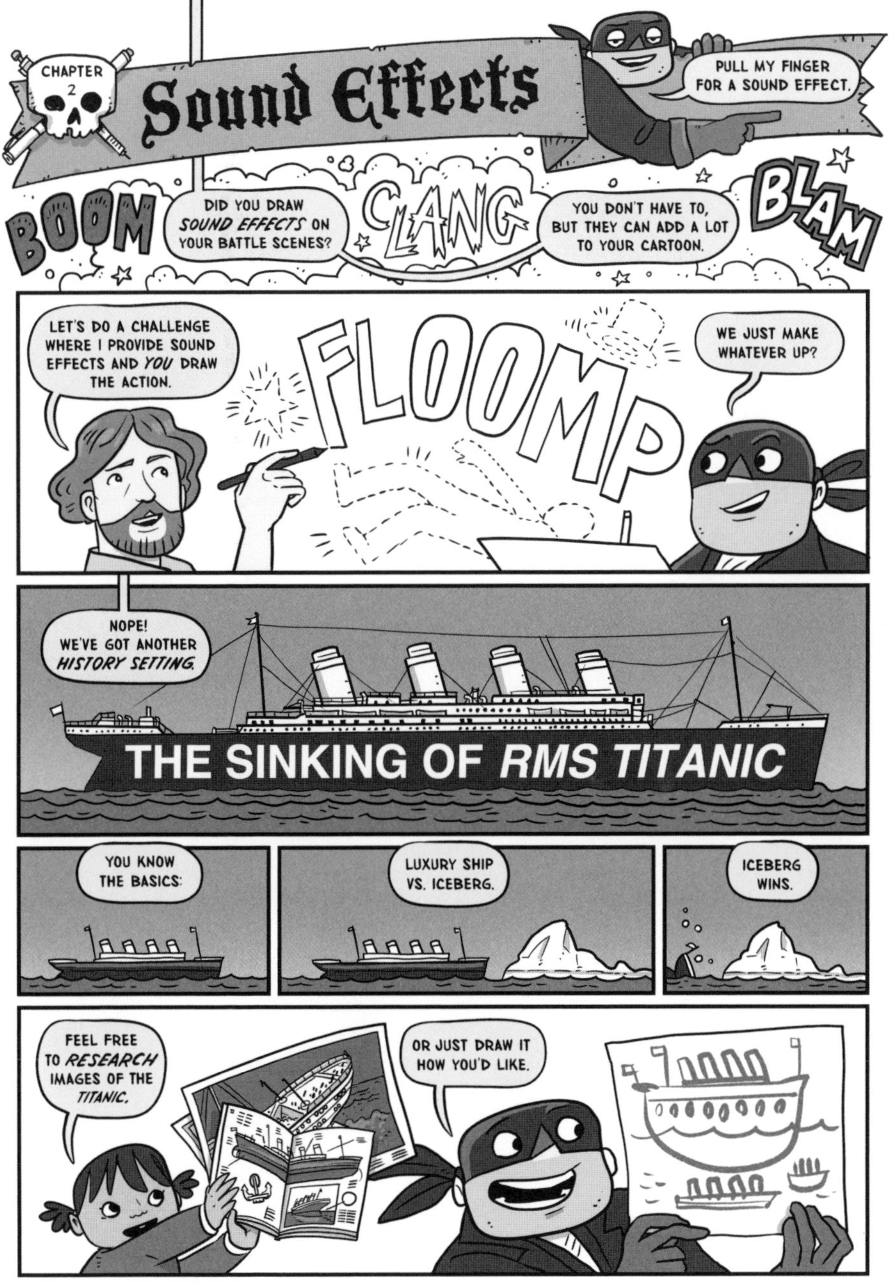
CHAPTER 2
Sound Effects
PULL MY FINGER FOR A SOUND EFFECT.
BOOM
DID YOU DRAW SOUND EFFECTS ON YOUR BATTLE SCENES?
CLANG
YOU DON'T HAVE TO, BUT THEY CAN ADD A LOT TO YOUR CARTOON.
BLAM
LET'S DO A CHALLENGE WHERE I PROVIDE SOUND EFFECTS AND YOU DRAW THE ACTION.
FLOOMP
WE JUST MAKE WHATEVER UP?
NOPE! WE'VE GOT ANOTHER HISTORY SETTING.
THE SINKING OF RMS TITANIC
YOU KNOW THE BASICS:
LUXURY SHIP VS. ICEBERG.
ICEBERG WINS.
FEEL FREE TO RESEARCH IMAGES OF THE TITANIC.
OR JUST DRAW IT HOW YOU'D LIKE.

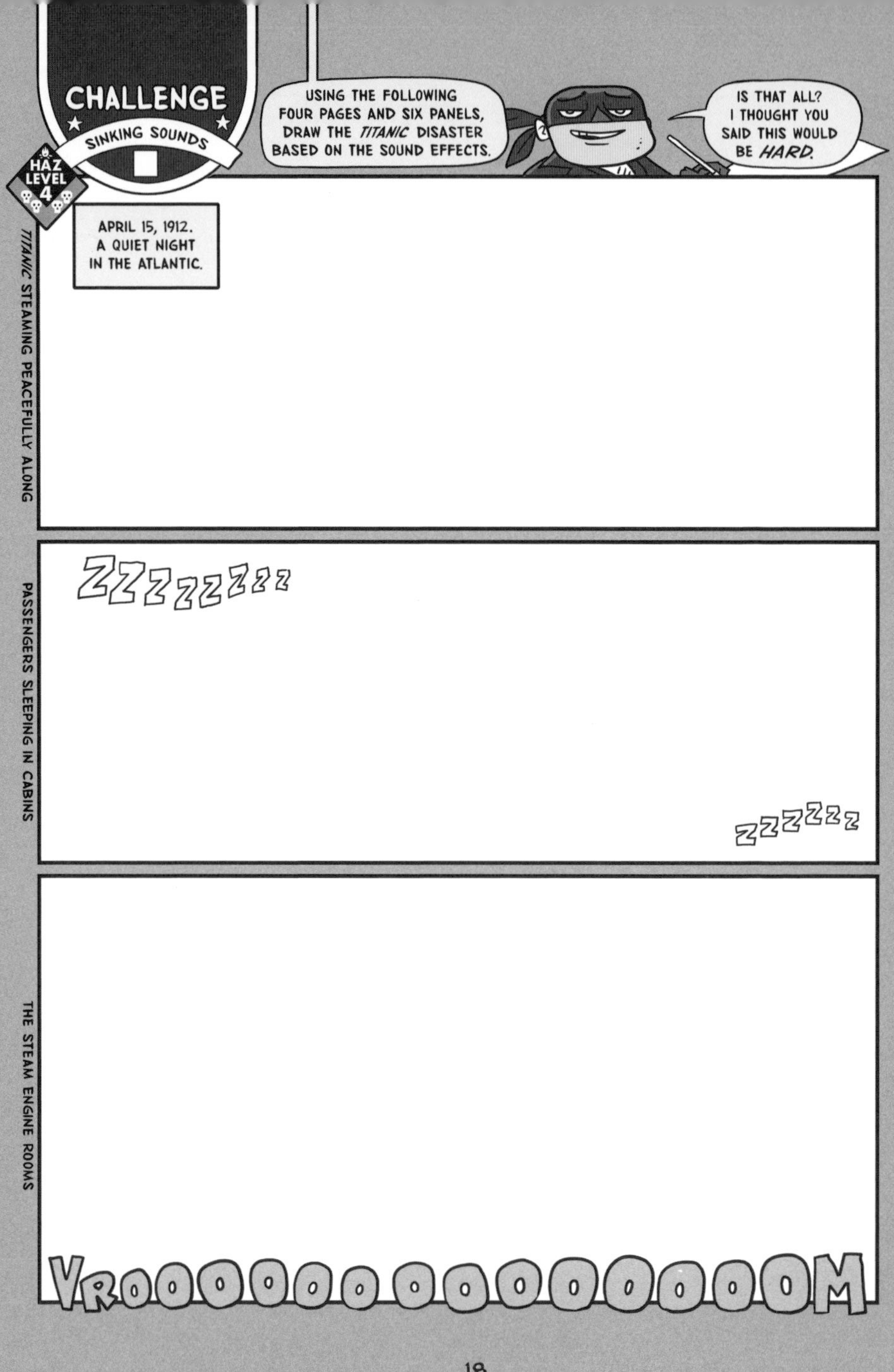
CHALLENGE
SINKING SOUNDS
HAZ LEVEL 4
USING THE FOLLOWING FOUR PAGES AND SIX PANELS, DRAW THE *TITANIC* DISASTER BASED ON THE SOUND EFFECTS.
IS THAT ALL? I THOUGHT YOU SAID THIS WOULD BE *HARD*.
APRIL 15, 1912. A QUIET NIGHT IN THE ATLANTIC.
TITANIC STEAMING PEACEFULLY ALONG
ZZZZZZZZ
ZZZZZZ
PASSENGERS SLEEPING IN CABINS
THE STEAM ENGINE ROOMS
VROOOOOOOOOOOOOOOOM

ICE SCRAPES THE HULL

THE SHIP HITS THE ICEBERG

FURNITURE SLIDES AND BREAKS, CABLES SNAP

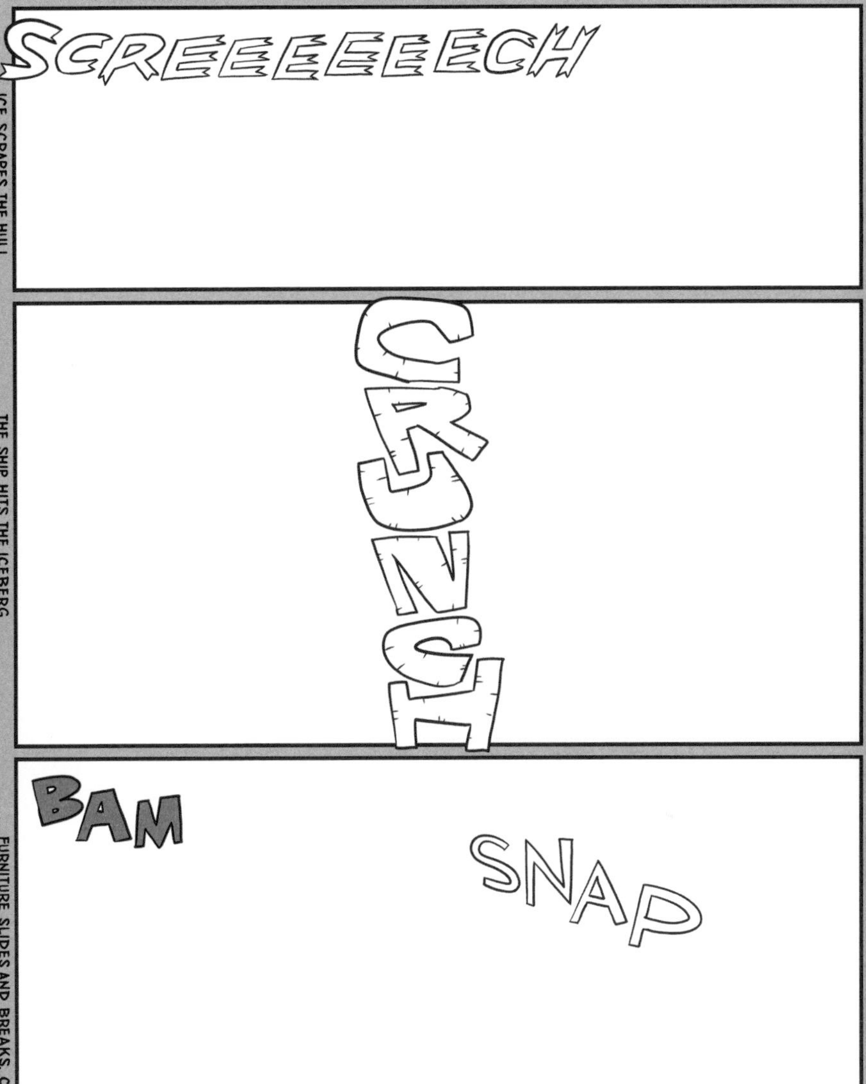
SCREEEEEECH
CRUNCH
BAM
SNAP
BAM

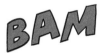

STEAM BLASTS FROM THE BOILERS

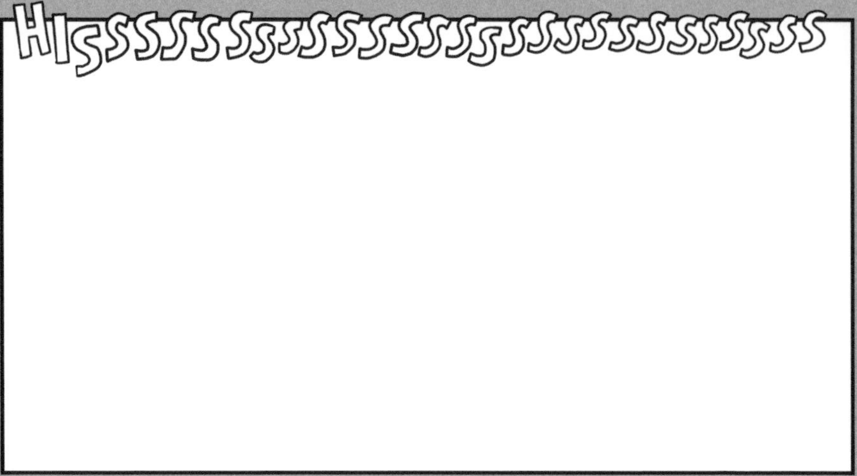
HISSSSSSSSSSSSSSSSSSSSSSSSSSSS

PASSENGERS FALL OVERBOARD

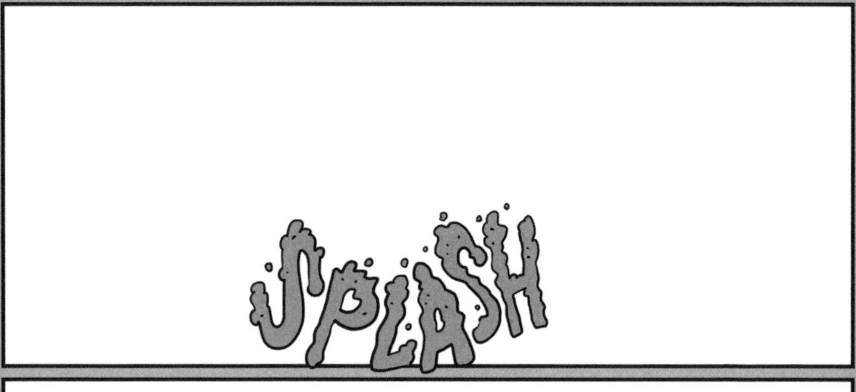
SPLASH

THE SHIP BEGINS TO FILL WITH WATER

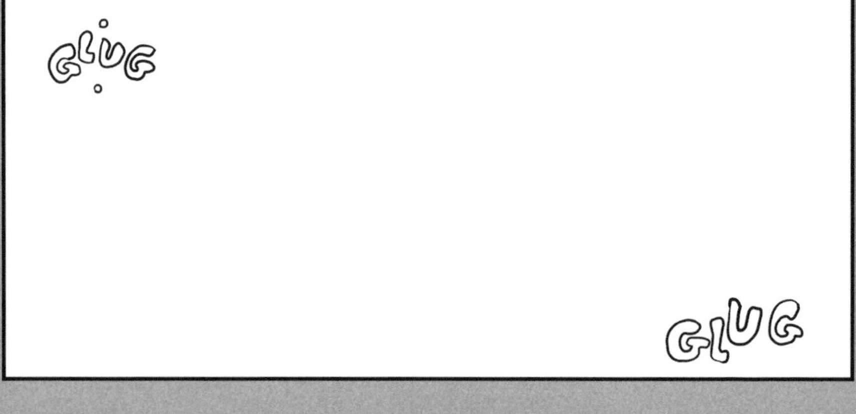
GLUG
GLUG

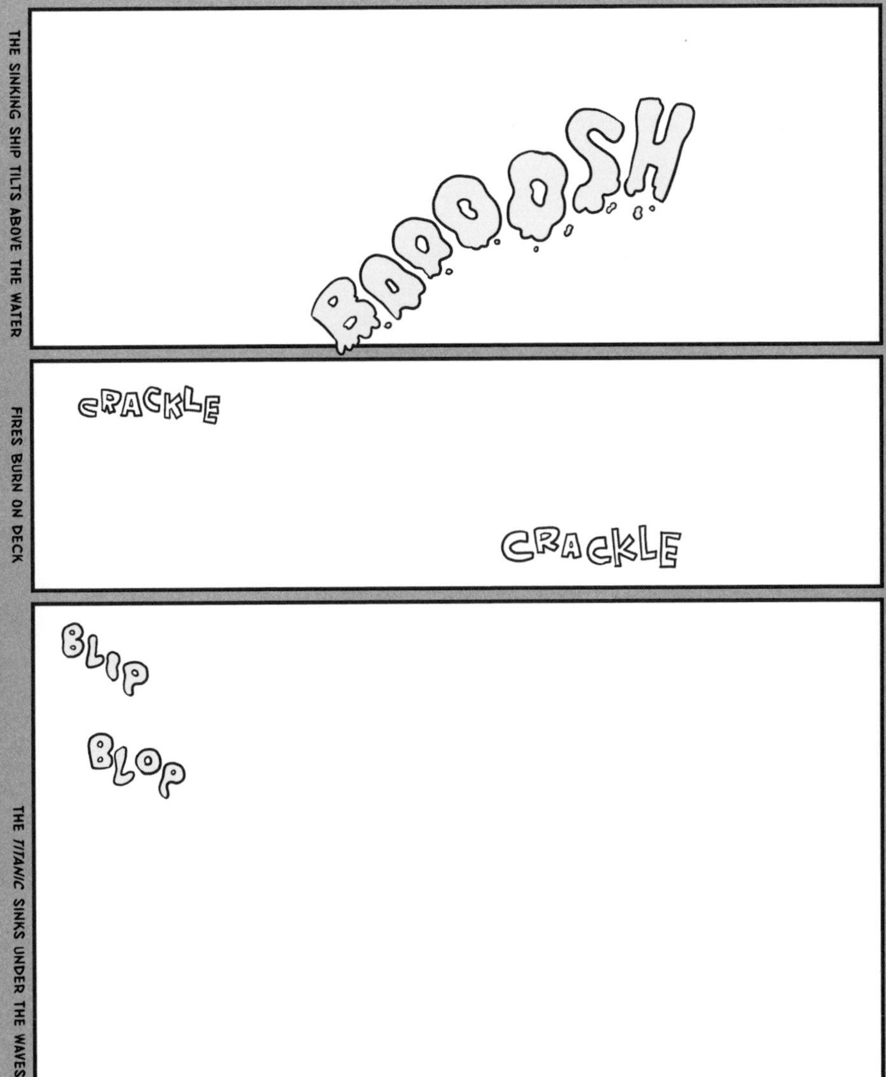
THE SINKING SHIP TILTS ABOVE THE WATER
BOOOOSH
FIRES BURN ON DECK
CRACKLE
CRACKLE
THE *TITANIC* SINKS UNDER THE WAVES
BLIP
BLOP
BLOOP

THE END

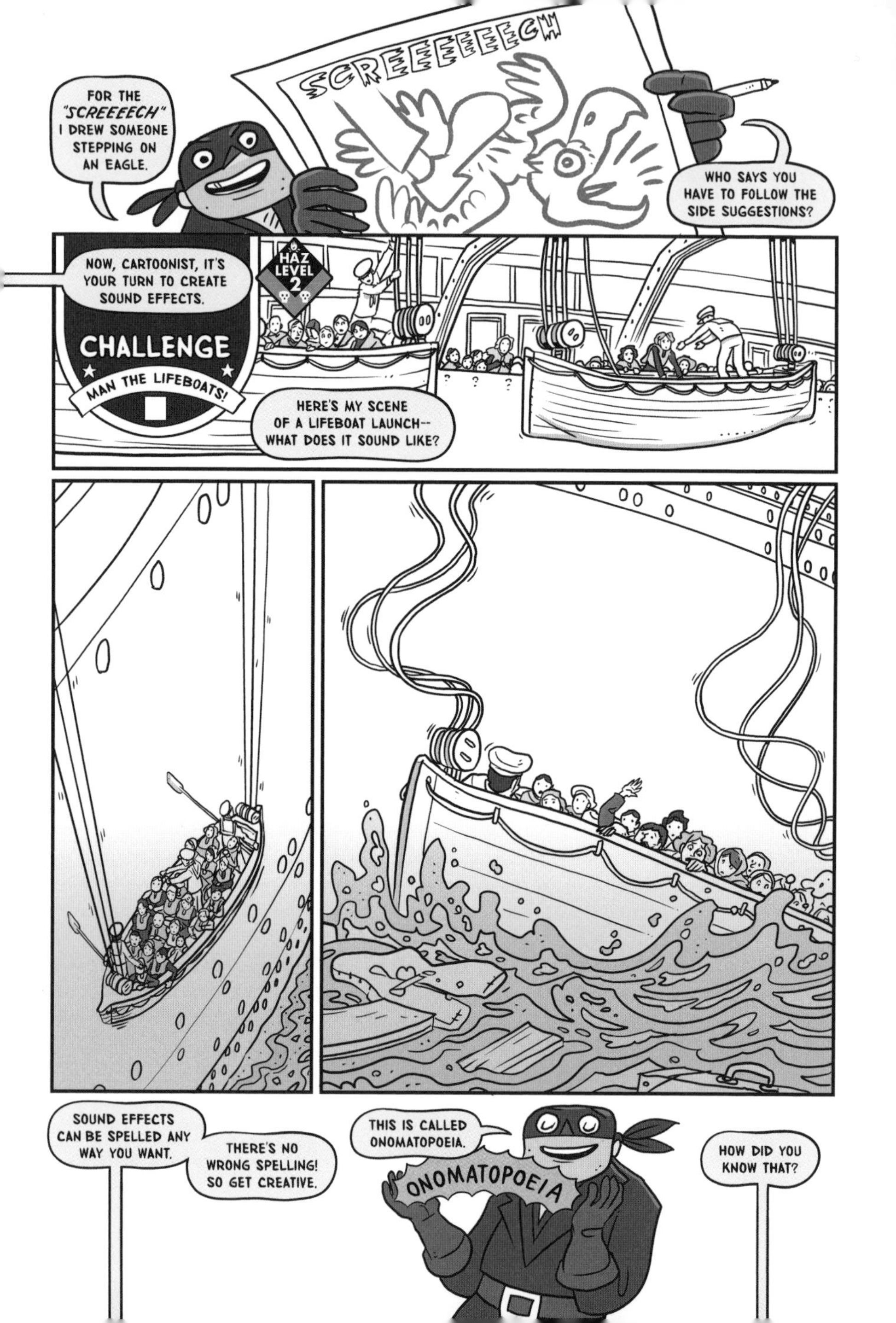
SCREEEEEEECH
FOR THE "SCREEEECH" I DREW SOMEONE STEPPING ON AN EAGLE.
WHO SAYS YOU HAVE TO FOLLOW THE SIDE SUGGESTIONS?
NOW, CARTOONIST, IT'S YOUR TURN TO CREATE SOUND EFFECTS.
CHALLENGE
MAN THE LIFEBOATS!
HAZ LEVEL 2
HERE'S MY SCENE OF A LIFEBOAT LAUNCH-- WHAT DOES IT SOUND LIKE?
SOUND EFFECTS CAN BE SPELLED ANY WAY YOU WANT.
THERE'S NO WRONG SPELLING! SO GET CREATIVE.
THIS IS CALLED ONOMATOPOEIA.
ONOMATOPOEIA
HOW DID YOU KNOW THAT?

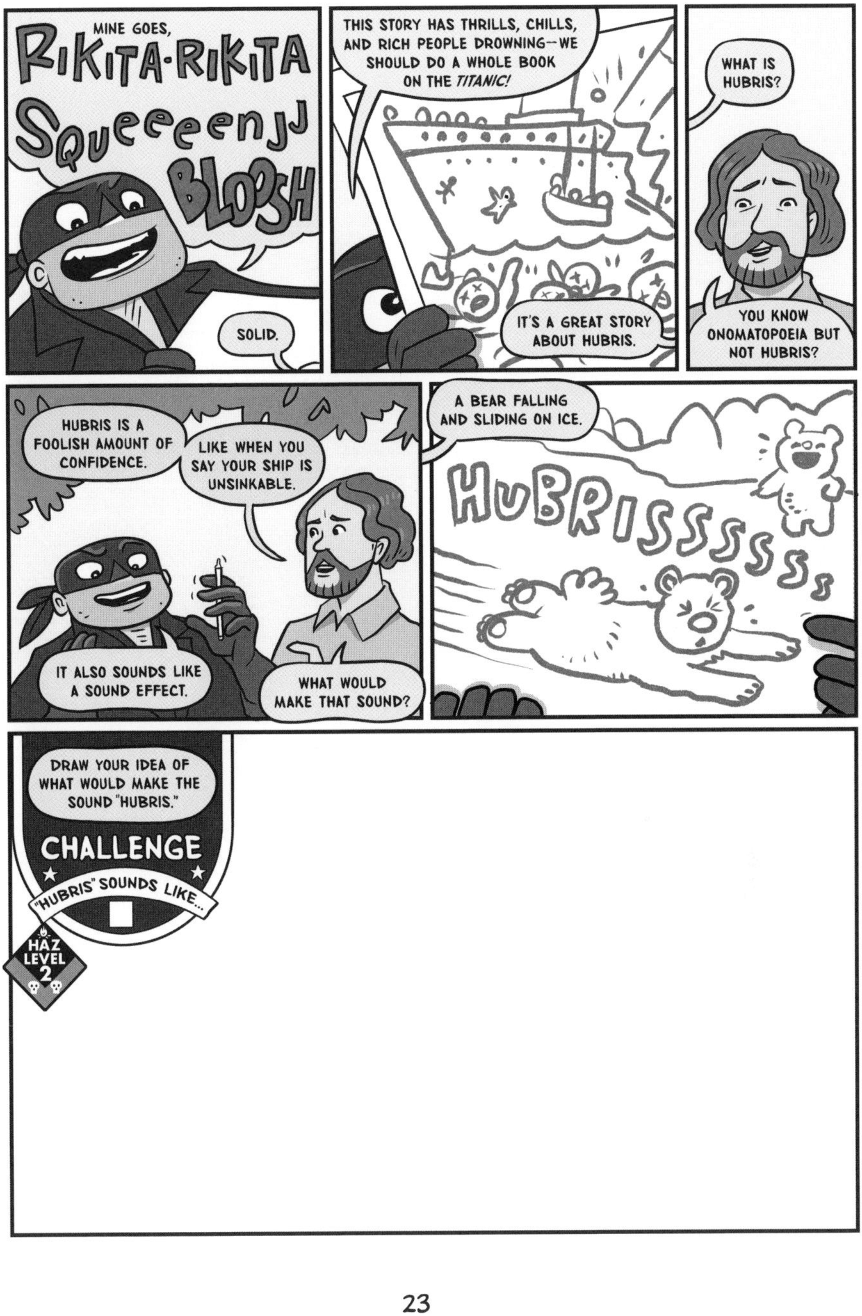
MINE GOES,
RIKITA-RIKITA
SQUEEEENJJ
BLOOSH
SOLID.
THIS STORY HAS THRILLS, CHILLS, AND RICH PEOPLE DROWNING--WE SHOULD DO A WHOLE BOOK ON THE *TITANIC!*
IT'S A GREAT STORY ABOUT HUBRIS.
WHAT IS HUBRIS?
YOU KNOW ONOMATOPOEIA BUT NOT HUBRIS?
HUBRIS IS A FOOLISH AMOUNT OF CONFIDENCE.
LIKE WHEN YOU SAY YOUR SHIP IS UNSINKABLE.
IT ALSO SOUNDS LIKE A SOUND EFFECT.
WHAT WOULD MAKE THAT SOUND?
A BEAR FALLING AND SLIDING ON ICE.
HUBRISSSSSSS
DRAW YOUR IDEA OF WHAT WOULD MAKE THE SOUND "HUBRIS."
CHALLENGE
"HUBRIS" SOUNDS LIKE...
HAZ LEVEL 2

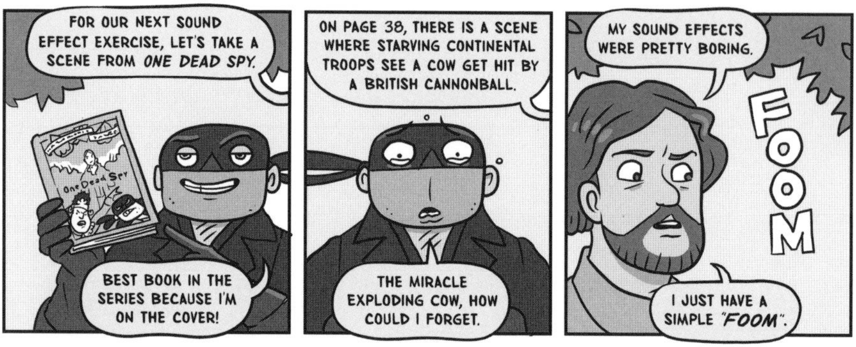
FOR OUR NEXT SOUND EFFECT EXERCISE, LET'S TAKE A SCENE FROM *ONE DEAD SPY.*
One Dead Spy
BEST BOOK IN THE SERIES BECAUSE I'M ON THE COVER!
ON PAGE 38, THERE IS A SCENE WHERE STARVING CONTINENTAL TROOPS SEE A COW GET HIT BY A BRITISH CANNONBALL.
THE MIRACLE EXPLODING COW, HOW COULD I FORGET.
MY SOUND EFFECTS WERE PRETTY BORING.
FOOM
I JUST HAVE A SIMPLE *"FOOM"*.

EXCERPT FROM *ONE DEAD SPY*, PAGE 38:

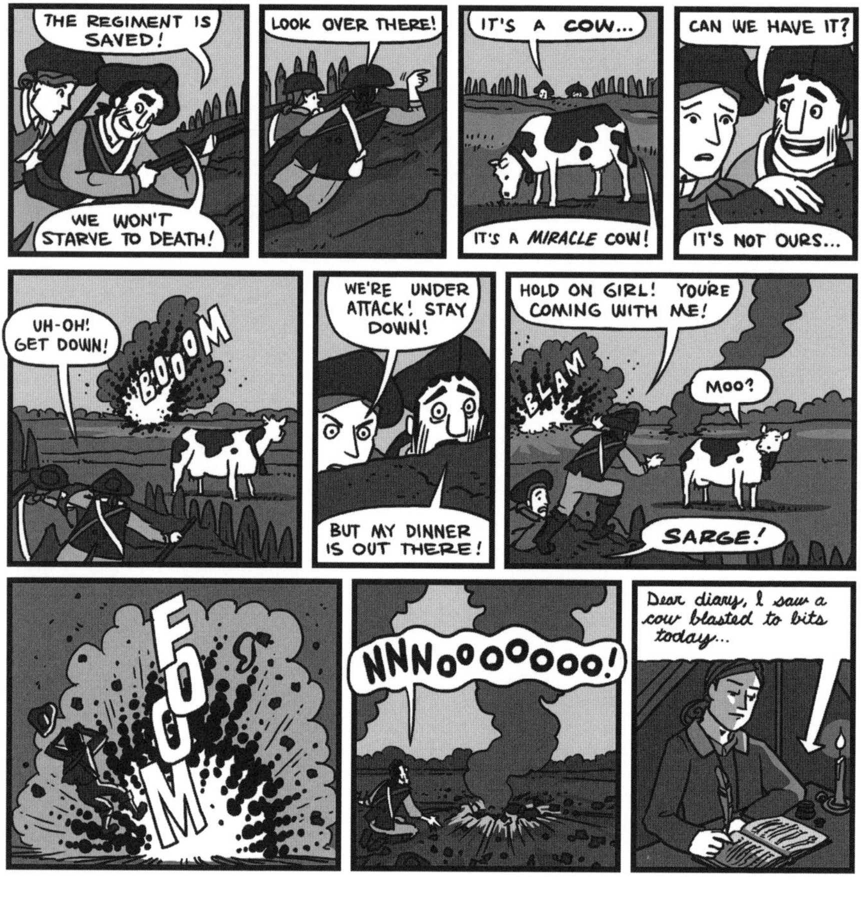
THE REGIMENT IS SAVED!
WE WON'T STARVE TO DEATH!
LOOK OVER THERE!
IT'S A COW...
IT'S A *MIRACLE* COW!
CAN WE HAVE IT?
IT'S NOT OURS...
UH-OH! GET DOWN!
BOOOOM
WE'RE UNDER ATTACK! STAY DOWN!
BUT MY DINNER IS OUT THERE!
HOLD ON GIRL! YOU'RE COMING WITH ME!
BLAM
MOO?
SARGE!
FOOM
NNNOOOOOOO!
Dear diary, I saw a cow blasted to bits today...

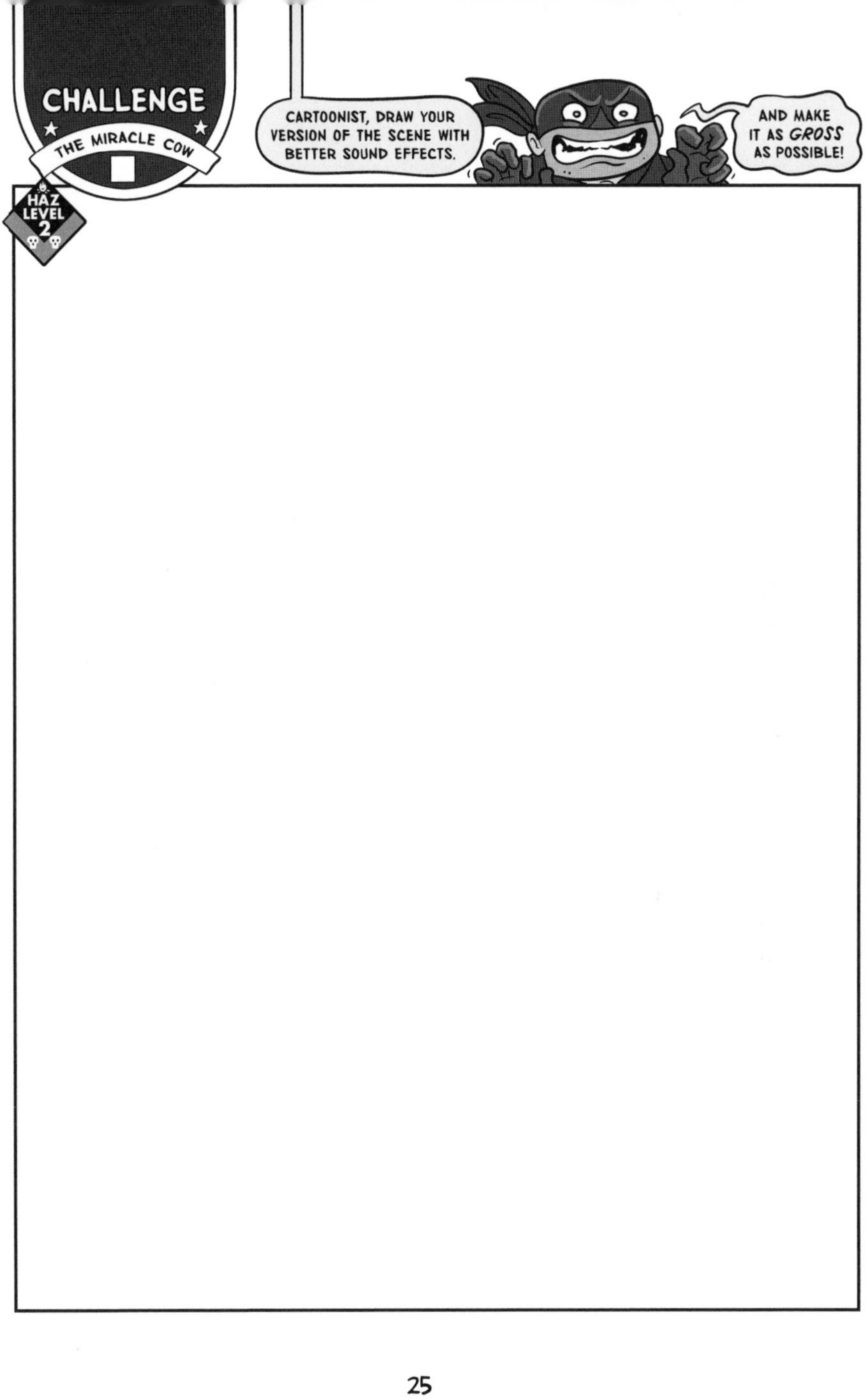
CHALLENGE
THE MIRACLE COW
HAZ LEVEL 2
CARTOONIST, DRAW YOUR VERSION OF THE SCENE WITH BETTER SOUND EFFECTS.
AND MAKE IT AS *GROSS* AS POSSIBLE!

FOR A FUN AND DISGUSTING CHALLENGE, DRAW THE EXPLODING COW SCENE AGAIN, BUT THIS TIME, USE THE *GUTS* TO SPELL OUT THE SOUND EFFECTS!

CHALLENGE
★ THE SOUND OF GUTS ★

HAZ LEVEL 2

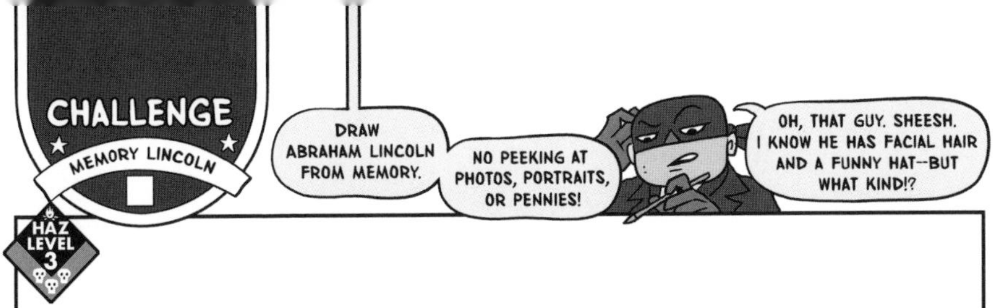
CHALLENGE
MEMORY LINCOLN
HAZ LEVEL 3
DRAW ABRAHAM LINCOLN FROM MEMORY.
NO PEEKING AT PHOTOS, PORTRAITS, OR PENNIES!
OH, THAT GUY. SHEESH. I KNOW HE HAS FACIAL HAIR AND A FUNNY HAT--BUT WHAT KIND!?

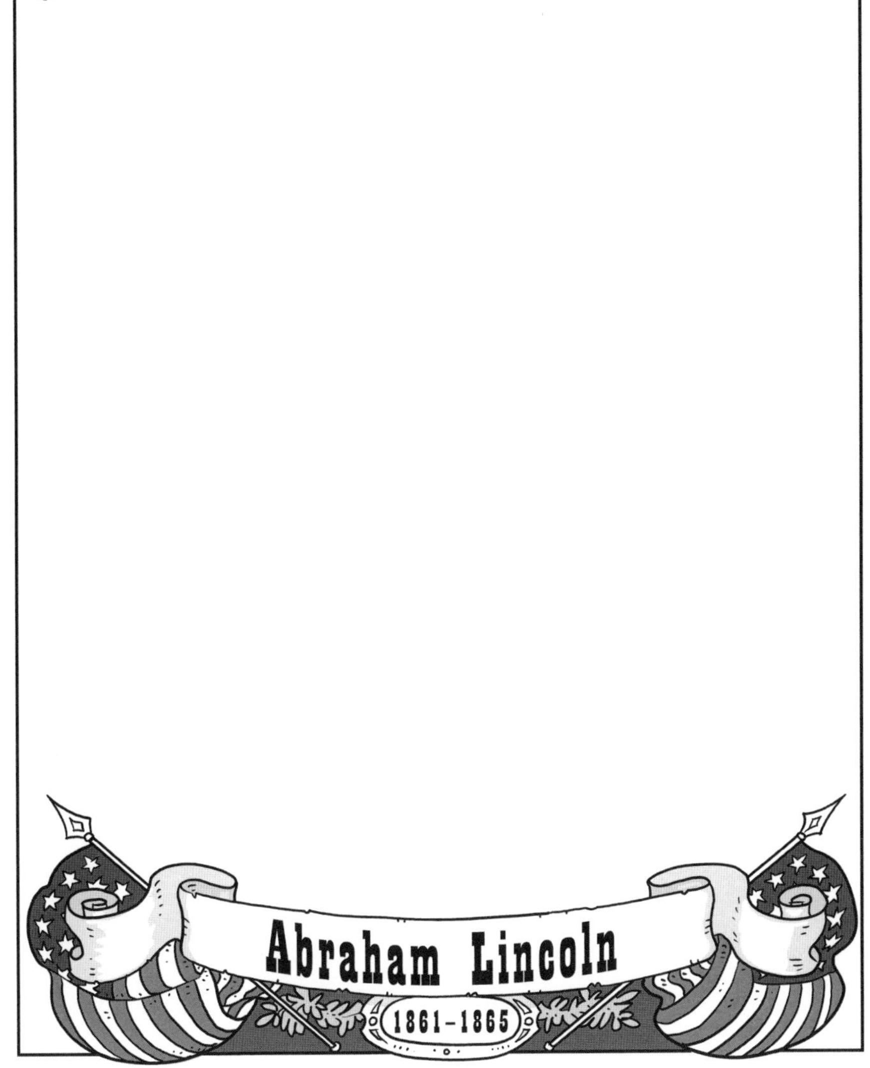
Abraham Lincoln
1861-1865

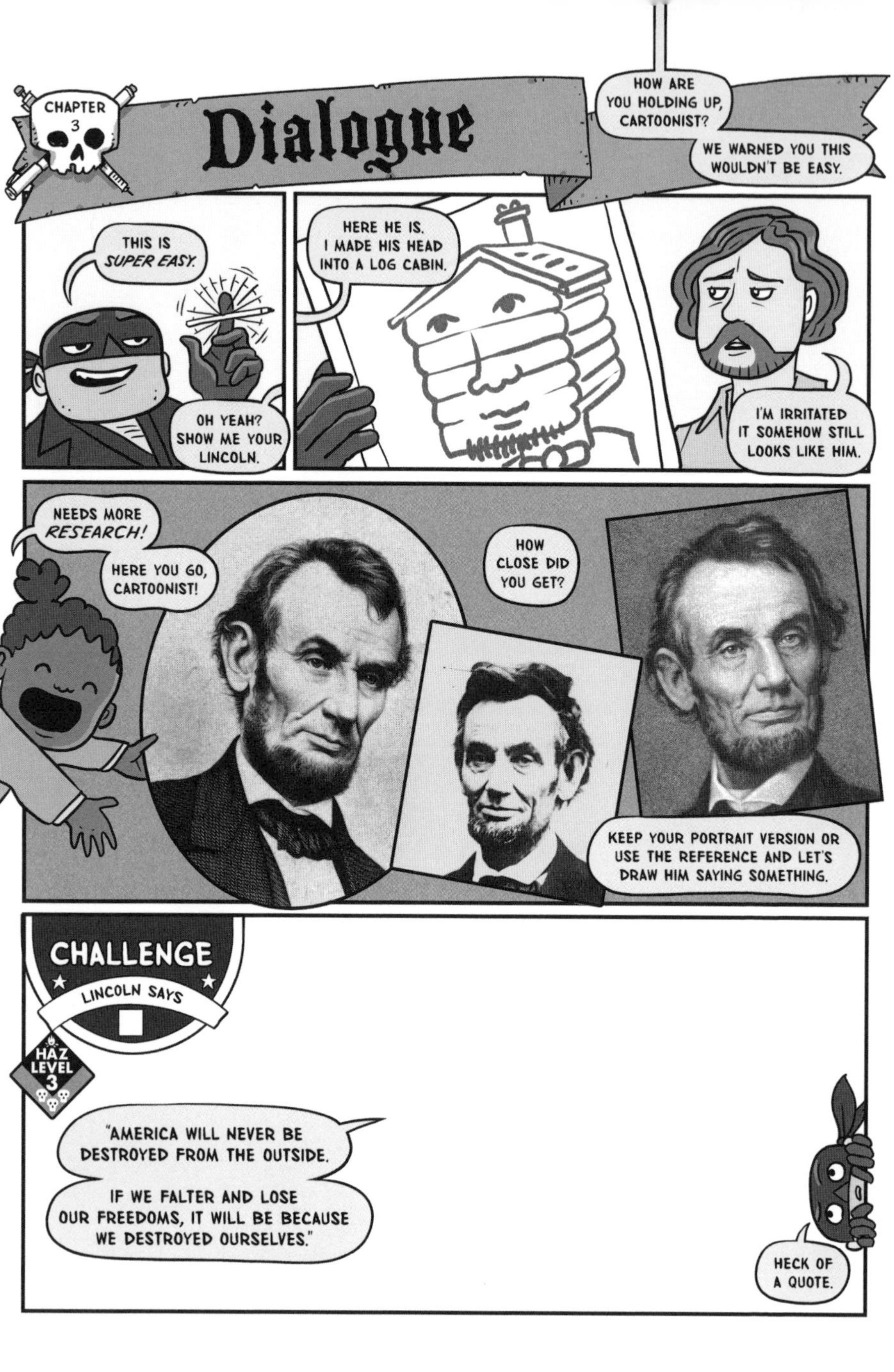
CHAPTER 3
Dialogue
HOW ARE YOU HOLDING UP, CARTOONIST?
WE WARNED YOU THIS WOULDN'T BE EASY.
THIS IS *SUPER EASY.*
OH YEAH? SHOW ME YOUR LINCOLN.
HERE HE IS. I MADE HIS HEAD INTO A LOG CABIN.
I'M IRRITATED IT SOMEHOW STILL LOOKS LIKE HIM.
NEEDS MORE *RESEARCH!*
HERE YOU GO, CARTOONIST!
HOW CLOSE DID YOU GET?
KEEP YOUR PORTRAIT VERSION OR USE THE REFERENCE AND LET'S DRAW HIM SAYING SOMETHING.
CHALLENGE
LINCOLN SAYS
HAZ LEVEL 3
"AMERICA WILL NEVER BE DESTROYED FROM THE OUTSIDE.
IF WE FALTER AND LOSE OUR FREEDOMS, IT WILL BE BECAUSE WE DESTROYED OURSELVES."
HECK OF A QUOTE.

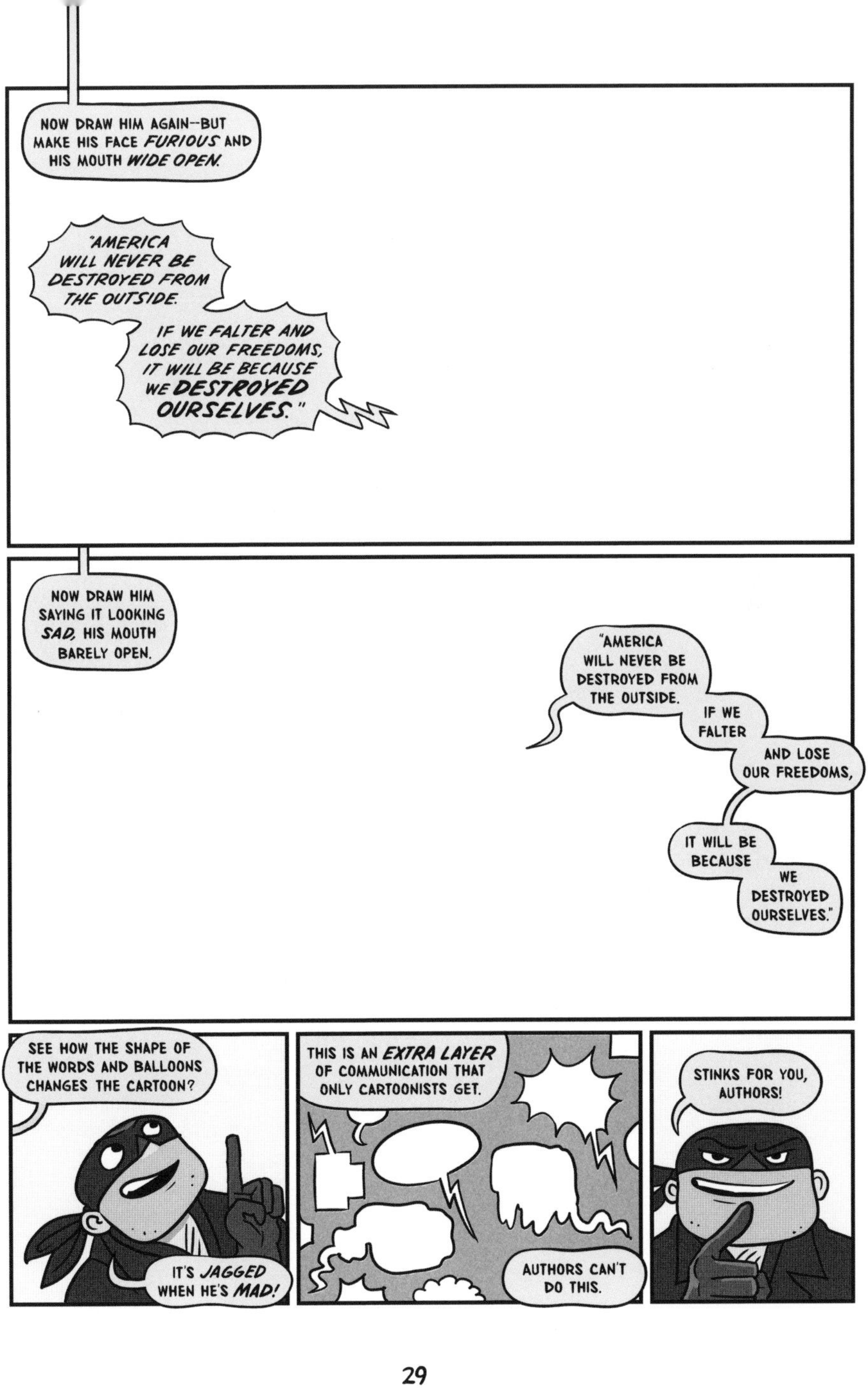
NOW DRAW HIM AGAIN--BUT MAKE HIS FACE *FURIOUS* AND HIS MOUTH *WIDE OPEN.*
"AMERICA WILL NEVER BE DESTROYED FROM THE OUTSIDE.
IF WE FALTER AND LOSE OUR FREEDOMS, IT WILL BE BECAUSE WE ***DESTROYED OURSELVES."***
NOW DRAW HIM SAYING IT LOOKING *SAD,* HIS MOUTH BARELY OPEN.
"AMERICA WILL NEVER BE DESTROYED FROM THE OUTSIDE.
IF WE FALTER
AND LOSE OUR FREEDOMS,
IT WILL BE BECAUSE
WE DESTROYED OURSELVES."
SEE HOW THE SHAPE OF THE WORDS AND BALLOONS CHANGES THE CARTOON?
IT'S *JAGGED* WHEN HE'S *MAD!*
THIS IS AN *EXTRA LAYER* OF COMMUNICATION THAT ONLY CARTOONISTS GET.
AUTHORS CAN'T DO THIS.
STINKS FOR YOU, AUTHORS!

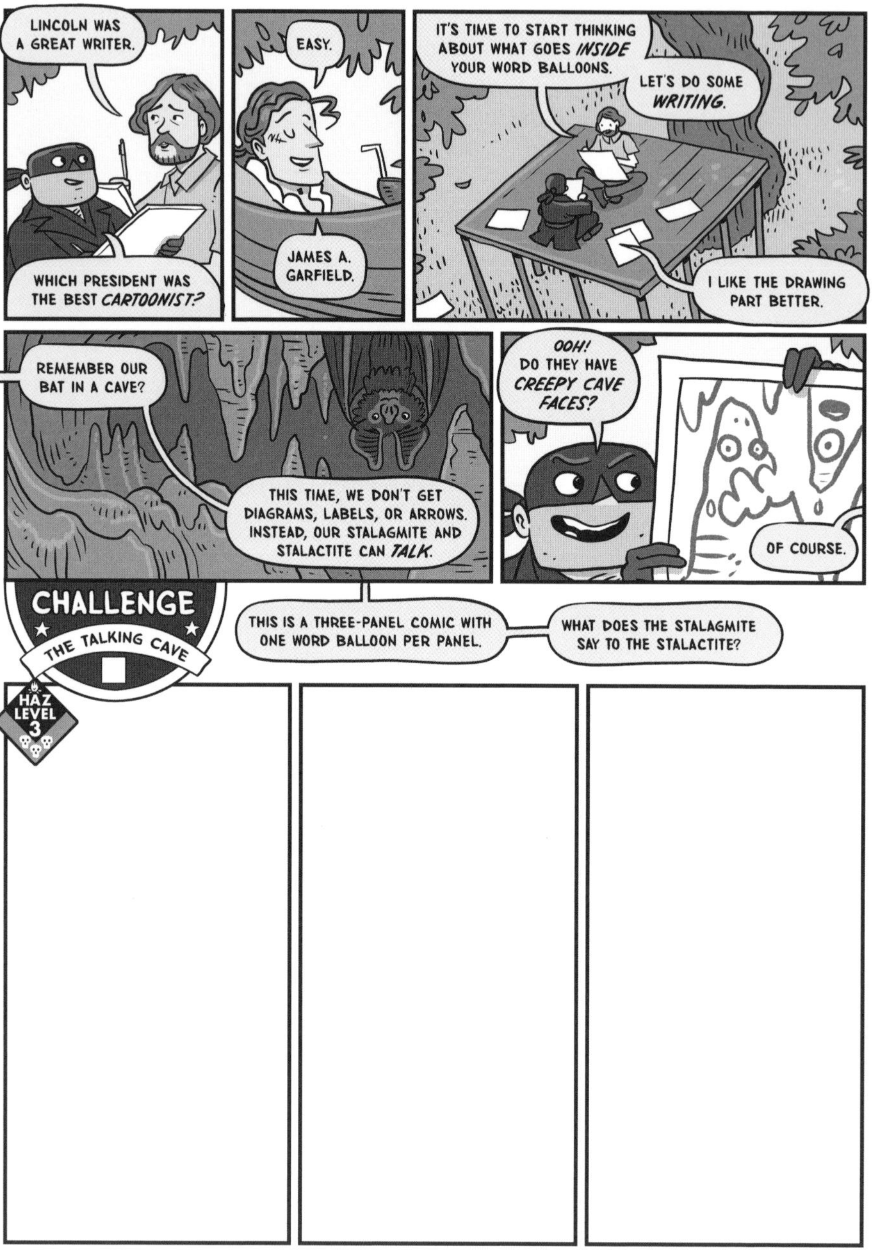

LINCOLN WAS A GREAT WRITER.
WHICH PRESIDENT WAS THE BEST *CARTOONIST?*
EASY.
JAMES A. GARFIELD.
IT'S TIME TO START THINKING ABOUT WHAT GOES *INSIDE* YOUR WORD BALLOONS.
LET'S DO SOME *WRITING.*
I LIKE THE DRAWING PART BETTER.
REMEMBER OUR BAT IN A CAVE?
THIS TIME, WE DON'T GET DIAGRAMS, LABELS, OR ARROWS. INSTEAD, OUR STALAGMITE AND STALACTITE CAN *TALK.*
OOH! DO THEY HAVE *CREEPY CAVE FACES?*
OF COURSE.
CHALLENGE
THE TALKING CAVE
HAZ LEVEL 3
THIS IS A THREE-PANEL COMIC WITH ONE WORD BALLOON PER PANEL.
WHAT DOES THE STALAGMITE SAY TO THE STALACTITE?

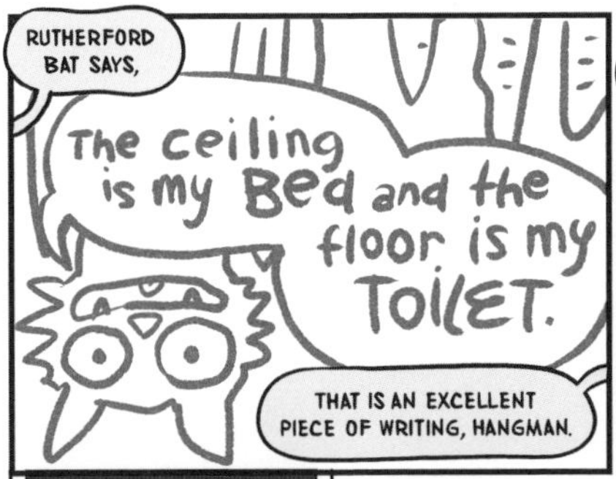
RUTHERFORD BAT SAYS,
The ceiling is my Bed and the floor is my TOILET.
THAT IS AN EXCELLENT PIECE OF WRITING, HANGMAN.

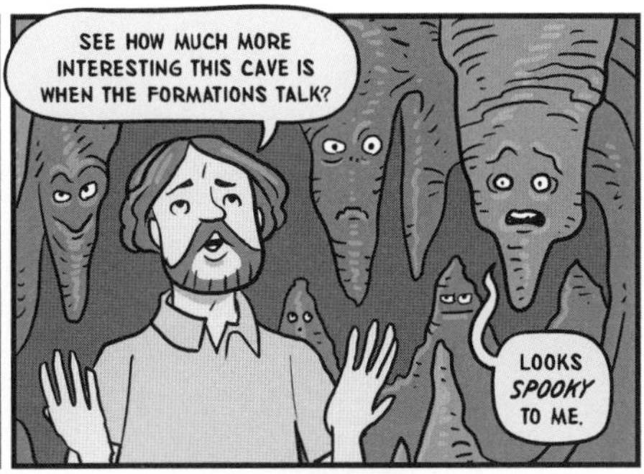
SEE HOW MUCH MORE INTERESTING THIS CAVE IS WHEN THE FORMATIONS TALK?
LOOKS *SPOOKY* TO ME.

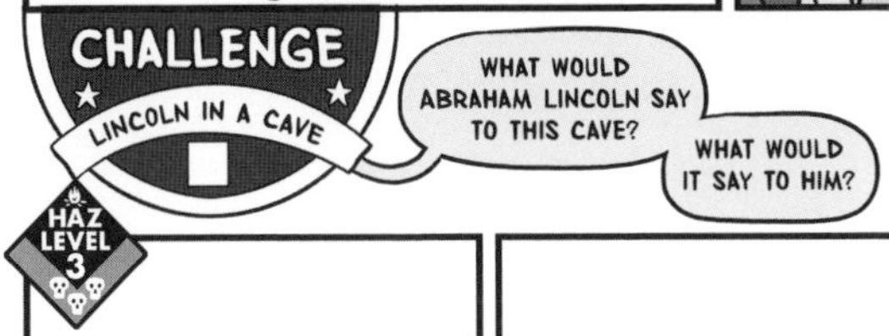
CHALLENGE
LINCOLN IN A CAVE
HAZ LEVEL 3
WHAT WOULD ABRAHAM LINCOLN SAY TO THIS CAVE?
WHAT WOULD IT SAY TO HIM?

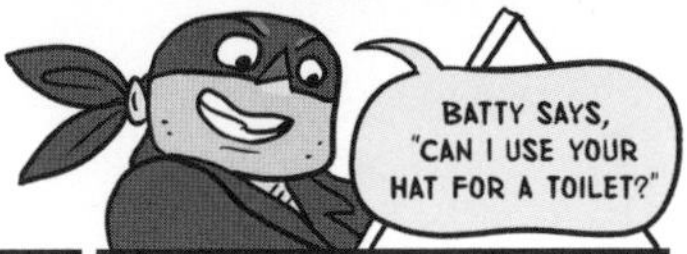
BATTY SAYS, "CAN I USE YOUR HAT FOR A TOILET?"

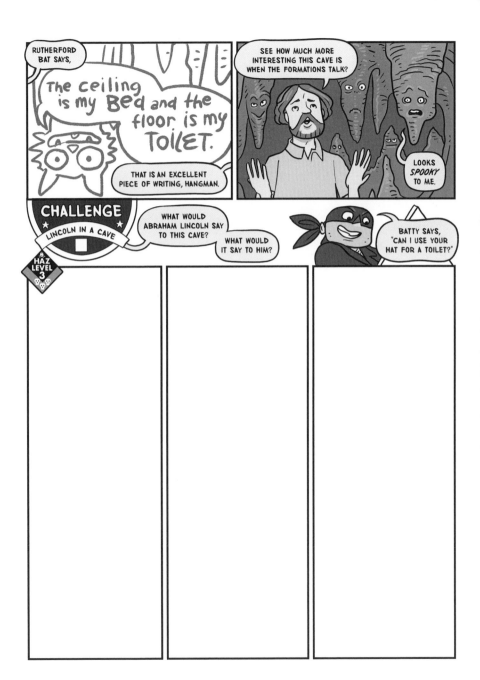

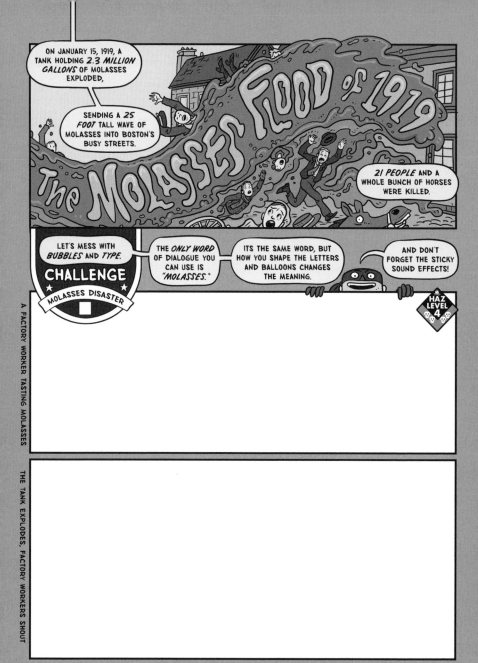

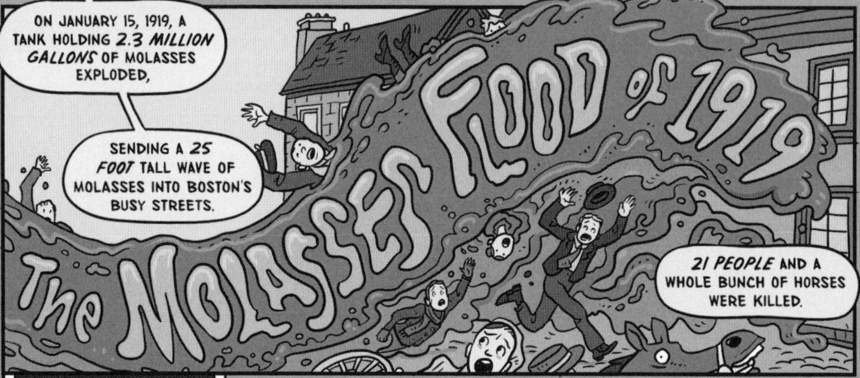
ON JANUARY 15, 1919, A TANK HOLDING 2.3 MILLION GALLONS OF MOLASSES EXPLODED,
SENDING A 25 FOOT TALL WAVE OF MOLASSES INTO BOSTON'S BUSY STREETS.
The Molasses Flood of 1919
21 PEOPLE AND A WHOLE BUNCH OF HORSES WERE KILLED.

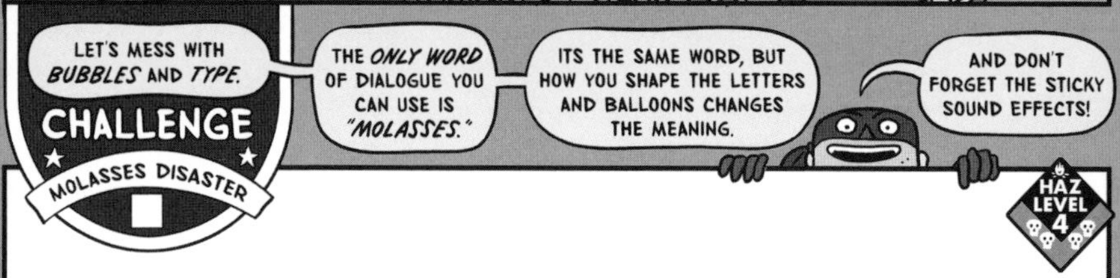
LET'S MESS WITH BUBBLES AND TYPE.
CHALLENGE
MOLASSES DISASTER
THE ONLY WORD OF DIALOGUE YOU CAN USE IS "MOLASSES."
ITS THE SAME WORD, BUT HOW YOU SHAPE THE LETTERS AND BALLOONS CHANGES THE MEANING.
AND DON'T FORGET THE STICKY SOUND EFFECTS!
HAZ LEVEL 4

A FACTORY WORKER TASTING MOLASSES

THE TANK EXPLODES, FACTORY WORKERS SHOUT

THE WAVE HITS A BUSY STREET, CIVILIANS ARE CONFUSED

AN ELEVATED TRAIN COLLAPSES INTO THE GOO

SURVIVORS LOOK AT THE AFTERMATH

THE END

I DREW A GIANT ABRAHAM LINCOLN EATING ALL THE MOLASSES.
THAT'S NOT HISTORICALLY *ACCURATE!*

CARTOONIST, DRAW A GIANT ABRAHAM LINCOLN BATTLING THE MOLASSES.
CHALLENGE
MOLASSES VS. LINCOLN
HAZ LEVEL 3
MAKE SURE THE PEOPLE AND THE GIANT LINCOLN HAVE *DIALOGUE!*
AND GIVE THE *MOLASSES* SOMETHING TO SAY TOO.

THE END

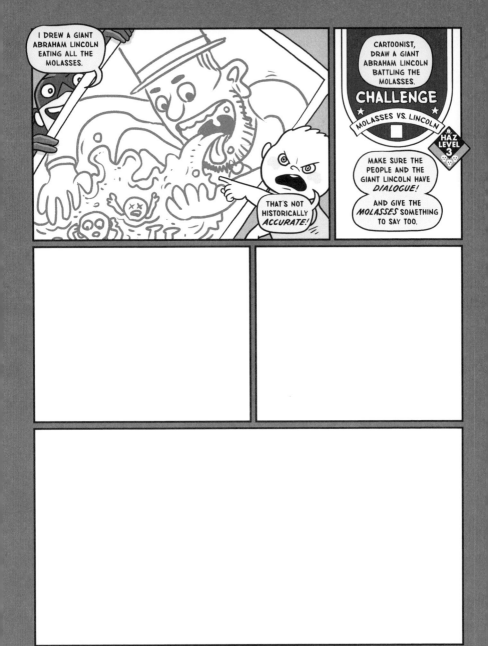

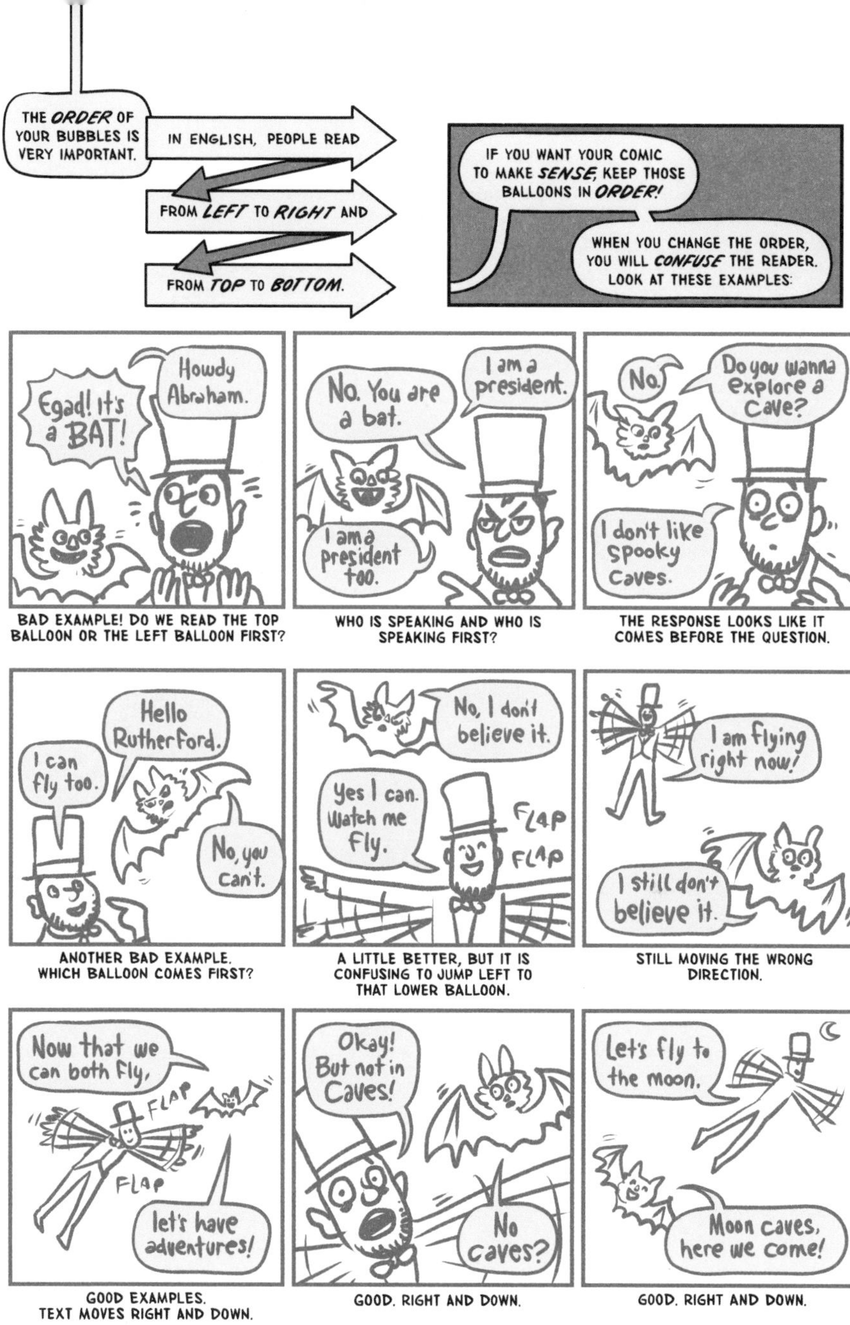
THE *ORDER* OF YOUR BUBBLES IS VERY IMPORTANT.
IN ENGLISH, PEOPLE READ
FROM *LEFT* TO *RIGHT* AND
FROM *TOP* TO *BOTTOM*.
IF YOU WANT YOUR COMIC TO MAKE *SENSE*, KEEP THOSE BALLOONS IN *ORDER!*
WHEN YOU CHANGE THE ORDER, YOU WILL *CONFUSE* THE READER. LOOK AT THESE EXAMPLES:
Egad! It's a BAT!
Howdy Abraham.
BAD EXAMPLE! DO WE READ THE TOP BALLOON OR THE LEFT BALLOON FIRST?
No. You are a bat.
I am a president.
I am a president too.
WHO IS SPEAKING AND WHO IS SPEAKING FIRST?
No.
Do you wanna explore a cave?
I don't like spooky caves.
THE RESPONSE LOOKS LIKE IT COMES BEFORE THE QUESTION.
I can fly too.
Hello Rutherford.
No, you can't.
ANOTHER BAD EXAMPLE. WHICH BALLOON COMES FIRST?
No, I don't believe it.
Yes I can. Watch me fly.
FLAP
FLAP
A LITTLE BETTER, BUT IT IS CONFUSING TO JUMP LEFT TO THAT LOWER BALLOON.
I am flying right now!
I still don't believe it.
STILL MOVING THE WRONG DIRECTION.
Now that we can both fly,
FLAP
FLAP
let's have adventures!
GOOD EXAMPLES. TEXT MOVES RIGHT AND DOWN.
Okay! But not in caves!
No caves?
GOOD. RIGHT AND DOWN.
Let's fly to the moon.
Moon caves, here we come!
GOOD. RIGHT AND DOWN.

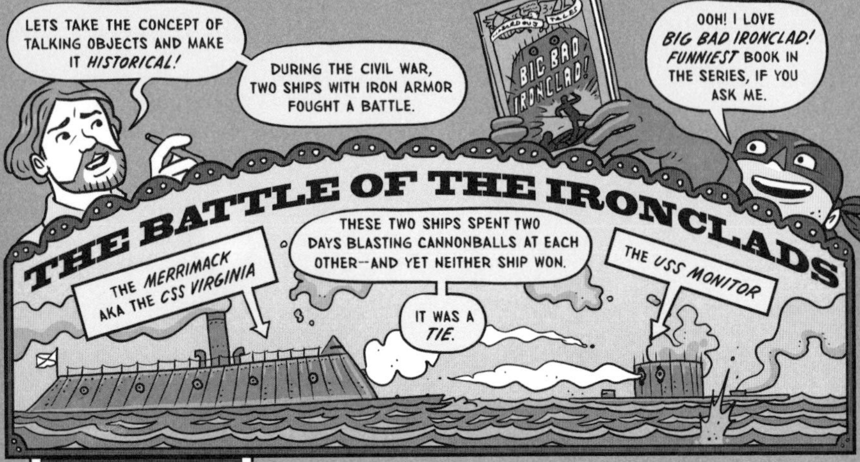

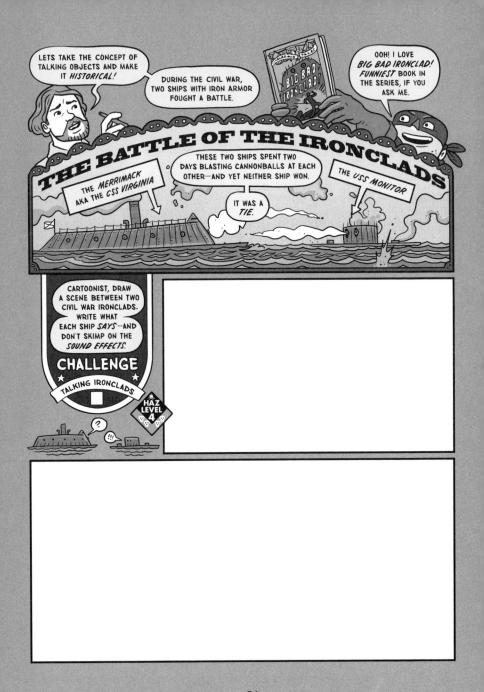

LETS TAKE THE CONCEPT OF TALKING OBJECTS AND MAKE IT *HISTORICAL!*
DURING THE CIVIL WAR, TWO SHIPS WITH IRON ARMOR FOUGHT A BATTLE.
BIG BAD IRONCLAD!
OOH! I LOVE *BIG BAD IRONCLAD! FUNNIEST* BOOK IN THE SERIES, IF YOU ASK ME.
THE BATTLE OF THE IRONCLADS
THE *MERRIMACK* AKA THE *CSS VIRGINIA*
THESE TWO SHIPS SPENT TWO DAYS BLASTING CANNONBALLS AT EACH OTHER--AND YET NEITHER SHIP WON.
IT WAS A *TIE*.
THE *USS MONITOR*

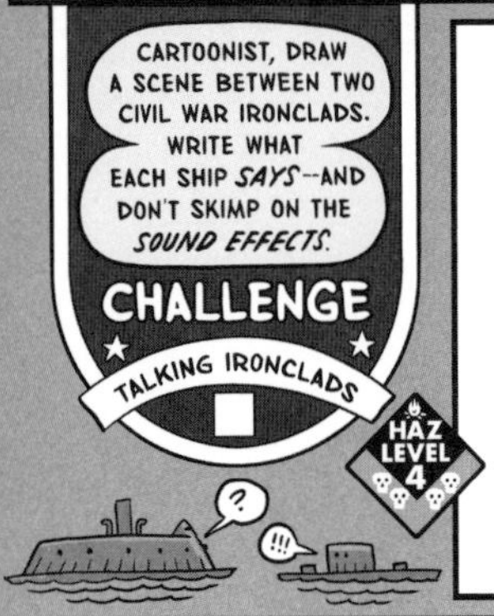

CARTOONIST, DRAW A SCENE BETWEEN TWO CIVIL WAR IRONCLADS. WRITE WHAT EACH SHIP *SAYS*--AND DON'T SKIMP ON THE *SOUND EFFECTS*.
CHALLENGE
TALKING IRONCLADS
HAZ LEVEL 4
?
!!!

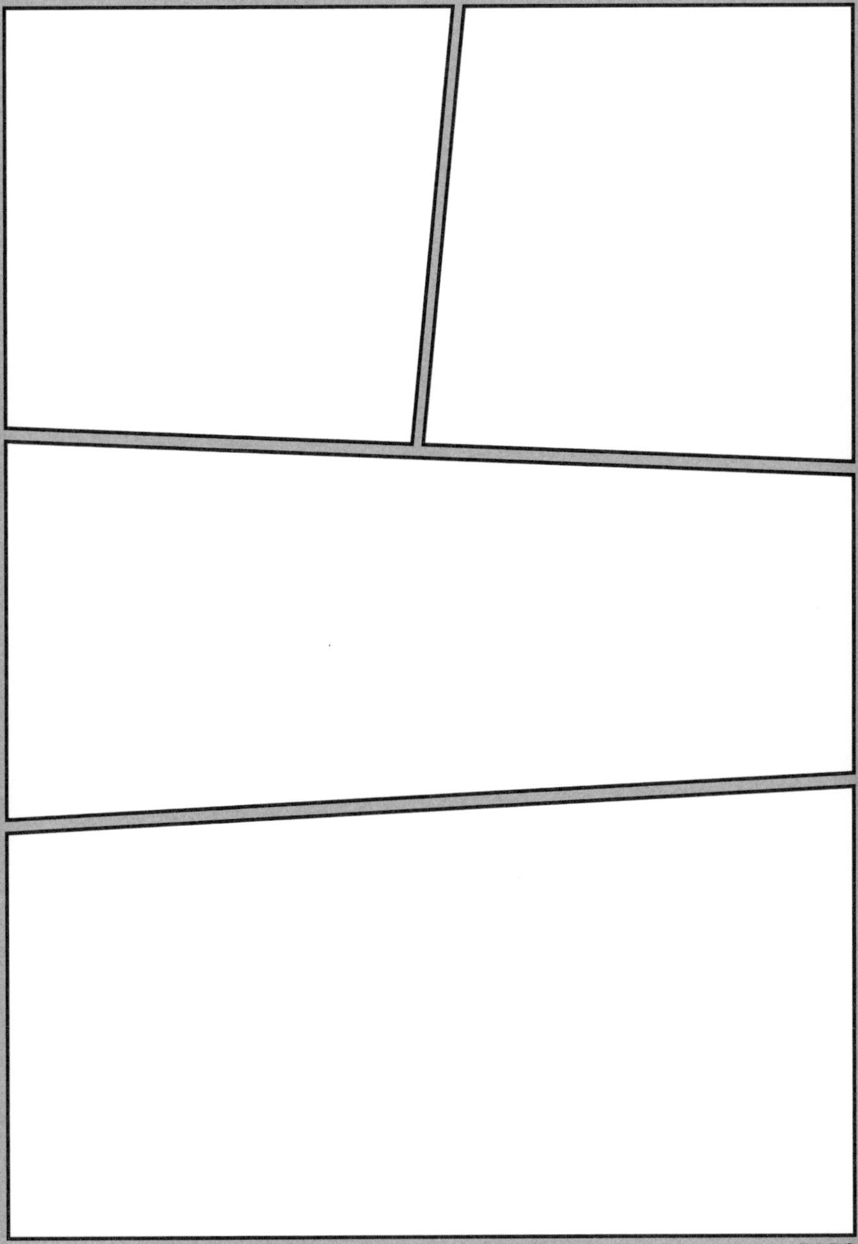

THE END

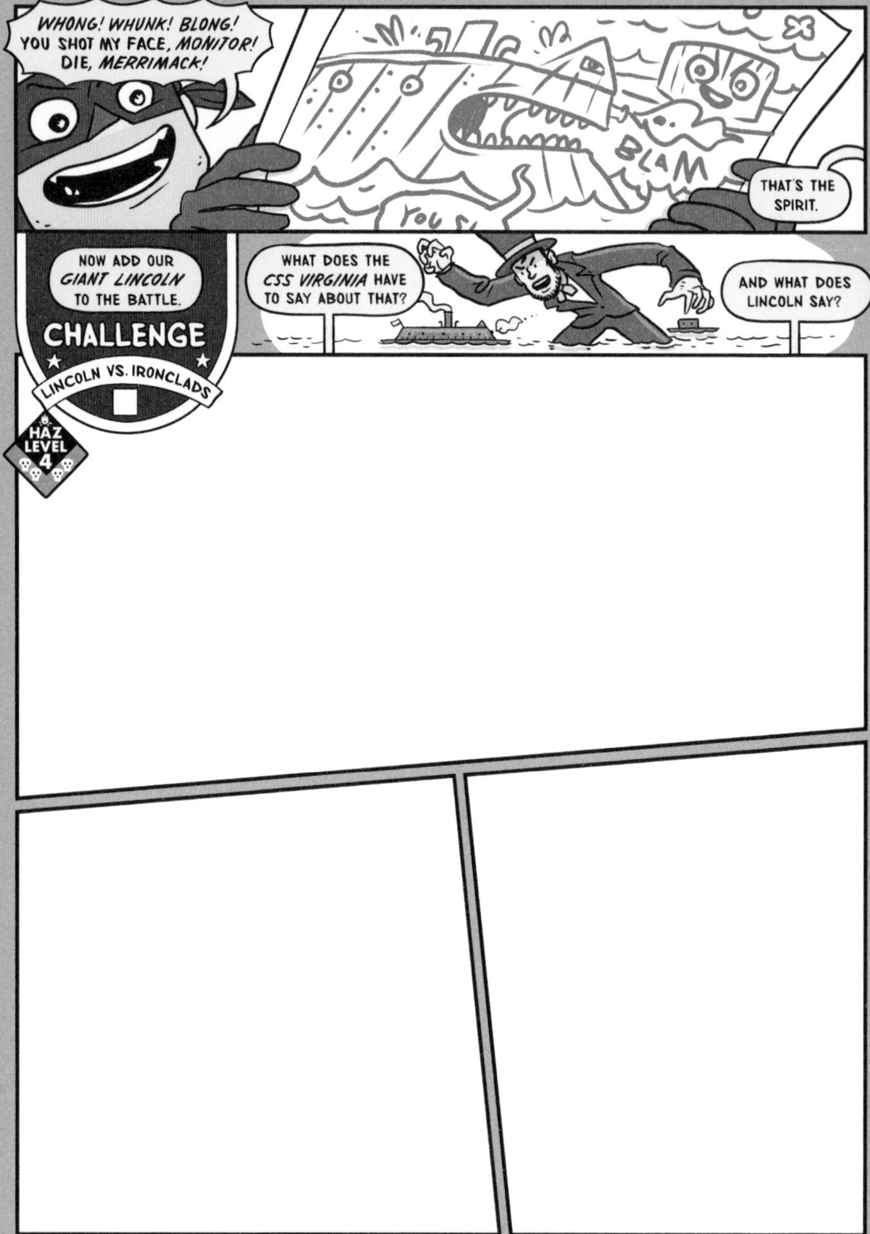

WHONG! WHUNK! BLONG! YOU SHOT MY FACE, *MONITOR*! DIE, *MERRIMACK*!
BLAM
THAT'S THE SPIRIT.
NOW ADD OUR *GIANT LINCOLN* TO THE BATTLE.
CHALLENGE
LINCOLN VS. IRONCLADS
HAZ LEVEL 4
WHAT DOES THE *CSS VIRGINIA* HAVE TO SAY ABOUT THAT?
AND WHAT DOES LINCOLN SAY?

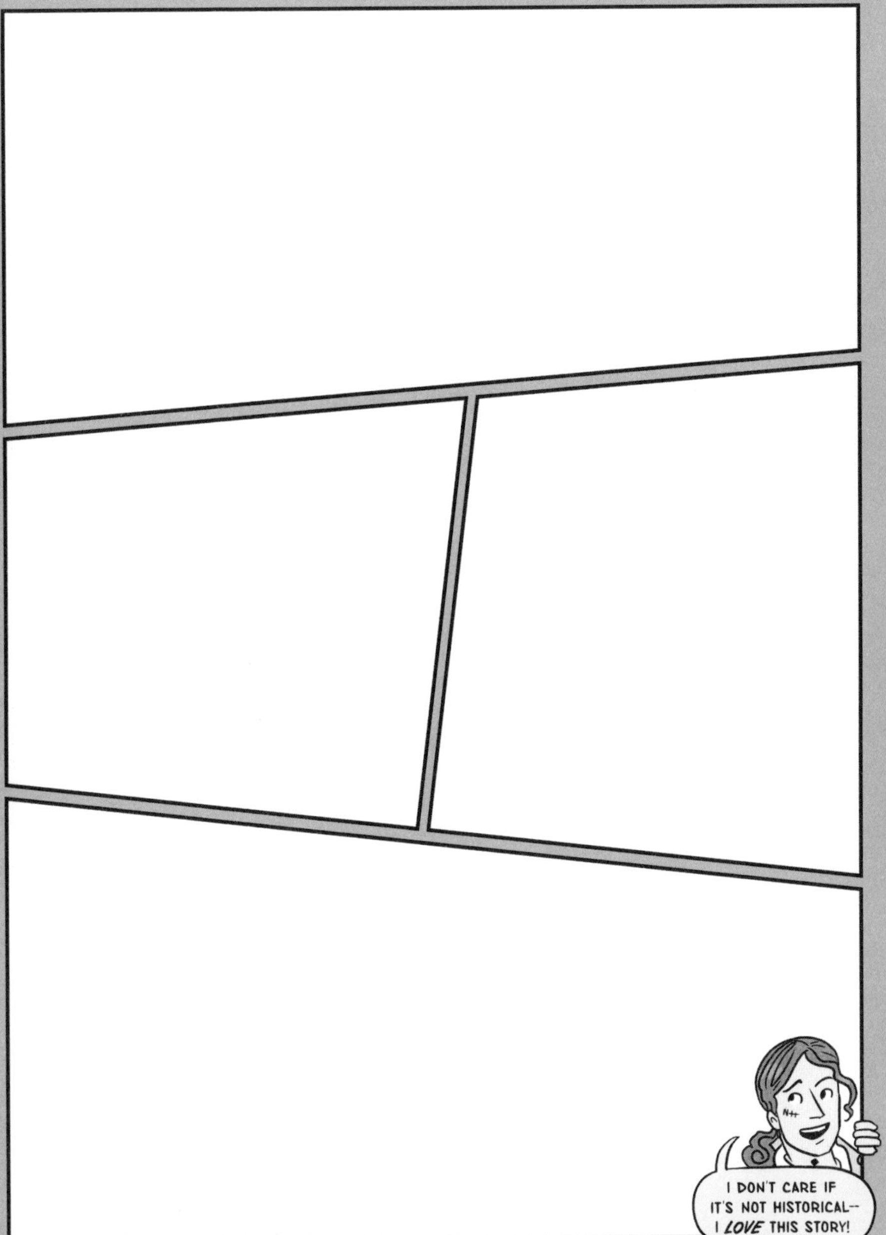
I DON'T CARE IF IT'S NOT HISTORICAL-- I *LOVE* THIS STORY!

THE END

DRAW AN IRONCLAD ABRAHAM LINCOLN.

CHALLENGE

★ IRON ABRAHAM ★

HAZ LEVEL 2

ABE IN A SUIT OF *ARMOR?*

ABE AS A *METAL MAN?*

ABE AS A *METAL BOAT?*

USE YOUR *IMAGINATION!*

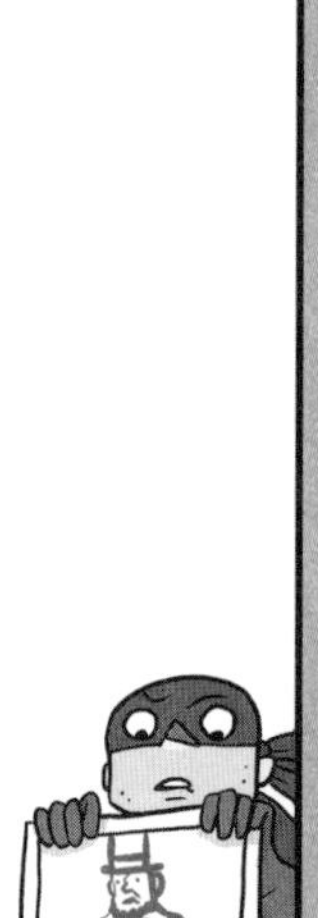

I DREW LINCOLN IRONING A SHIRT.

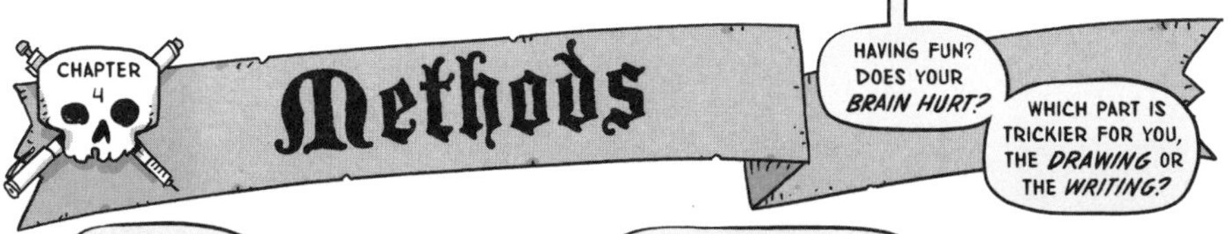
CHAPTER 4
Methods
HAVING FUN? DOES YOUR BRAIN HURT?
WHICH PART IS TRICKIER FOR YOU, THE DRAWING OR THE WRITING?

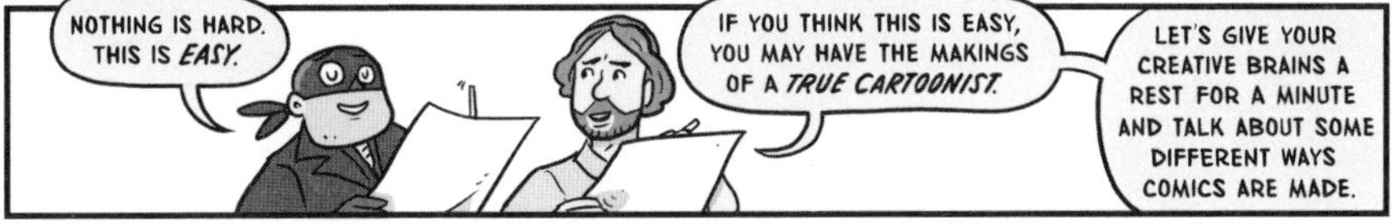
NOTHING IS HARD. THIS IS EASY.
IF YOU THINK THIS IS EASY, YOU MAY HAVE THE MAKINGS OF A TRUE CARTOONIST.
LET'S GIVE YOUR CREATIVE BRAINS A REST FOR A MINUTE AND TALK ABOUT SOME DIFFERENT WAYS COMICS ARE MADE.

THE AMERICAN SUPER METHOD

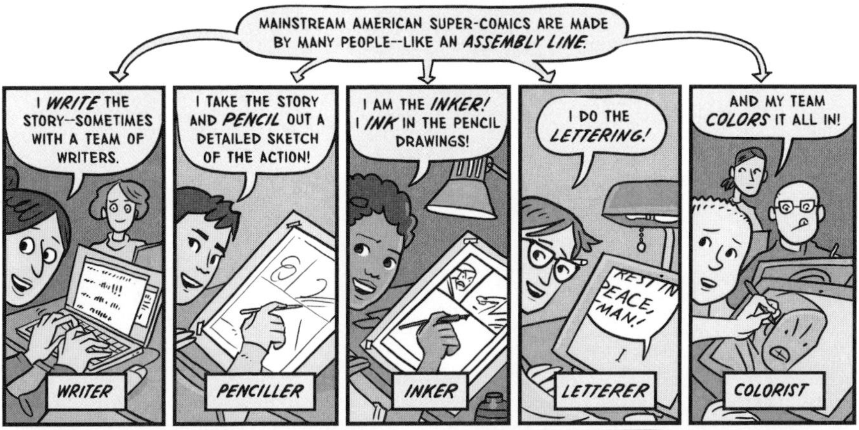
MAINSTREAM AMERICAN SUPER-COMICS ARE MADE BY MANY PEOPLE--LIKE AN ASSEMBLY LINE.
I WRITE THE STORY--SOMETIMES WITH A TEAM OF WRITERS.
WRITER
I TAKE THE STORY AND PENCIL OUT A DETAILED SKETCH OF THE ACTION!
PENCILLER
I AM THE INKER! I INK IN THE PENCIL DRAWINGS!
INKER
I DO THE LETTERING!
REST IN PEACE, MAN!
LETTERER
AND MY TEAM COLORS IT ALL IN!
COLORIST

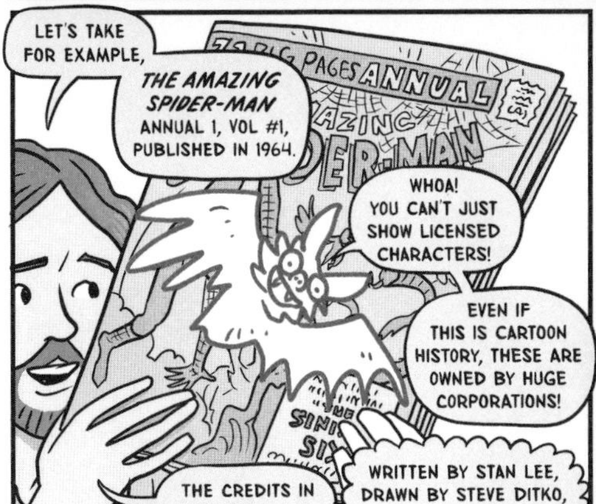
LET'S TAKE FOR EXAMPLE,
THE AMAZING SPIDER-MAN ANNUAL 1, VOL #1, PUBLISHED IN 1964.
PAGES ANNUAL
WHOA! YOU CAN'T JUST SHOW LICENSED CHARACTERS!
EVEN IF THIS IS CARTOON HISTORY, THESE ARE OWNED BY HUGE CORPORATIONS!
THE CREDITS IN THIS ISSUE SAY:
WRITTEN BY STAN LEE, DRAWN BY STEVE DITKO, LETTERED BY SAM ROSEN, COLORED BY A. YANCHUS.

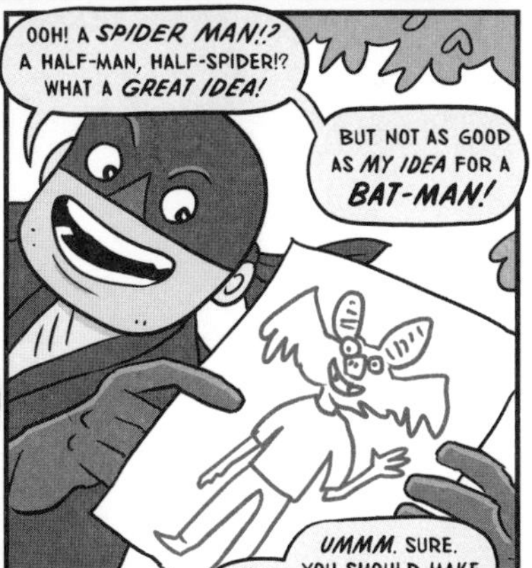
OOH! A SPIDER MAN!? A HALF-MAN, HALF-SPIDER!? WHAT A GREAT IDEA!
BUT NOT AS GOOD AS MY IDEA FOR A BAT-MAN!
UMMM. SURE. YOU SHOULD MAKE THAT CHARACTER.

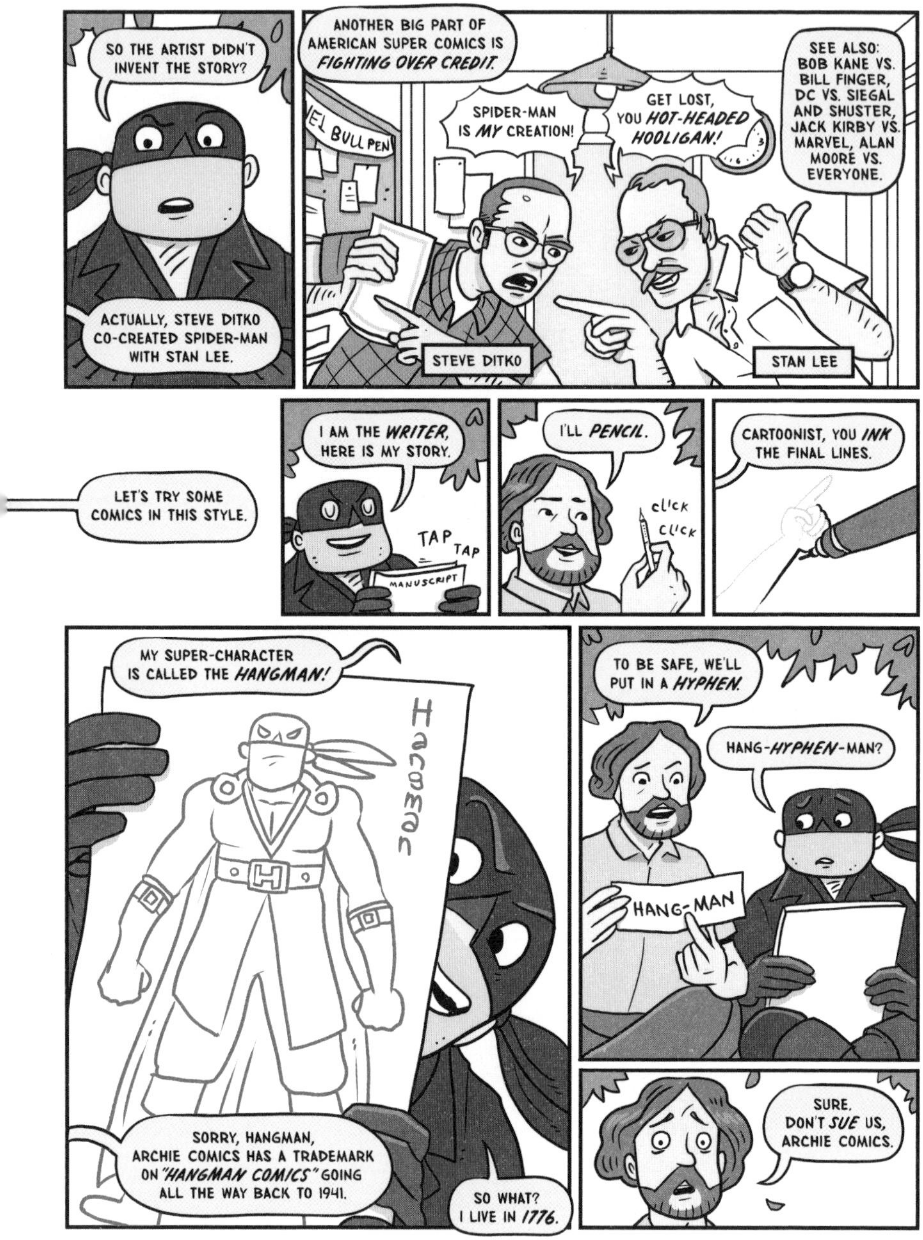
SO THE ARTIST DIDN'T INVENT THE STORY?
ACTUALLY, STEVE DITKO CO-CREATED SPIDER-MAN WITH STAN LEE.
ANOTHER BIG PART OF AMERICAN SUPER COMICS IS *FIGHTING OVER CREDIT.*
EL BULLPEN
SPIDER-MAN IS *MY* CREATION!
GET LOST, YOU *HOT-HEADED HOOLIGAN!*
SEE ALSO: BOB KANE VS. BILL FINGER, DC VS. SIEGAL AND SHUSTER, JACK KIRBY VS. MARVEL, ALAN MOORE VS. EVERYONE.
STEVE DITKO
STAN LEE
LET'S TRY SOME COMICS IN THIS STYLE.
I AM THE *WRITER,* HERE IS MY STORY.
TAP TAP
MANUSCRIPT
I'LL *PENCIL.*
CLICK CLICK
CARTOONIST, YOU *INK* THE FINAL LINES.
MY SUPER-CHARACTER IS CALLED THE *HANGMAN!*
HANGMAN
SORRY, HANGMAN, ARCHIE COMICS HAS A TRADEMARK ON *"HANGMAN COMICS"* GOING ALL THE WAY BACK TO 1941.
SO WHAT? I LIVE IN *1776.*
TO BE SAFE, WE'LL PUT IN A *HYPHEN.*
HANG-*HYPHEN*-MAN?
HANG-MAN
SURE. DON'T *SUE* US, ARCHIE COMICS.

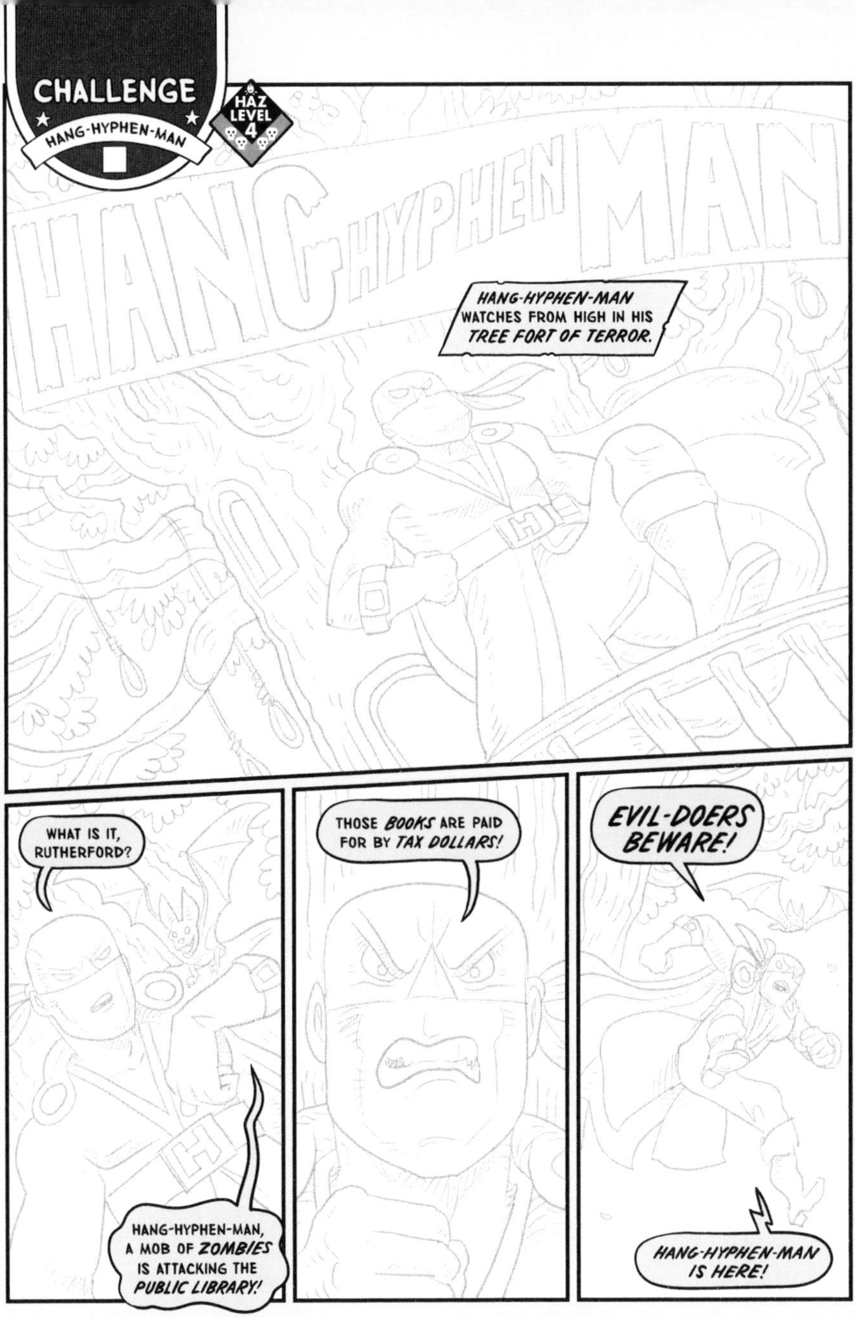
CHALLENGE
HANG-HYPHEN-MAN
HAZ LEVEL 4
HANG-HYPHEN-MAN
HANG-HYPHEN-MAN WATCHES FROM HIGH IN HIS TREE FORT OF TERROR.
WHAT IS IT, RUTHERFORD?
HANG-HYPHEN-MAN, A MOB OF ZOMBIES IS ATTACKING THE PUBLIC LIBRARY!
THOSE BOOKS ARE PAID FOR BY TAX DOLLARS!
EVIL-DOERS BEWARE!
HANG-HYPHEN-MAN IS HERE!

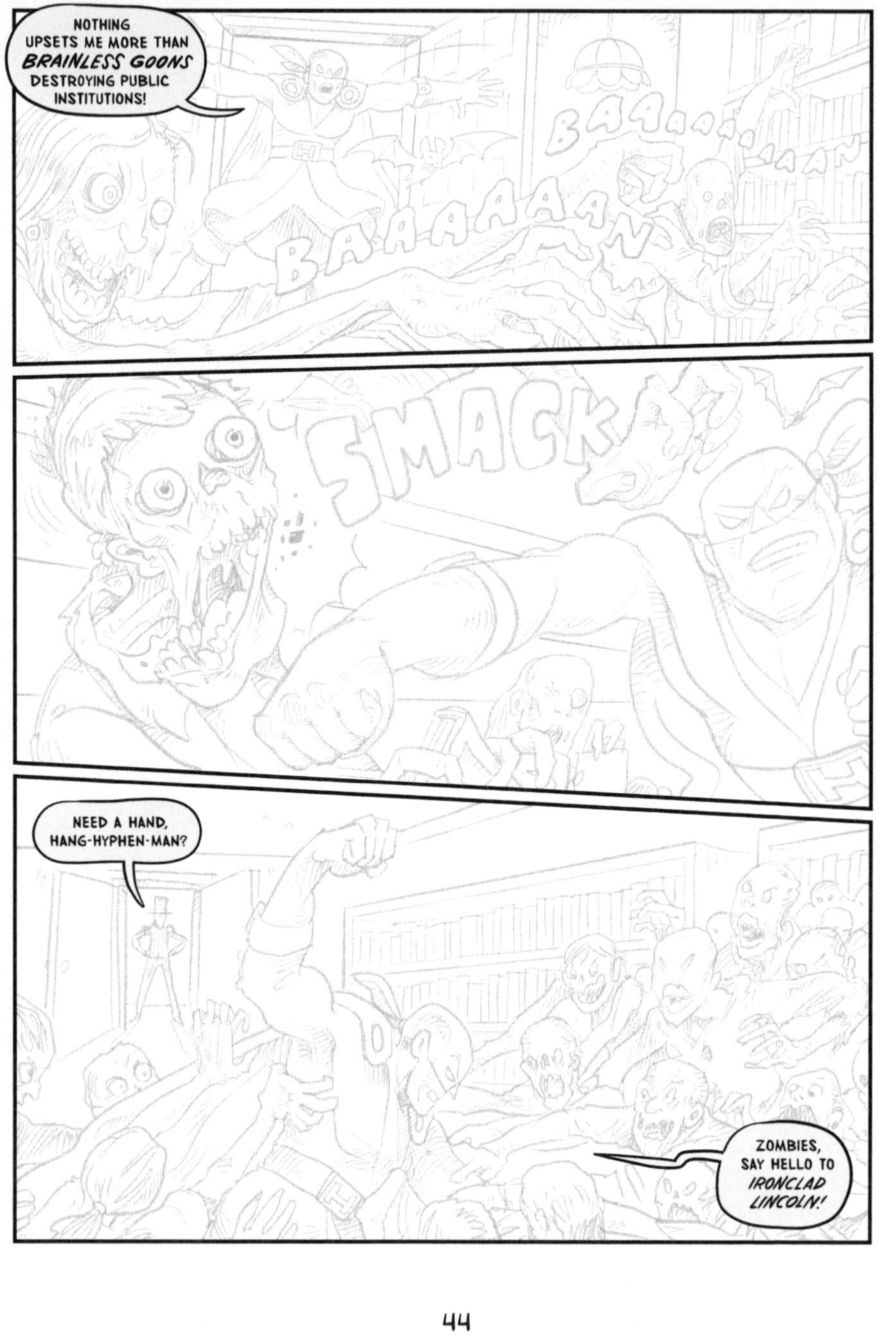
NOTHING UPSETS ME MORE THAN *BRAINLESS GOONS* DESTROYING PUBLIC INSTITUTIONS!
BAAAAAAN
SMACK
NEED A HAND, HANG-HYPHEN-MAN?
ZOMBIES, SAY HELLO TO *IRONCLAD LINCOLN!*

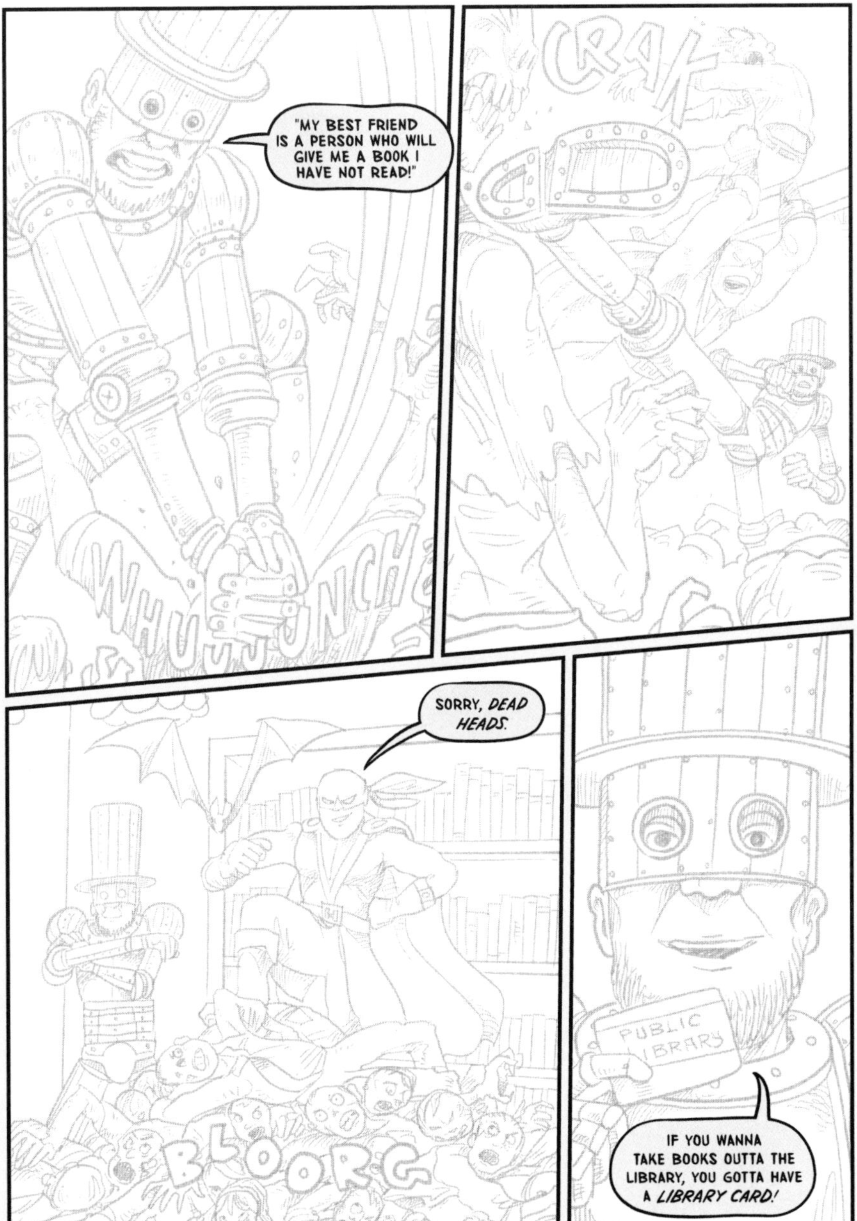
"MY BEST FRIEND IS A PERSON WHO WILL GIVE ME A BOOK I HAVE NOT READ!"
CRAK
SORRY, *DEAD HEADS.*
BLOORG
PUBLIC LIBRARY
IF YOU WANNA TAKE BOOKS OUTTA THE LIBRARY, YOU GOTTA HAVE A *LIBRARY CARD!*

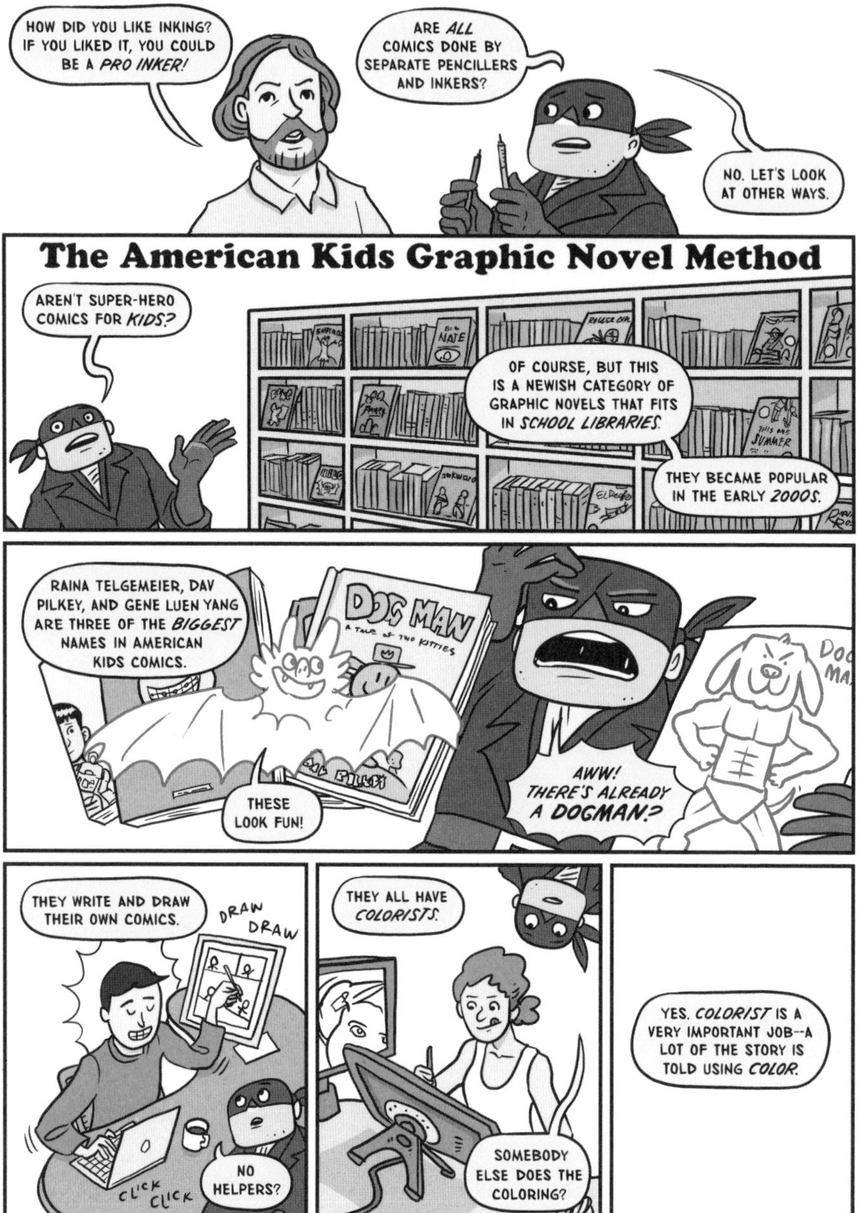
HOW DID YOU LIKE INKING? IF YOU LIKED IT, YOU COULD BE A *PRO INKER!*
ARE *ALL* COMICS DONE BY SEPARATE PENCILLERS AND INKERS?
NO. LET'S LOOK AT OTHER WAYS.
The American Kids Graphic Novel Method
AREN'T SUPER-HERO COMICS FOR *KIDS?*
OF COURSE, BUT THIS IS A NEWISH CATEGORY OF GRAPHIC NOVELS THAT FITS IN *SCHOOL LIBRARIES.*
THEY BECAME POPULAR IN THE EARLY *2000S.*
RAINA TELGEMEIER, DAV PILKEY, AND GENE LUEN YANG ARE THREE OF THE *BIGGEST* NAMES IN AMERICAN KIDS COMICS.
DOG MAN
THESE LOOK FUN!
AWW! THERE'S ALREADY A **DOGMAN?**
THEY WRITE AND DRAW THEIR OWN COMICS.
DRAW DRAW
CLICK CLICK
NO HELPERS?
THEY ALL HAVE *COLORISTS.*
SOMEBODY ELSE DOES THE COLORING?
YES. *COLORIST* IS A VERY IMPORTANT JOB--A LOT OF THE STORY IS TOLD USING *COLOR.*

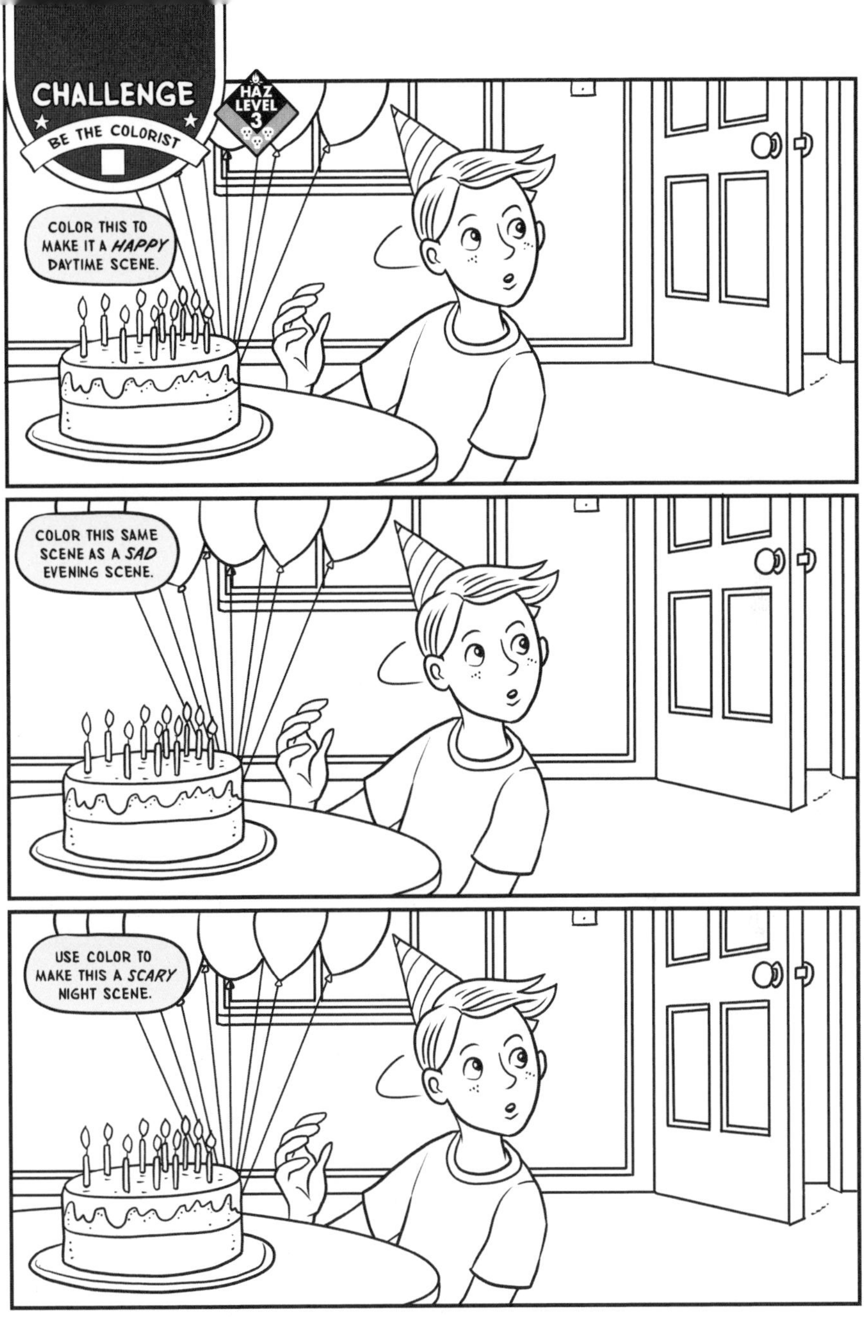
CHALLENGE
BE THE COLORIST
HAZ LEVEL 3
COLOR THIS TO MAKE IT A *HAPPY* DAYTIME SCENE.
COLOR THIS SAME SCENE AS A *SAD* EVENING SCENE.
USE COLOR TO MAKE THIS A *SCARY* NIGHT SCENE.

The Manga Method

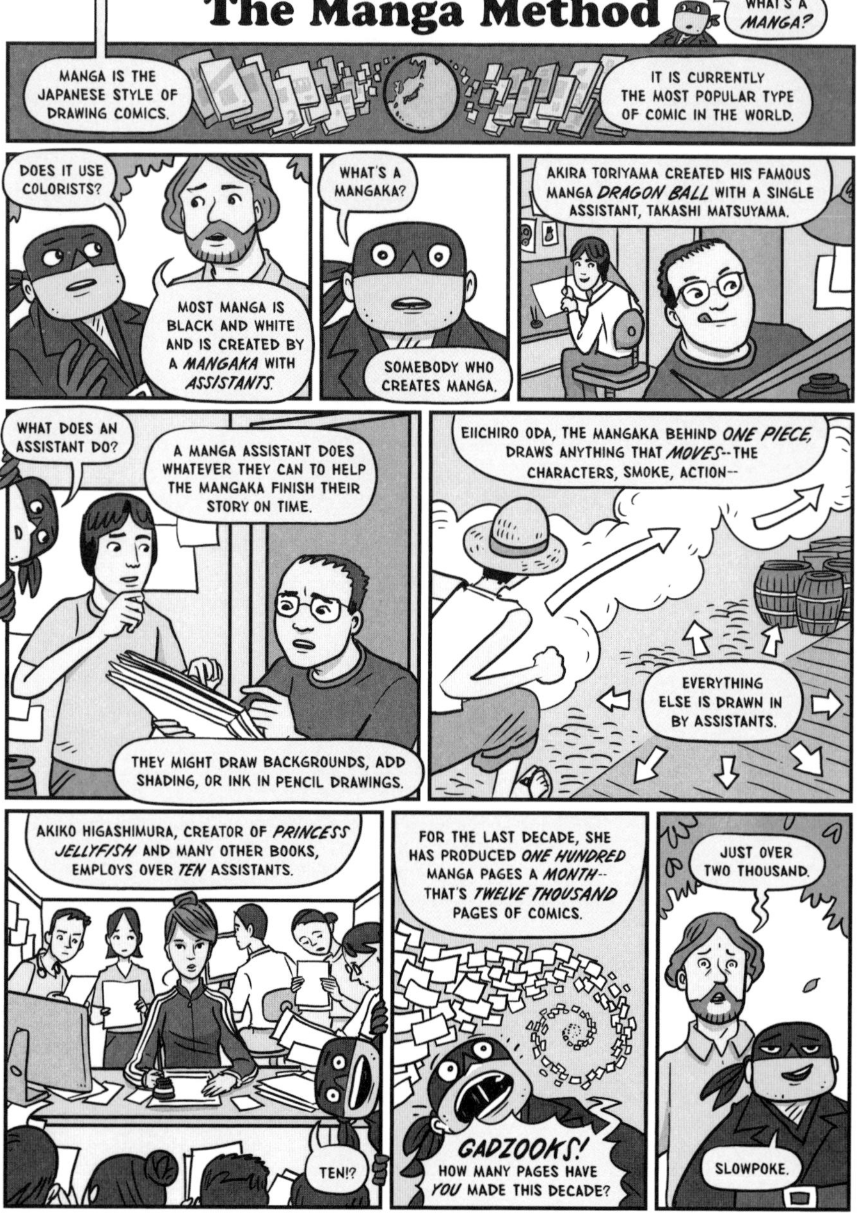

WHAT'S A *MANGA?*
MANGA IS THE JAPANESE STYLE OF DRAWING COMICS.
IT IS CURRENTLY THE MOST POPULAR TYPE OF COMIC IN THE WORLD.
DOES IT USE COLORISTS?
MOST MANGA IS BLACK AND WHITE AND IS CREATED BY A *MANGAKA* WITH *ASSISTANTS.*
WHAT'S A MANGAKA?
SOMEBODY WHO CREATES MANGA.
AKIRA TORIYAMA CREATED HIS FAMOUS MANGA *DRAGON BALL* WITH A SINGLE ASSISTANT, TAKASHI MATSUYAMA.
WHAT DOES AN ASSISTANT DO?
A MANGA ASSISTANT DOES WHATEVER THEY CAN TO HELP THE MANGAKA FINISH THEIR STORY ON TIME.
THEY MIGHT DRAW BACKGROUNDS, ADD SHADING, OR INK IN PENCIL DRAWINGS.
EIICHIRO ODA, THE MANGAKA BEHIND *ONE PIECE,* DRAWS ANYTHING THAT *MOVES*--THE CHARACTERS, SMOKE, ACTION--
EVERYTHING ELSE IS DRAWN IN BY ASSISTANTS.
AKIKO HIGASHIMURA, CREATOR OF *PRINCESS JELLYFISH* AND MANY OTHER BOOKS, EMPLOYS OVER *TEN* ASSISTANTS.
TEN!?
FOR THE LAST DECADE, SHE HAS PRODUCED *ONE HUNDRED* MANGA PAGES A *MONTH*-- THAT'S *TWELVE THOUSAND* PAGES OF COMICS.
GADZOOKS!
HOW MANY PAGES HAVE *YOU* MADE THIS DECADE?
JUST OVER TWO THOUSAND.
SLOWPOKE.

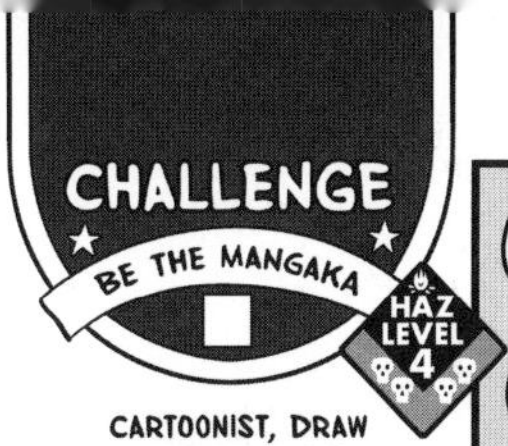

CHALLENGE
BE THE MANGAKA
HAZ LEVEL 4

CARTOONIST, DRAW ***IRONCLAD LINCOLN*** FIGHTING ***CHESTER ALLIGATOR ARTHUR*** *KAIJU STYLE* IN *NEO-TOKYO.*

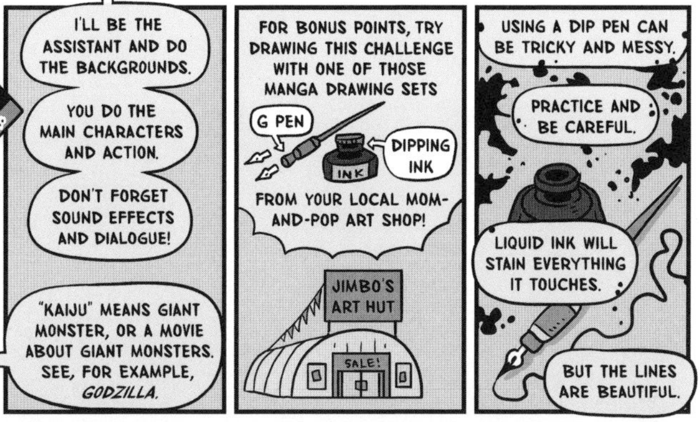

I'LL BE THE ASSISTANT AND DO THE BACKGROUNDS.
YOU DO THE MAIN CHARACTERS AND ACTION.
DON'T FORGET SOUND EFFECTS AND DIALOGUE!
"KAIJU" MEANS GIANT MONSTER, OR A MOVIE ABOUT GIANT MONSTERS. SEE, FOR EXAMPLE, *GODZILLA.*
FOR BONUS POINTS, TRY DRAWING THIS CHALLENGE WITH ONE OF THOSE MANGA DRAWING SETS
G PEN
DIPPING INK
INK
FROM YOUR LOCAL MOM-AND-POP ART SHOP!
JIMBO'S ART HUT
SALE!
USING A DIP PEN CAN BE TRICKY AND MESSY.
PRACTICE AND BE CAREFUL.
LIQUID INK WILL STAIN EVERYTHING IT TOUCHES.
BUT THE LINES ARE BEAUTIFUL.

MANGA TITLE MAKER FIGURE OUT THE NAME OF YOUR MANGA, AND DRAW IT BELOW.

BIRTH MONTH
JAN--TOTAL
FEB--POWER
MARCH--LOST
APRIL--FIRE
MAY--GHOST
JUNE--FINAL
JULY--BEAUTIFUL
AUG--CROSS
SEPT--MEGA
OCT--STAR
NOV--MIDNIGHT
DEC--ULTIMATE

BIRTH DATE		
1--DRAGON	11--SPACE	22--BOX
2--FIGHT	12--SPY	23--EVENT
3--CASTLE	13--HAT	24--MONKEY
4--SCHOOL	14--BOOK	25--SLAM
5--WAVE	15--TIME	26--LUCK
6--CAT	16--TOWER	27--TIGER
7--VISION	17--BUNNY	28--BITE
8--COWBOY	18--BLOCK	29--MILLION
9--FINDER	19--BANANA	30--VAMPIRE
10--MAGIC	20--ROBO	31--PUNCH
	21--TRIP	

FAVORITE BREAKFAST
CEREAL--SAGA
PANCAKES--QUEST
WAFFLES--TEAM
EGGS--GAME
OMELETTE--TALE
YOGURT--TRICK
FRUIT--BLAST
CANDY--CLUB
MUFFINS--SOUL
OATMEAL--SWORD

HAIR COLOR
BLACK--Z
BROWN--D
RED--ONE
BLONDE--X
BALD--99

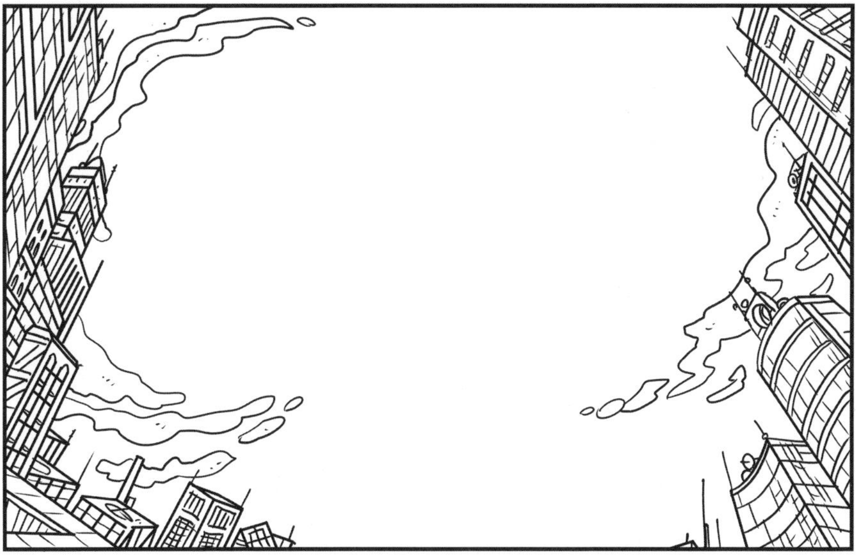

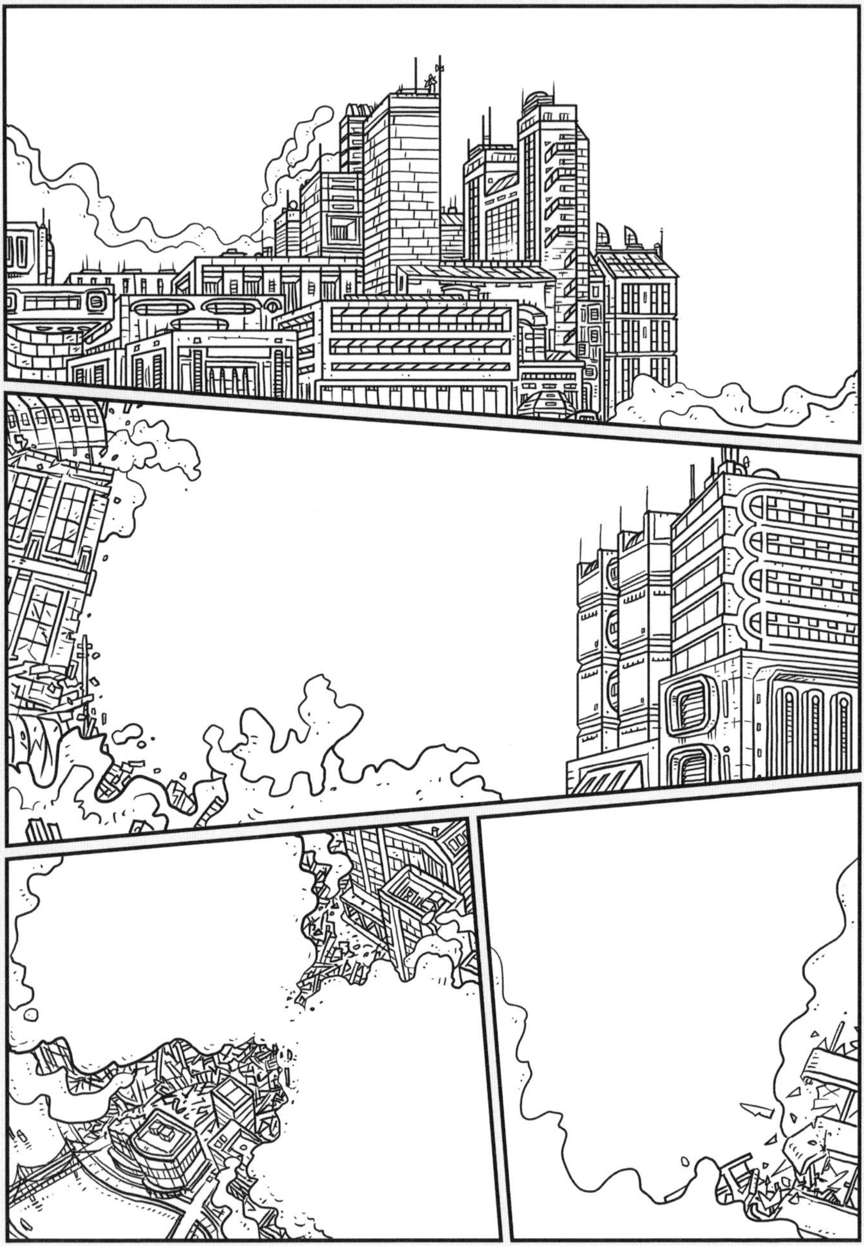

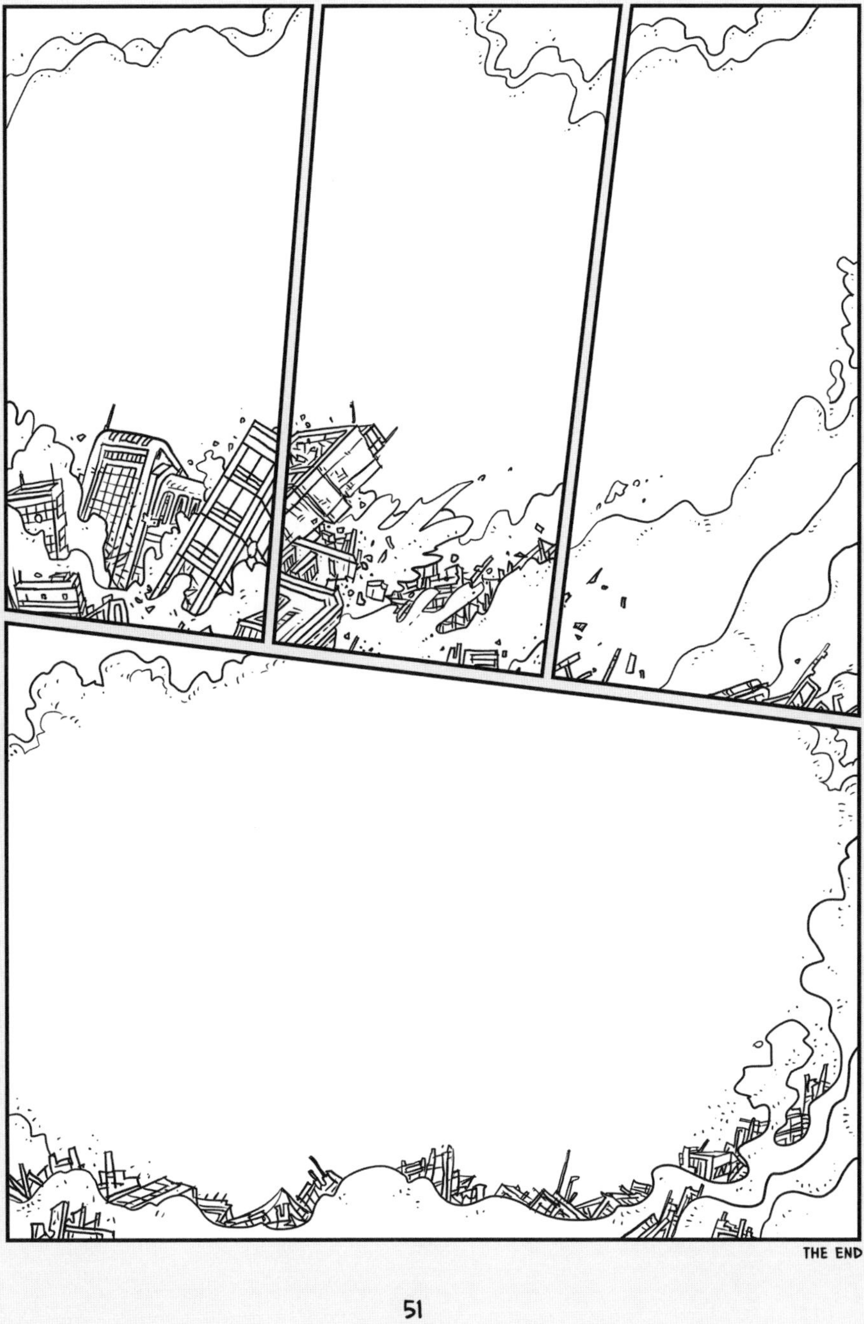

THE END

The Daily Strip Method

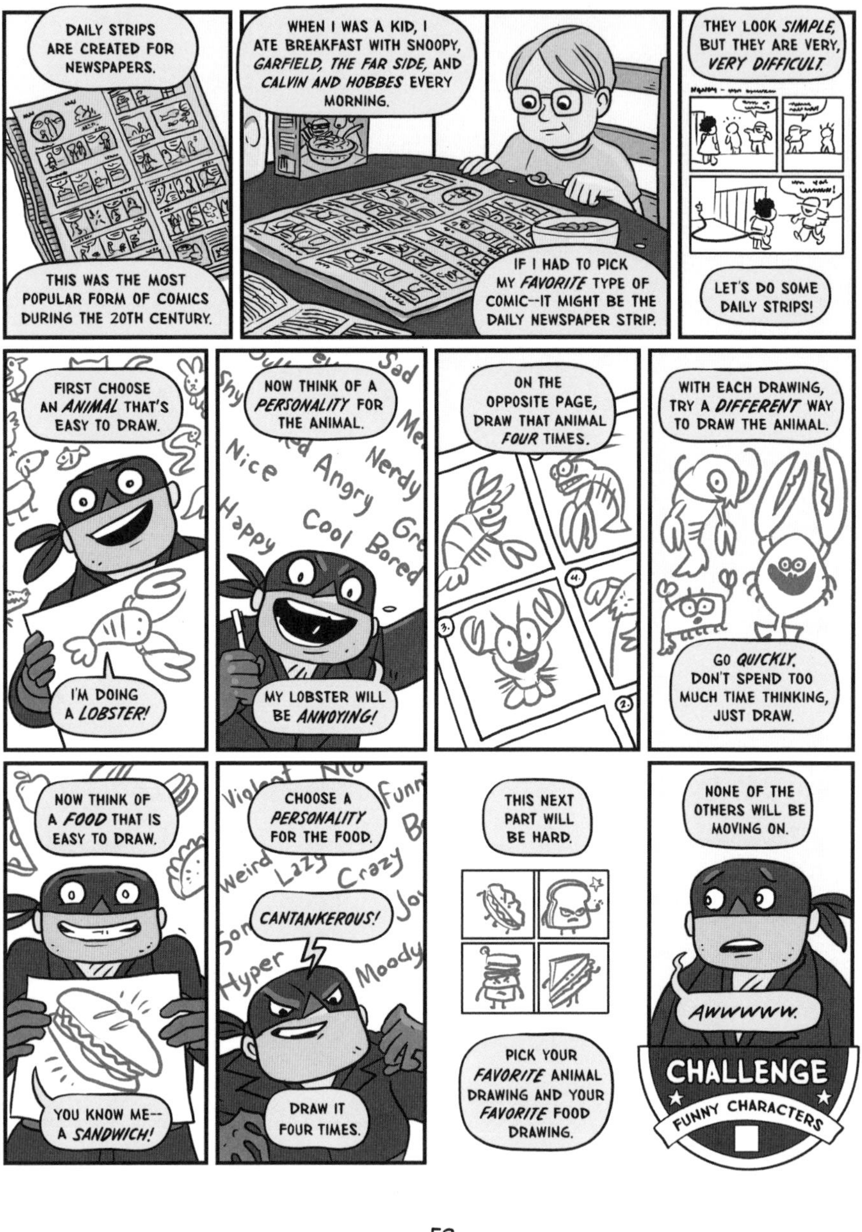
DAILY STRIPS ARE CREATED FOR NEWSPAPERS.
THIS WAS THE MOST POPULAR FORM OF COMICS DURING THE 20TH CENTURY.
WHEN I WAS A KID, I ATE BREAKFAST WITH SNOOPY, *GARFIELD, THE FAR SIDE,* AND *CALVIN AND HOBBES* EVERY MORNING.
IF I HAD TO PICK MY *FAVORITE* TYPE OF COMIC--IT MIGHT BE THE DAILY NEWSPAPER STRIP.
THEY LOOK *SIMPLE,* BUT THEY ARE VERY, *VERY DIFFICULT.*
LET'S DO SOME DAILY STRIPS!
FIRST CHOOSE AN *ANIMAL* THAT'S EASY TO DRAW.
I'M DOING A *LOBSTER!*
NOW THINK OF A *PERSONALITY* FOR THE ANIMAL.
Nice
Angry
Nerdy
Happy
Cool
Bored
Sad
MY LOBSTER WILL BE *ANNOYING!*
ON THE OPPOSITE PAGE, DRAW THAT ANIMAL *FOUR* TIMES.
WITH EACH DRAWING, TRY A *DIFFERENT* WAY TO DRAW THE ANIMAL.
GO *QUICKLY.* DON'T SPEND TOO MUCH TIME THINKING, JUST DRAW.
NOW THINK OF A *FOOD* THAT IS EASY TO DRAW.
YOU KNOW ME-- A *SANDWICH!*
CHOOSE A *PERSONALITY* FOR THE FOOD.
Weird
Lazy
Crazy
Hyper
Moody
CANTANKEROUS!
DRAW IT FOUR TIMES.
THIS NEXT PART WILL BE HARD.
PICK YOUR *FAVORITE* ANIMAL DRAWING AND YOUR *FAVORITE* FOOD DRAWING.
NONE OF THE OTHERS WILL BE MOVING ON.
AWWWWW.
CHALLENGE
FUNNY CHARACTERS

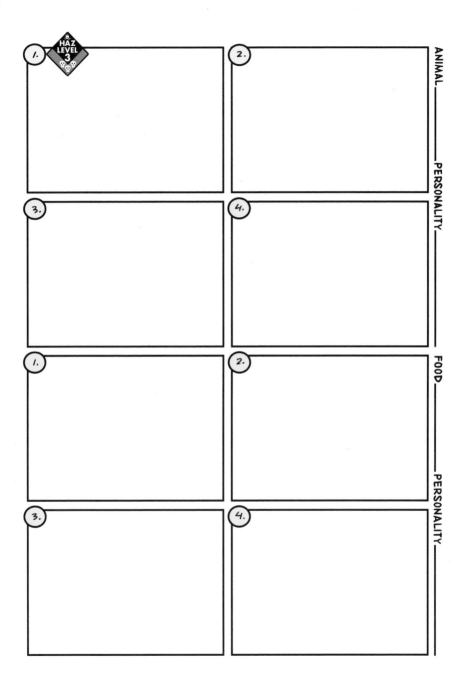

1.

2.

3.

4.

1.

2.

3.

4.

ANIMAL —————— PERSONALITY ——————

FOOD —————— PERSONALITY ——————

HAZ LEVEL 3

CHALLENGE

HAZ LEVEL 2

DRAW A FULL VERSION OF YOUR ANIMAL.

GIVE IT A NAME.

FIGURE OUT WHAT IT LOVES AND WHAT IT'S MOST AFRAID OF.

FRONT

BACK

NAME: _____

WHAT DOES IT *LOVE*: _____

WHAT IS IT *AFRAID OF*: _____

CHALLENGE

FOOD CHARACTER

HAZ LEVEL 2

DRAW YOUR FOOD CHARACTER.

IF YOU ARE HAVING TROUBLE THINKING OF A NAME,

ASK THE DRAWING AND LISTEN FOR AN ANSWER. IT WORKS.

FRONT	BACK

NAME: ______________________________

WHAT DOES IT ***LOVE:*** ______________________________

WHAT IS IT ***AFRAID OF:*** ______________________________

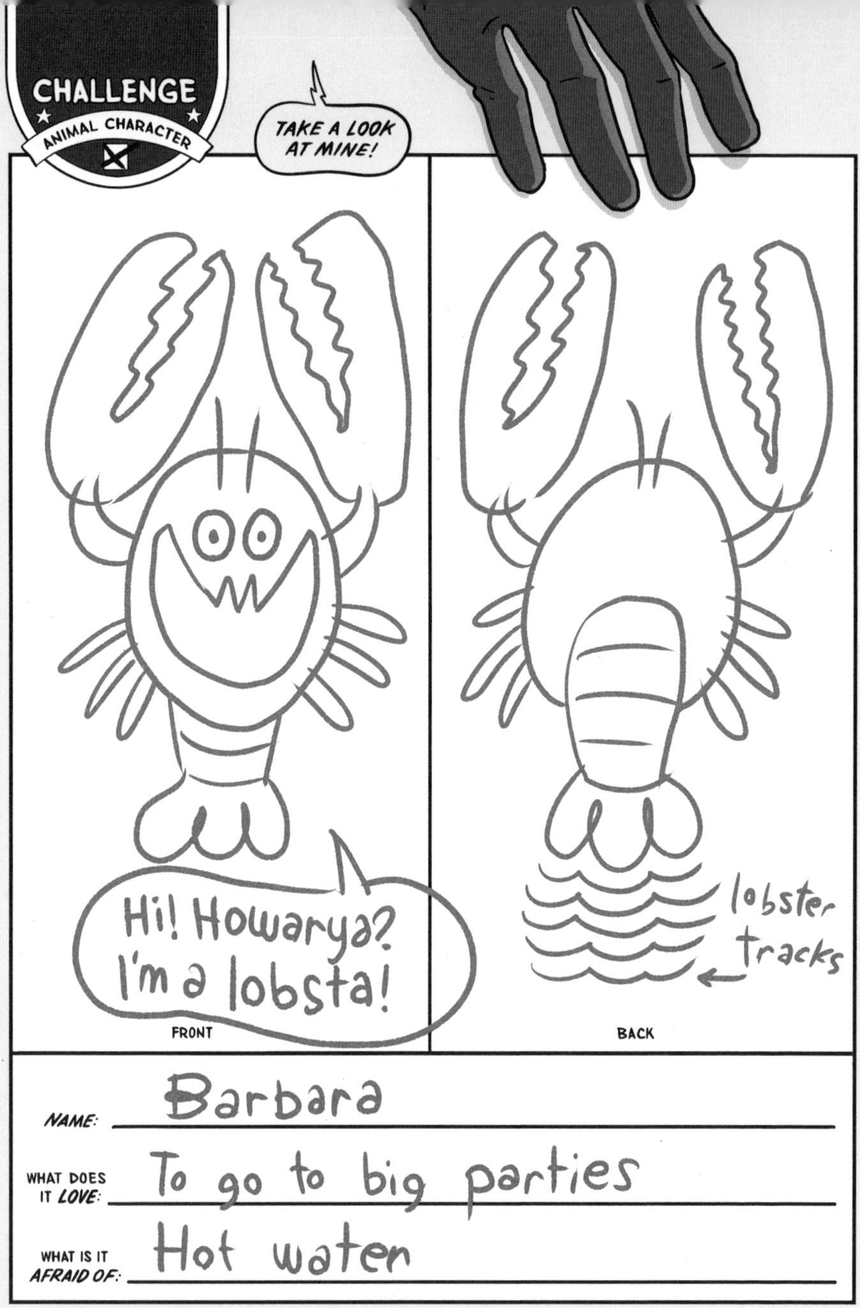
CHALLENGE
ANIMAL CHARACTER
TAKE A LOOK AT MINE!
Hi! Howarya? I'm a lobsta!
FRONT
lobster tracks
BACK
NAME: Barbara
WHAT DOES IT LOVE: To go to big parties
WHAT IS IT AFRAID OF: Hot water

CHALLENGE

★ FOOD CHARACTER ★

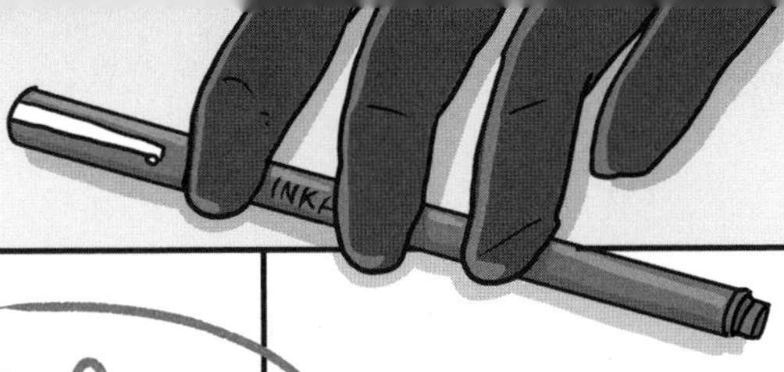

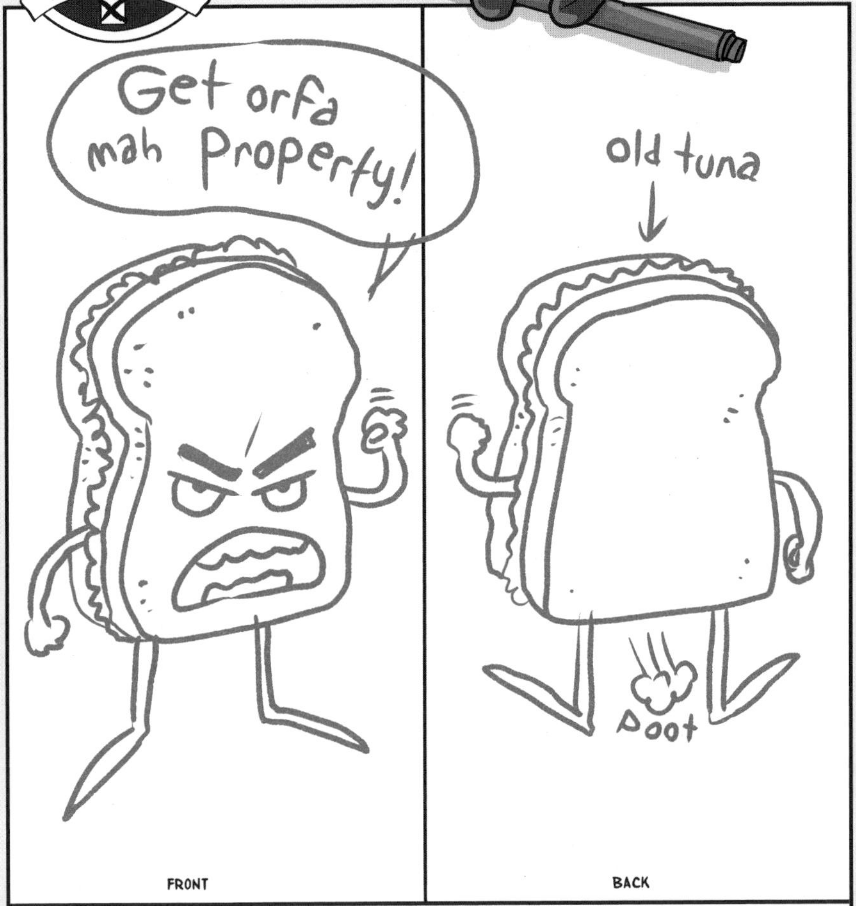
Get orfa mah Property!
old tuna
Poot
FRONT
BACK

NAME: Toop

WHAT DOES IT ***LOVE:*** His Property

WHAT IS IT ***AFRAID OF:*** Alien Invasion

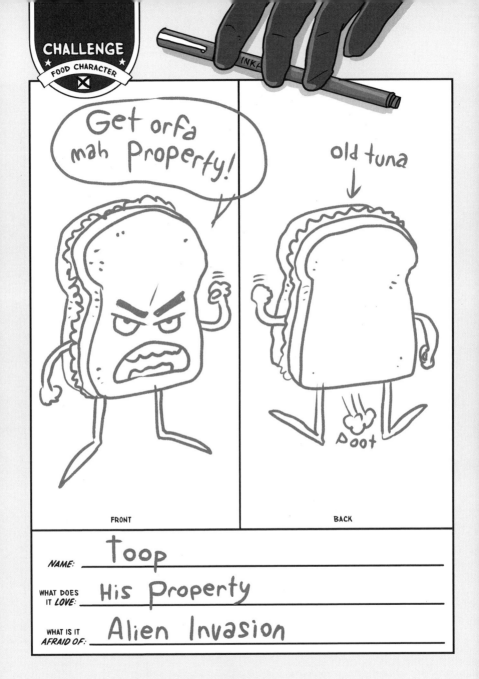

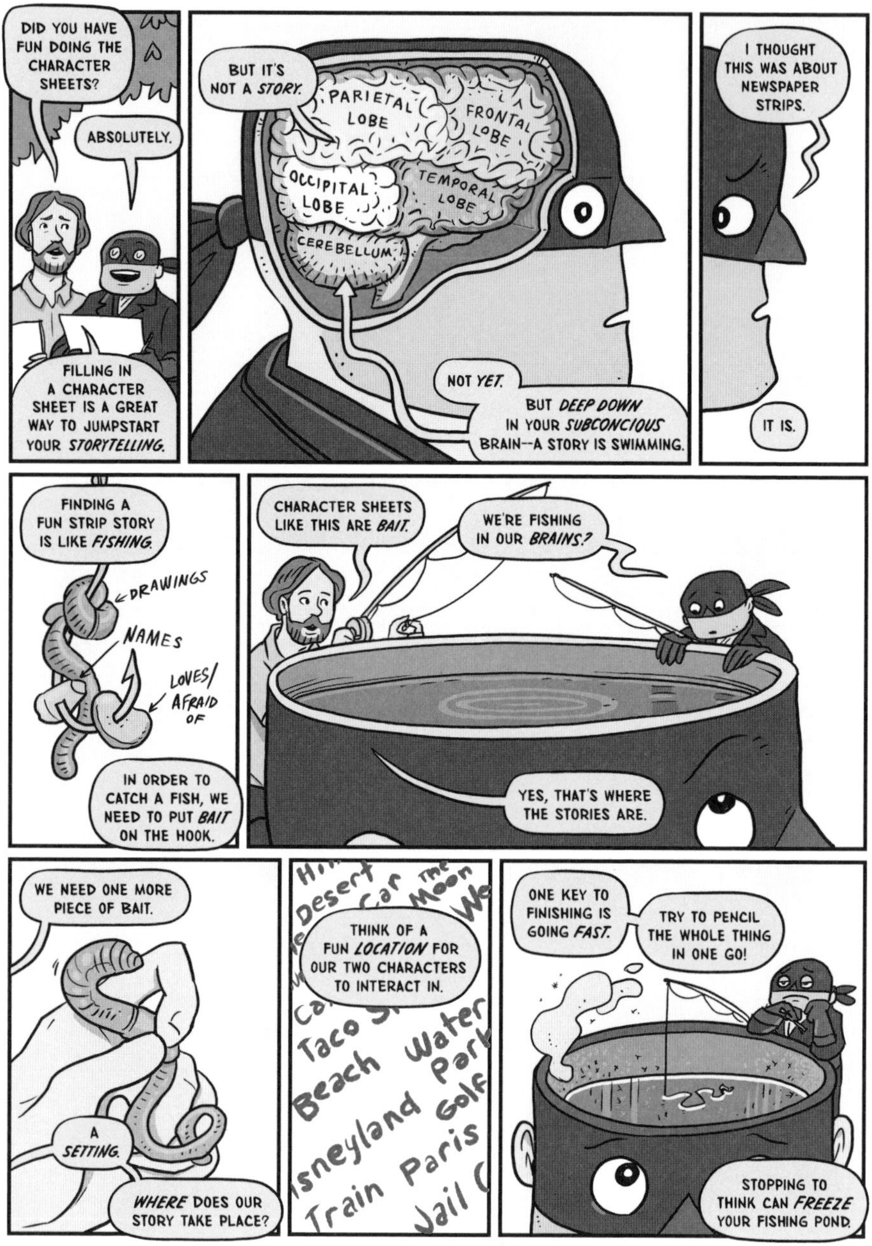

DID YOU HAVE FUN DOING THE CHARACTER SHEETS?
ABSOLUTELY.
FILLING IN A CHARACTER SHEET IS A GREAT WAY TO JUMPSTART YOUR *STORYTELLING.*
BUT IT'S NOT A *STORY.*
PARIETAL LOBE
FRONTAL LOBE
OCCIPITAL LOBE
TEMPORAL LOBE
CEREBELLUM
NOT *YET.*
BUT *DEEP DOWN* IN YOUR *SUBCONCIOUS* BRAIN--A STORY IS SWIMMING.
I THOUGHT THIS WAS ABOUT NEWSPAPER STRIPS.
IT IS.
FINDING A FUN STRIP STORY IS LIKE *FISHING.*
DRAWINGS
NAMES
LOVES/ AFRAID OF
IN ORDER TO CATCH A FISH, WE NEED TO PUT *BAIT* ON THE HOOK.
CHARACTER SHEETS LIKE THIS ARE *BAIT.*
WE'RE FISHING IN OUR *BRAINS?*
YES, THAT'S WHERE THE STORIES ARE.
WE NEED ONE MORE PIECE OF BAIT.
A *SETTING.*
WHERE DOES OUR STORY TAKE PLACE?
Desert
Car
The Moon
THINK OF A FUN *LOCATION* FOR OUR TWO CHARACTERS TO INTERACT IN.
Taco
Water
Beach
Park
Golf
Paris
Train
Jail
ONE KEY TO FINISHING IS GOING *FAST.*
TRY TO PENCIL THE WHOLE THING IN ONE GO!
STOPPING TO THINK CAN *FREEZE* YOUR FISHING POND.

CHALLENGE

ANIMALS AND FOOD 1

HAZ LEVEL 4

THE FIRST PANEL IS THE EASIEST:

IT'S JUST THE *TITLE*, WHICH IS THE *TWO NAMES* PLUS THE *SETTING*.

START THE COMIC WITH *ONE* CHARACTER SPEAKING.

WHICH ONE WILL YOU START WITH, *FOOD* OR *ANIMAL?*

DRAW IN BACKGROUND DETAILS TO SHOW THE SETTING.

IN THIS PANEL, BOTH CHARACTERS SHOULD INTERACT.

DO BOTH SPEAK?

YOU DECIDE.

THIS IS THE *END*. HOW DOES IT END?

DID YOU CATCH A *FISH?*

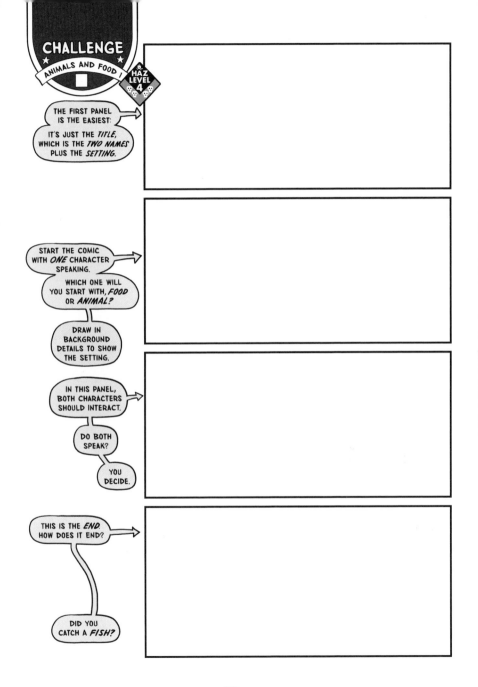

CHALLENGE

ANIMALS AND FOOD 2

HAZ LEVEL 4

THE *KEY* TO THE DAILY STRIP IS DOING IT AGAIN AND AGAIN.

SO LET'S DO IT *AGAIN!*

THIS TIME, START WITH THE *OTHER* CHARACTER.

IF YOU STARTED WITH THE FOOD CHARACTER, SWITCH TO THE ANIMAL, AND VICE VERSA.

FEEL FREE TO *WAIT A DAY* BETWEEN EACH OF THESE CHALLENGES.

REMEMBER, IT'S A *DAILY* STRIP.

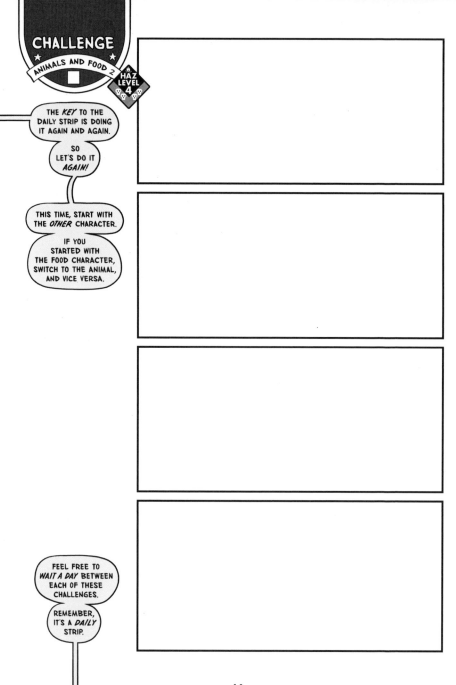

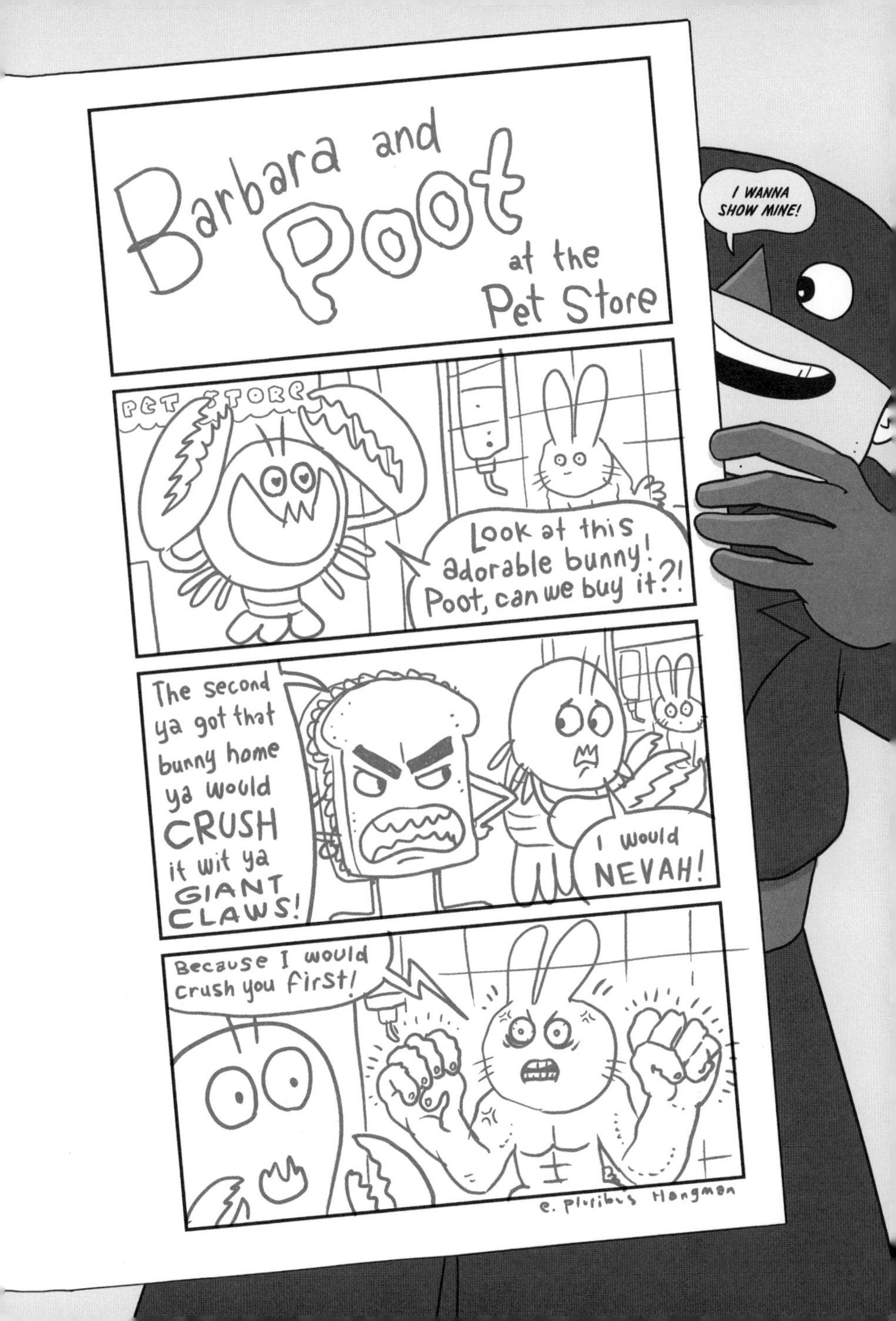
I WANNA SHOW MINE!
Barbara and Poot at the Pet Store
PET STORE
Look at this adorable bunny! Poot, can we buy it?!
The second ya got that bunny home ya would CRUSH it wit ya GIANT CLAWS!
I would NEVAH!
Because I would crush you first!
e. pluribus Hangman

CHALLENGE

THE SUNDAY STRIP

HAZ LEVEL 4

IN NEWSPAPERS, SUNDAY CAME WITH A *LARGE* SHEET OF *COLOR* COMICS.

NOW YOU HAVE *EIGHT* PANELS.

WHAT DO YOUR ANIMAL AND FOOD DO IN A LONGER STORY?

MAKE SURE TO COLOR THE FINAL.

TITLE

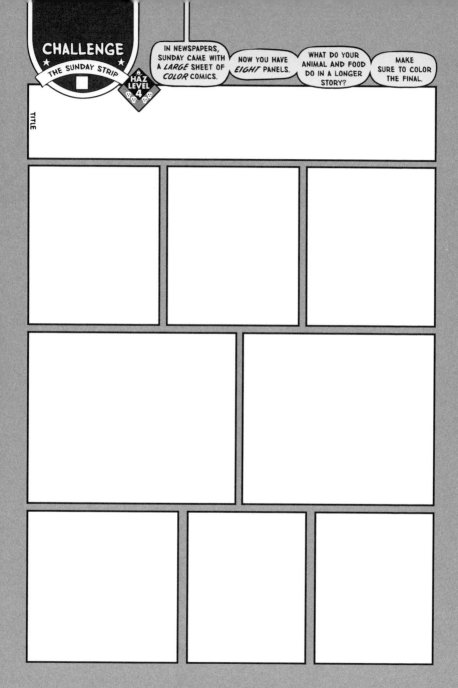

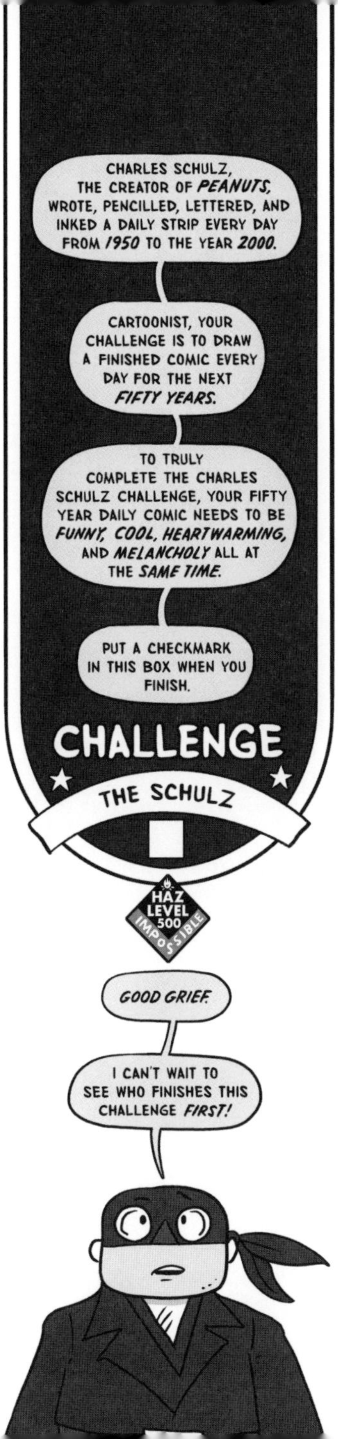

CHARLES SCHULZ, THE CREATOR OF *PEANUTS,* WROTE, PENCILLED, LETTERED, AND INKED A DAILY STRIP EVERY DAY FROM *1950* TO THE YEAR *2000.*
CARTOONIST, YOUR CHALLENGE IS TO DRAW A FINISHED COMIC EVERY DAY FOR THE NEXT *FIFTY YEARS.*
TO TRULY COMPLETE THE CHARLES SCHULZ CHALLENGE, YOUR FIFTY YEAR DAILY COMIC NEEDS TO BE *FUNNY, COOL, HEARTWARMING,* AND *MELANCHOLY* ALL AT THE *SAME TIME.*
PUT A CHECKMARK IN THIS BOX WHEN YOU FINISH.
CHALLENGE
THE SCHULZ
HAZ LEVEL 500 IMPOSSIBLE
GOOD GRIEF.
I CAN'T WAIT TO SEE WHO FINISHES THIS CHALLENGE *FIRST!*

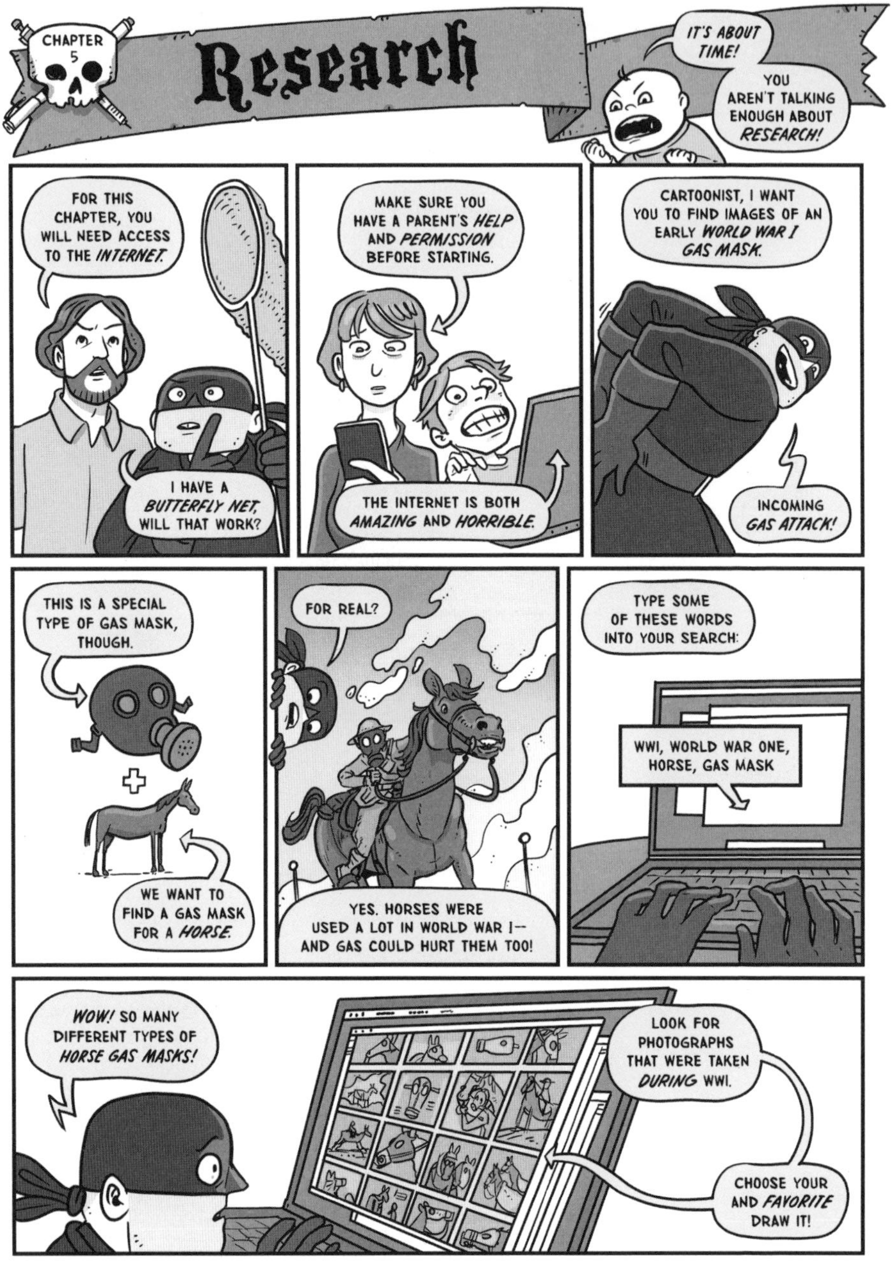
CHAPTER 5
Research
IT'S ABOUT TIME!
YOU AREN'T TALKING ENOUGH ABOUT RESEARCH!
FOR THIS CHAPTER, YOU WILL NEED ACCESS TO THE INTERNET.
I HAVE A BUTTERFLY NET. WILL THAT WORK?
MAKE SURE YOU HAVE A PARENT'S HELP AND PERMISSION BEFORE STARTING.
THE INTERNET IS BOTH AMAZING AND HORRIBLE.
CARTOONIST, I WANT YOU TO FIND IMAGES OF AN EARLY WORLD WAR I GAS MASK.
INCOMING GAS ATTACK!
THIS IS A SPECIAL TYPE OF GAS MASK, THOUGH.
WE WANT TO FIND A GAS MASK FOR A HORSE.
FOR REAL?
YES. HORSES WERE USED A LOT IN WORLD WAR I— AND GAS COULD HURT THEM TOO!
TYPE SOME OF THESE WORDS INTO YOUR SEARCH:
WWI, WORLD WAR ONE, HORSE, GAS MASK
WOW! SO MANY DIFFERENT TYPES OF HORSE GAS MASKS!
LOOK FOR PHOTOGRAPHS THAT WERE TAKEN DURING WWI.
CHOOSE YOUR AND FAVORITE DRAW IT!

CHALLENGE

GAS MASK HORSE

HAZ LEVEL 4

WAS THERE *INFO* WITH THE PHOTO?

WHEN WAS THE PICTURE TAKEN?

WHICH *COUNTRY* IS THE HORSE FROM?

ADD ANY INFO YOU FIND.

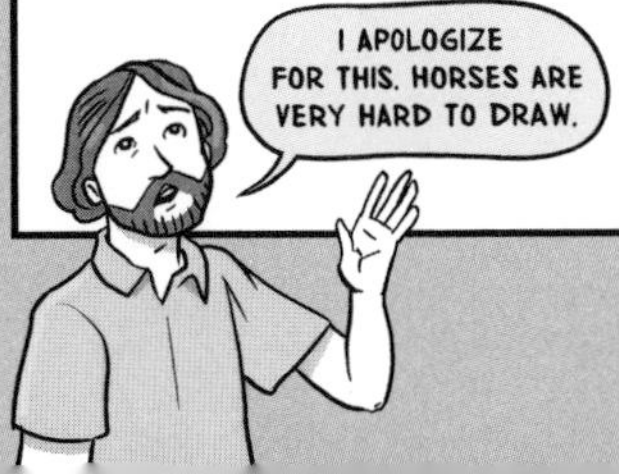
I APOLOGIZE FOR THIS. HORSES ARE VERY HARD TO DRAW.

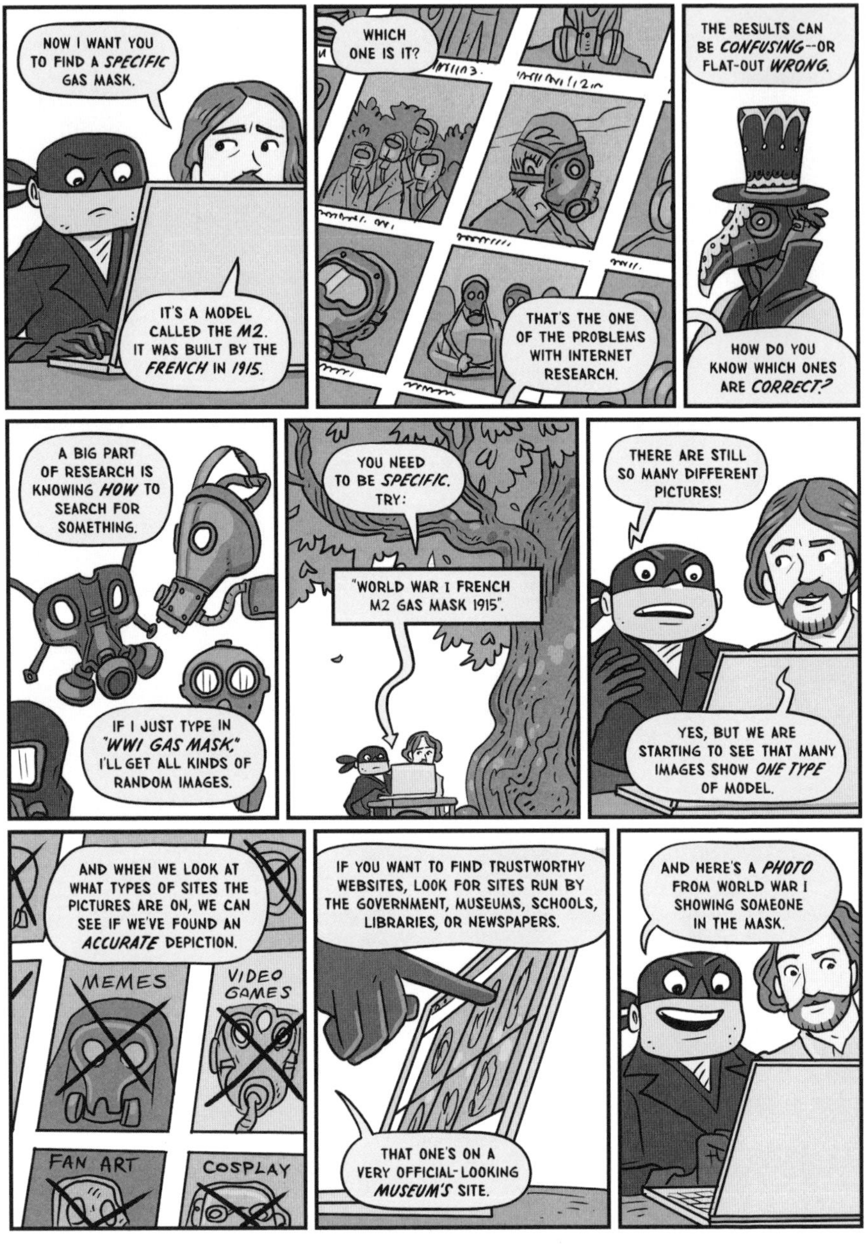

NOW I WANT YOU TO FIND A *SPECIFIC* GAS MASK.
IT'S A MODEL CALLED THE *M2*. IT WAS BUILT BY THE *FRENCH* IN *1915*.
WHICH ONE IS IT?
THAT'S THE ONE OF THE PROBLEMS WITH INTERNET RESEARCH.
THE RESULTS CAN BE *CONFUSING*--OR FLAT-OUT *WRONG*.
HOW DO YOU KNOW WHICH ONES ARE *CORRECT?*
A BIG PART OF RESEARCH IS KNOWING *HOW* TO SEARCH FOR SOMETHING.
IF I JUST TYPE IN *"WWI GAS MASK,"* I'LL GET ALL KINDS OF RANDOM IMAGES.
YOU NEED TO BE *SPECIFIC*. TRY:
"WORLD WAR I FRENCH M2 GAS MASK 1915".
THERE ARE STILL SO MANY DIFFERENT PICTURES!
YES, BUT WE ARE STARTING TO SEE THAT MANY IMAGES SHOW *ONE TYPE* OF MODEL.
AND WHEN WE LOOK AT WHAT TYPES OF SITES THE PICTURES ARE ON, WE CAN SEE IF WE'VE FOUND AN *ACCURATE* DEPICTION.
MEMES
VIDEO GAMES
FAN ART
COSPLAY
IF YOU WANT TO FIND TRUSTWORTHY WEBSITES, LOOK FOR SITES RUN BY THE GOVERNMENT, MUSEUMS, SCHOOLS, LIBRARIES, OR NEWSPAPERS.
THAT ONE'S ON A VERY OFFICIAL-LOOKING *MUSEUM'S* SITE.
AND HERE'S A *PHOTO* FROM WORLD WAR I SHOWING SOMEONE IN THE MASK.

CHALLENGE
1915 FRENCH M2 MASK
☐

HAZ LEVEL 3

CARTOONIST, FIND AND DRAW THE 1915 FRENCH M2 GAS MASK!

CHALLENGE
LOOK AT THIS MASK!
☐

HAZ LEVEL 3

IN YOUR SEARCH, DID YOU STUMBLE ON AN INTERESTING GAS MASK THAT WASN'T THE M2?

DRAW THE INTERESTING MASK YOU FOUND, AND GIVE SOME INFORMATION ABOUT IT.

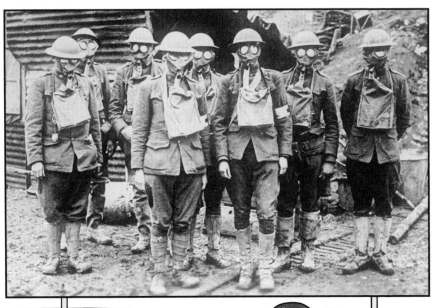

HERE'S AN IMAGE FROM THE NATIONAL PHOTO COMPANY COLLECTION IN THE LIBRARY OF CONGRESS.

DOESN'T SOUND LIKE A *TRUSTWORTHY* SOURCE TO ME.

YOU CAN TRUST THE LIBRARY OF CONGRESS.

EVEN THOUGH THIS IMAGE COMES FROM THE LIBRARY OF CONGRESS, THERE ISN'T MUCH *INFO* ON THE PHOTO.

ALL IT SAYS IS, IT WAS CREATED FROM GLASS NEGATIVES SOMETIME BETWEEN *1909* AND *1920*.

WE DON'T KNOW *WHO* TOOK THE PICTURE OR *WHERE* THEY TOOK IT.

WHAT CAN *YOU* FIGURE OUT ABOUT THIS IMAGE?

I'D SAY THIS PICTURE WAS TAKEN IN MY BACKYARD.

CHALLENGE
★ PHOTO DETECTIVE ★

JUDGING FROM THE *UNIFORMS* AND *GEAR*, WHAT COUNTRY ARE THESE SOLDIERS FROM?

ARE THERE ANY *CLUES* TO NARROW DOWN THE TIMELINE?

CAN YOU BEAT THE LIBRARY OF CONGRESS BY FIGURING OUT MORE ABOUT THIS PICTURE?

HAZ LEVEL 4

WHO?

WHERE?

WHEN?

THEORIES?

NOW THAT YOU'VE FOUND SOME INTERESTING VISUAL REFERENCE, IT'S TIME TO *DRAW* WITH IT!

A GOOD CARTOONIST DOESN'T JUST *COPY* THE IMAGE. YOU NEED TO *CHANGE* IT TO MAKE IT *YOURS*.

DRAW THIS GAS MASK GUY IN SOME DIFFERENT *POSES*.

CHALLENGE
★ POSE THAT SOLDIER ★

HAZ LEVEL 4

RUNNING

CROUCHING FOR COVER

LAYING FLAT IN THE MUD

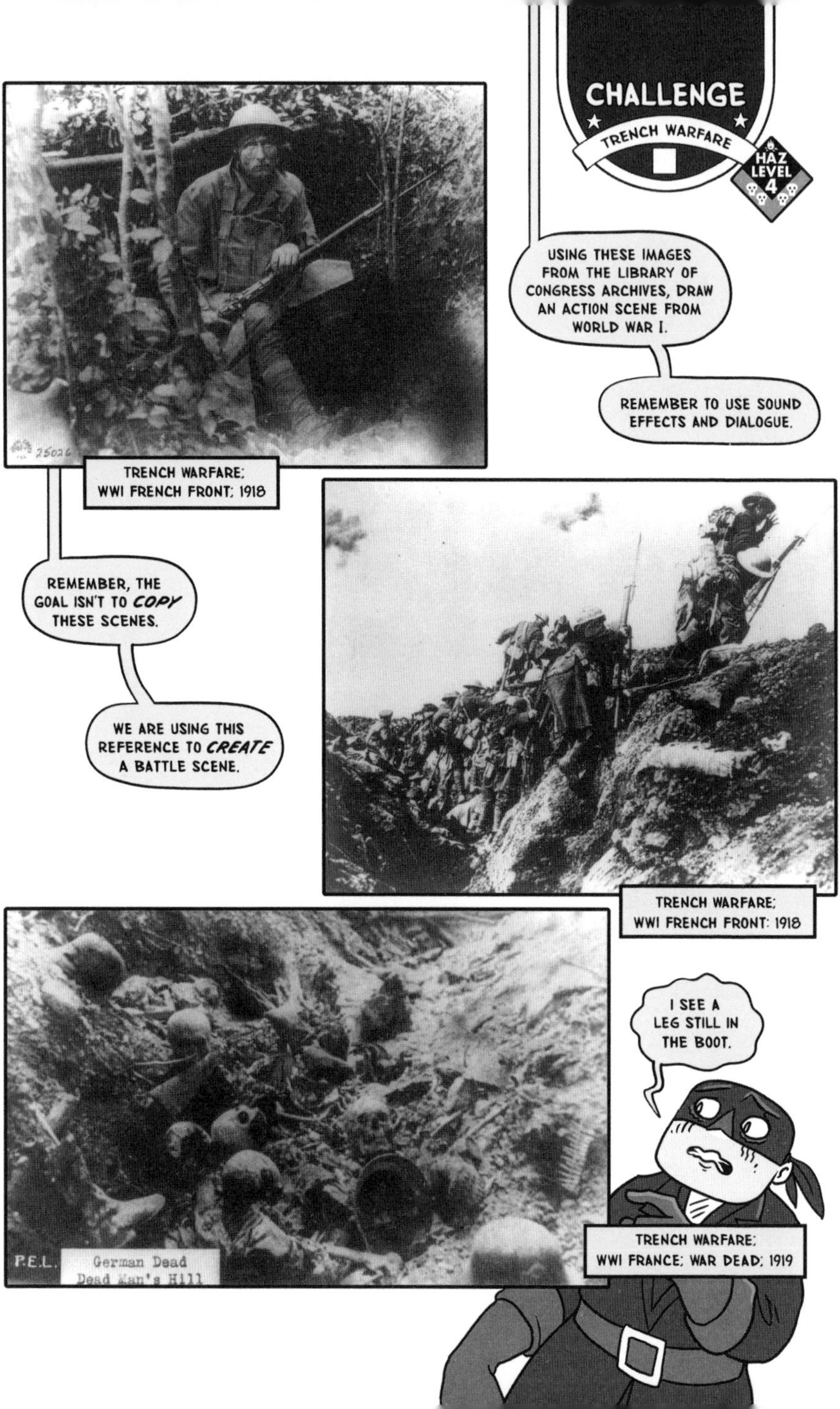
CHALLENGE
TRENCH WARFARE
HAZ LEVEL 4
USING THESE IMAGES FROM THE LIBRARY OF CONGRESS ARCHIVES, DRAW AN ACTION SCENE FROM WORLD WAR I.
REMEMBER TO USE SOUND EFFECTS AND DIALOGUE.
25026
TRENCH WARFARE: WWI FRENCH FRONT: 1918
REMEMBER, THE GOAL ISN'T TO COPY THESE SCENES.
WE ARE USING THIS REFERENCE TO CREATE A BATTLE SCENE.
TRENCH WARFARE: WWI FRENCH FRONT: 1918
P.E.L.
German Dead
Dead Man's Hill
I SEE A LEG STILL IN THE BOOT.
TRENCH WARFARE: WWI FRANCE: WAR DEAD: 1919

TITLE

THE END

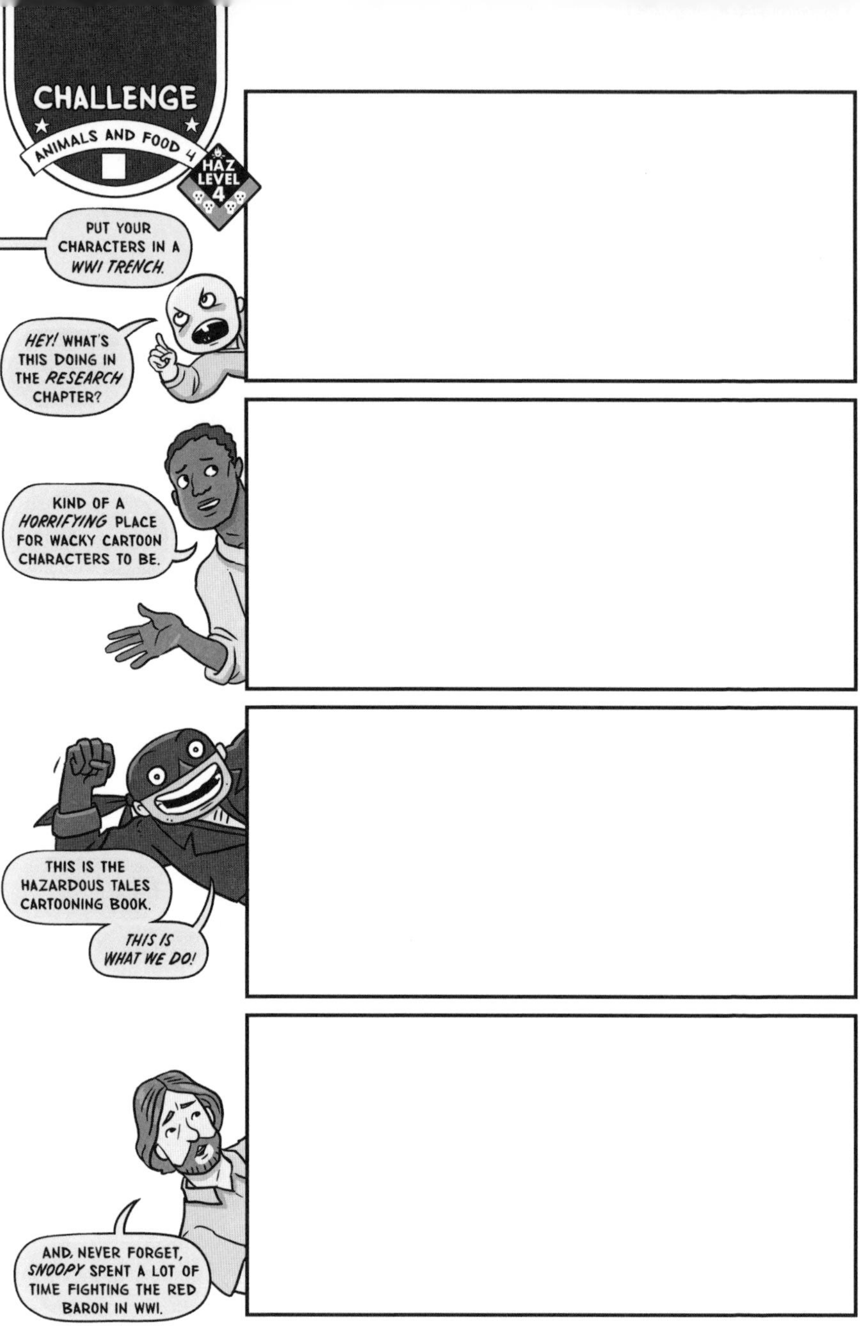
CHALLENGE
ANIMALS AND FOOD 4
HAZ LEVEL 4
PUT YOUR CHARACTERS IN A *WWI TRENCH.*
HEY! WHAT'S THIS DOING IN THE *RESEARCH* CHAPTER?
KIND OF A *HORRIFYING* PLACE FOR WACKY CARTOON CHARACTERS TO BE.
THIS IS THE HAZARDOUS TALES CARTOONING BOOK.
THIS IS WHAT WE DO!
AND, NEVER FORGET, *SNOOPY* SPENT A LOT OF TIME FIGHTING THE RED BARON IN WWI.

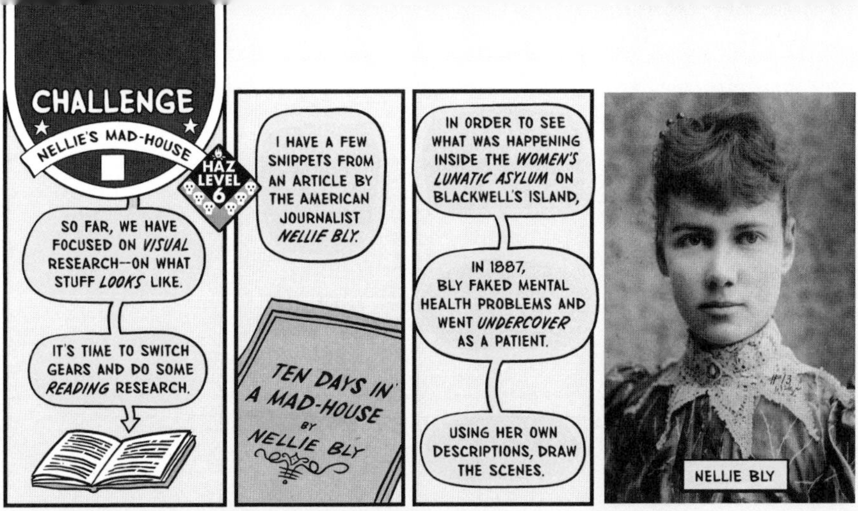
CHALLENGE
NELLIE'S MAD-HOUSE
HAZ LEVEL 6
SO FAR, WE HAVE FOCUSED ON *VISUAL* RESEARCH--ON WHAT STUFF *LOOKS* LIKE.
IT'S TIME TO SWITCH GEARS AND DO SOME *READING* RESEARCH.
I HAVE A FEW SNIPPETS FROM AN ARTICLE BY THE AMERICAN JOURNALIST *NELLIE BLY*.
TEN DAYS IN A MAD-HOUSE BY NELLIE BLY
IN ORDER TO SEE WHAT WAS HAPPENING INSIDE THE *WOMEN'S LUNATIC ASYLUM* ON BLACKWELL'S ISLAND,
IN 1887, BLY FAKED MENTAL HEALTH PROBLEMS AND WENT *UNDERCOVER* AS A PATIENT.
USING HER OWN DESCRIPTIONS, DRAW THE SCENES.
NELLIE BLY

The boat stopped and the old woman and the sick girl were taken off. The rest of us were told to sit still. At the next stop my companions were taken off, one at a time. I was last, and it seemed to require a man and a woman to lead me up the plank to reach the shore. An ambulance was standing there, and in it were the four other patients.

"What is this place?" I asked of the man, who had his fingers sunk into the flesh of my arm.

"Blackwell's Island, an insane place, where you'll never get out of."

With this I was shoved into the ambulance, the springboard was put up, an officer and a mail-carrier jumped on behind, and I was swiftly driven to the Insane Asylum on Blackwell's Island.

I looked at the poor crazy captives shivering, and added, emphatically, "It's horribly brutal." While they stood there I thought I would not relish supper that night. They looked so lost and hopeless. Some were chattering nonsense to invisible persons, others were laughing or crying aimlessly, and one old, gray-haired woman was nudging me, and, with winks and sage noddings of the head and pitiful uplifting of the eyes and hands, was assuring me that I must not mind the poor creatures, as they were all mad.

"Stop at the heater," was then ordered, "and get in line, two by two." "Mary, get a companion." "How many times must I tell you to keep in line?" "Stand still," and, as the orders were issued, a shove and a push were administered, and often a slap on the ears. After this third and final halt, we were marched into a long, narrow dining-room, where a rush was made for the table.

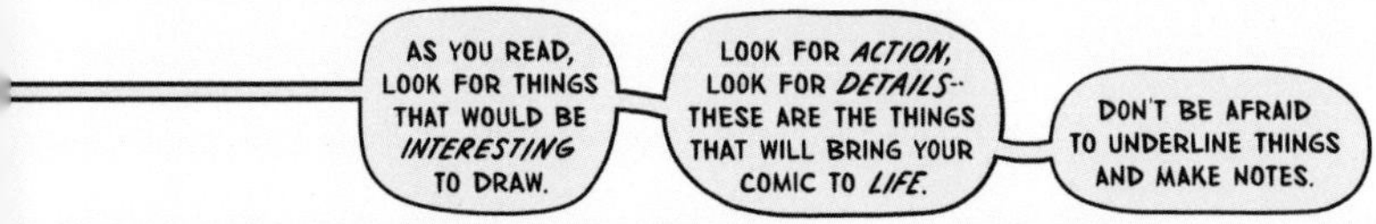
AS YOU READ, LOOK FOR THINGS THAT WOULD BE *INTERESTING* TO DRAW.
LOOK FOR *ACTION*, LOOK FOR *DETAILS*-- THESE ARE THE THINGS THAT WILL BRING YOUR COMIC TO *LIFE*.
DON'T BE AFRAID TO UNDERLINE THINGS AND MAKE NOTES.

The table reached the length of the room and was uncovered and uninviting. Long benches without backs were put for the patients to sit on, and over these they had to crawl in order to face the table. Placed close together all along the table were large dressing-bowls filled with a pinkish-looking stuff which the patients called tea. By each bowl was laid a piece of bread, cut thick and buttered. A small saucer containing five prunes accompanied the bread. One fat woman made a rush, and jerking up several saucers from those around her emptied their contents into her own saucer. Then while holding to her own bowl she lifted up another and drained its contents at one gulp. This she did to a second bowl in shorter time than it takes to tell it. Indeed, I was so amused at her successful grabbings that when I looked at my own share the woman opposite, without so much as by your leave, grabbed my bread and left me without any.

Another patient, seeing this, kindly offered me hers, but I declined with thanks and turned to the nurse and asked for more. As she flung a thick piece down on the table she made some remark about the fact that if I forgot where my home was I had not forgotten how to eat. I tried the bread, but the butter was so horrible that one could not eat it. A blue-eyed German girl on the opposite side of the table told me I could have bread unbuttered if I wished, and that very few were able to eat the butter. I turned my attention to the prunes and found that very few of them would be sufficient. A patient near asked me to give them to her. I did so. My bowl of tea was all that was left. I tasted, and one taste was enough. It had no sugar, and it tasted as if it had been made in copper. It was as weak as water. This was also transferred to a hungrier patient, in spite of the protest of Miss Neville.

"You must force the food down," she said, "else you will be sick, and who knows but what, with these surroundings, you may go crazy."

We had not gone many paces when I saw, proceeding from every walk, long lines of women guarded by nurses. How many there were! Every way I looked I could see them in the queer dresses, comical straw hats and shawls, marching slowly around. I eagerly watched the passing lines and a thrill of horror crept over me at the sight. Vacant eyes and meaningless faces, and their tongues uttered meaningless nonsense. One crowd passed and I noted, by nose as well as eyes, that they were fearfully dirty.

"Who are they?" I asked of a patient near me.

"They are considered the most violent on the island," she replied. "They are from the Lodge, the first building with the high steps." Some were yelling, some were cursing, others were singing or praying or preaching, as the fancy struck them, and they made up the most miserable collection of humanity I had ever seen. As the din of their passing faded in the distance there came another sight I can never forget:

DID SHE JUST SAY THEY SMELLED BAD?

A long cable rope fastened to wide leather belts, and these belts locked around the waists of fifty-two women. At the end of the rope was a heavy iron cart, and in it two women—one nursing a sore foot, another screaming at some nurse, saying: "You beat me and I shall not forget it. You want to kill me," and then she would sob and cry. The women "on the rope," as the patients call it, were each busy on their individual freaks. Some were yelling all the while. One who had blue eyes saw me look at her, and she turned as far as she could, talking and smiling, with that terrible, horrifying look of absolute insanity stamped on her. The doctors might safely judge on her case. The horror of that sight to one who had never been near an insane person before, was something unspeakable.

"God help them!" breathed Miss Neville, "It is so dreadful I cannot look."

On they passed, but for their places to be filled by more. Can you imagine the sight? According to one of the physicians there are 1600 insane women on Blackwell's Island.

Mad! What can be half so horrible? My heart thrilled with pity when I looked on old, gray-haired women talking aimlessly to space. One woman had on a straight-jacket, and two women had to drag her along. Crippled, blind, old, young, homely, and pretty; one senseless mass of humanity.

No fate could be worse.

THE END

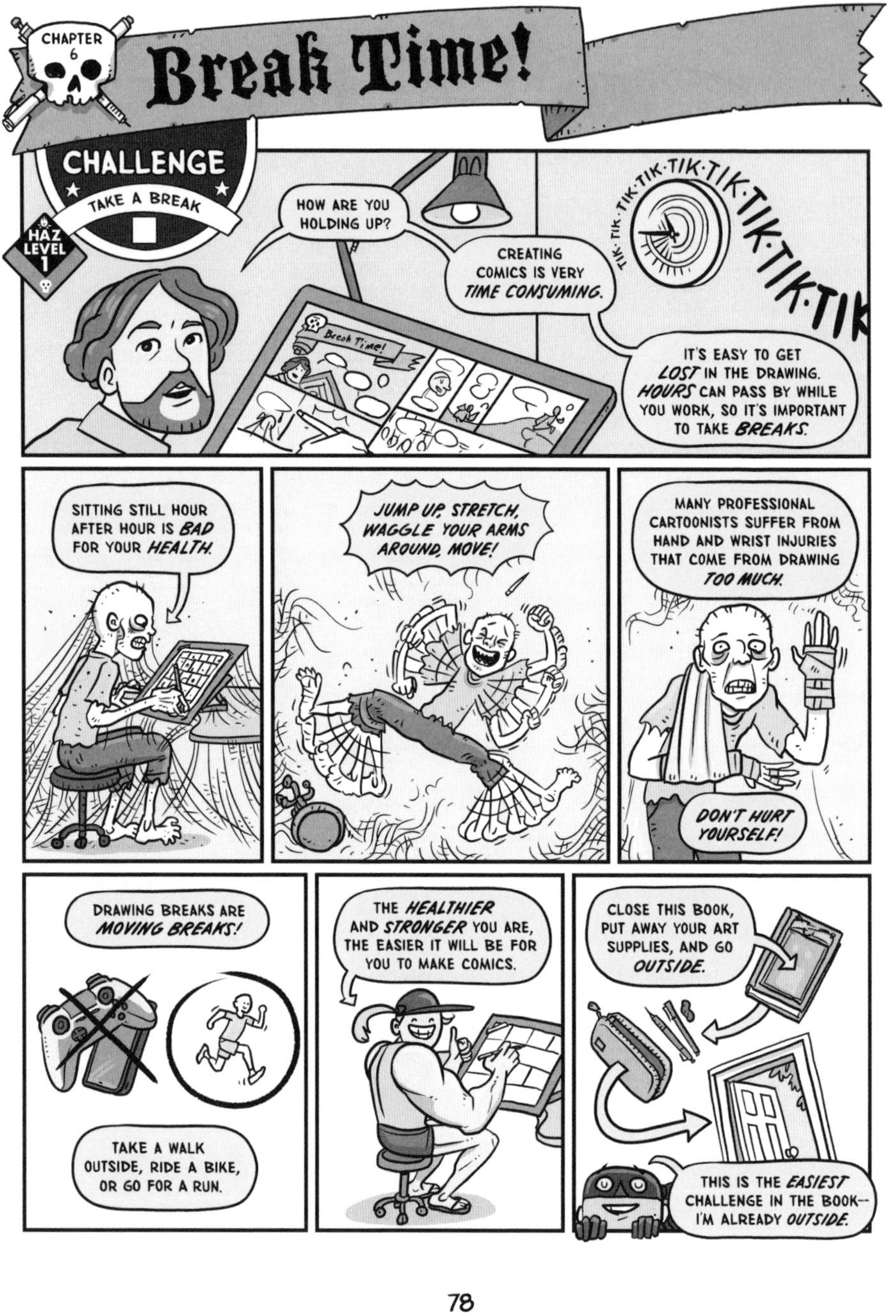

CHAPTER 6
Break Time!
CHALLENGE
TAKE A BREAK
HAZ LEVEL 1
HOW ARE YOU HOLDING UP?
CREATING COMICS IS VERY *TIME CONSUMING.*
Break Time!
TIK·TIK·TIK·TIK·TIK·TIK·TIK·TIK·TIK·TIK
IT'S EASY TO GET *LOST* IN THE DRAWING. *HOURS* CAN PASS BY WHILE YOU WORK, SO IT'S IMPORTANT TO TAKE *BREAKS.*
SITTING STILL HOUR AFTER HOUR IS *BAD* FOR YOUR *HEALTH.*
JUMP UP, STRETCH, WAGGLE YOUR ARMS AROUND, MOVE!
MANY PROFESSIONAL CARTOONISTS SUFFER FROM HAND AND WRIST INJURIES THAT COME FROM DRAWING *TOO MUCH.*
DON'T HURT YOURSELF!
DRAWING BREAKS ARE *MOVING BREAKS!*
TAKE A WALK OUTSIDE, RIDE A BIKE, OR GO FOR A RUN.
THE *HEALTHIER* AND *STRONGER* YOU ARE, THE EASIER IT WILL BE FOR YOU TO MAKE COMICS.
CLOSE THIS BOOK, PUT AWAY YOUR ART SUPPLIES, AND GO *OUTSIDE.*
THIS IS THE *EASIEST* CHALLENGE IN THE BOOK-- I'M ALREADY *OUTSIDE.*

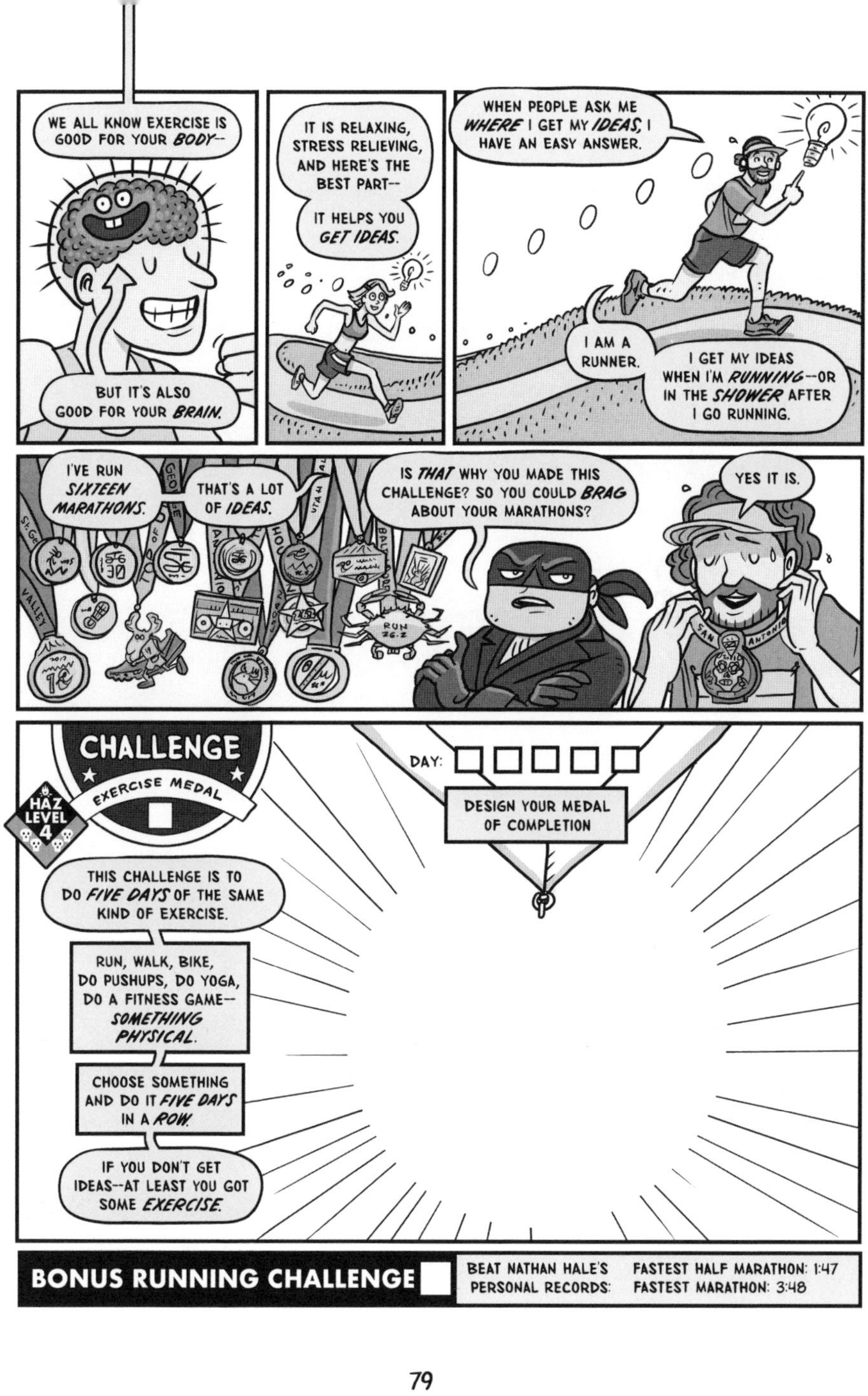
WE ALL KNOW EXERCISE IS GOOD FOR YOUR BODY--
BUT IT'S ALSO GOOD FOR YOUR BRAIN.
IT IS RELAXING, STRESS RELIEVING, AND HERE'S THE BEST PART--
IT HELPS YOU GET IDEAS.
WHEN PEOPLE ASK ME WHERE I GET MY IDEAS, I HAVE AN EASY ANSWER.
I AM A RUNNER.
I GET MY IDEAS WHEN I'M RUNNING--OR IN THE SHOWER AFTER I GO RUNNING.
I'VE RUN SIXTEEN MARATHONS.
THAT'S A LOT OF IDEAS.
IS THAT WHY YOU MADE THIS CHALLENGE? SO YOU COULD BRAG ABOUT YOUR MARATHONS?
YES IT IS.
RUN 26.2
SAN ANTONIO
CHALLENGE
EXERCISE MEDAL
HAZ LEVEL 4
DAY:
DESIGN YOUR MEDAL OF COMPLETION
THIS CHALLENGE IS TO DO FIVE DAYS OF THE SAME KIND OF EXERCISE.
RUN, WALK, BIKE, DO PUSHUPS, DO YOGA, DO A FITNESS GAME-- SOMETHING PHYSICAL.
CHOOSE SOMETHING AND DO IT FIVE DAYS IN A ROW.
IF YOU DON'T GET IDEAS--AT LEAST YOU GOT SOME EXERCISE.

BONUS RUNNING CHALLENGE ☐

BEAT NATHAN HALE'S PERSONAL RECORDS: FASTEST HALF MARATHON: 1:47 FASTEST MARATHON: 3:48

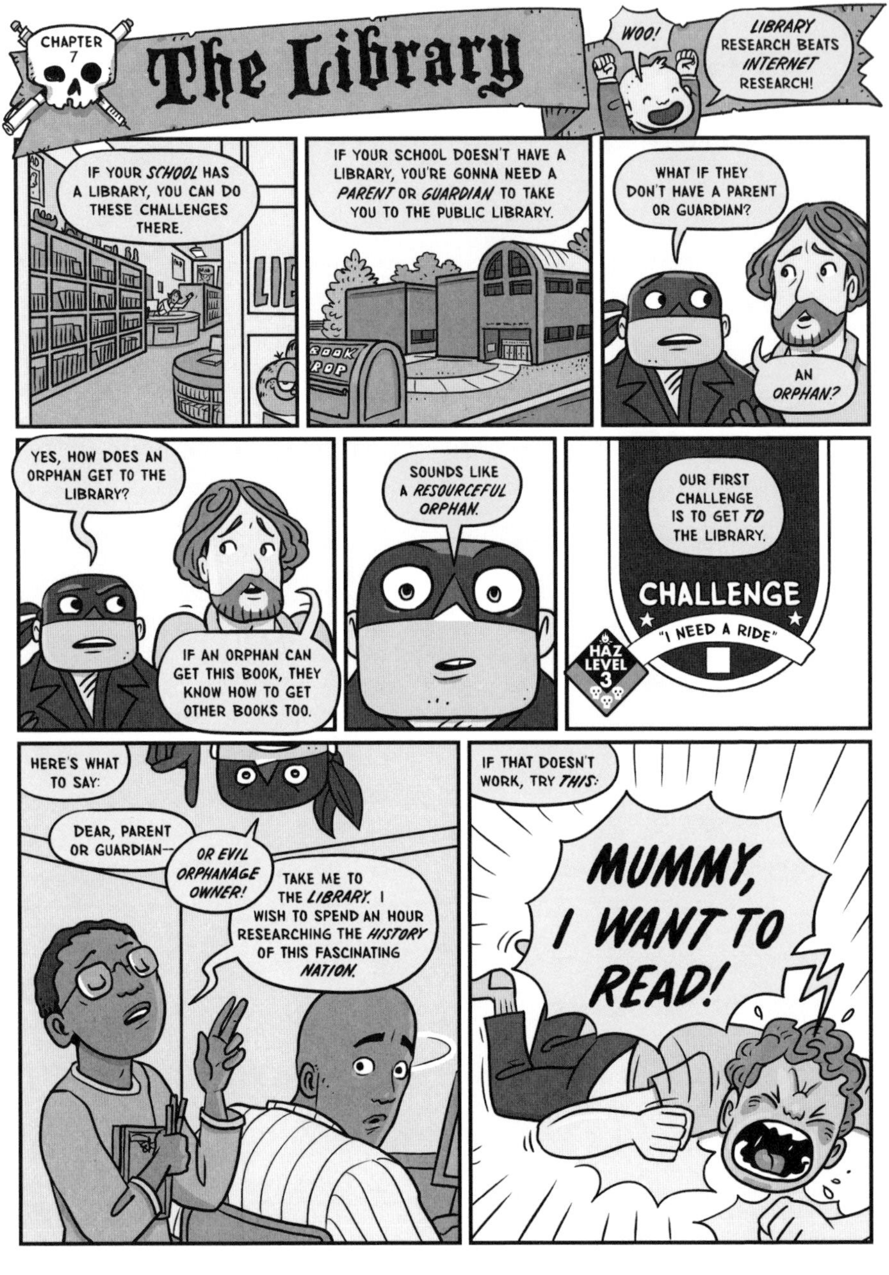

CHAPTER 7
The Library
WOO!
LIBRARY RESEARCH BEATS INTERNET RESEARCH!
IF YOUR SCHOOL HAS A LIBRARY, YOU CAN DO THESE CHALLENGES THERE.
IF YOUR SCHOOL DOESN'T HAVE A LIBRARY, YOU'RE GONNA NEED A PARENT OR GUARDIAN TO TAKE YOU TO THE PUBLIC LIBRARY.
WHAT IF THEY DON'T HAVE A PARENT OR GUARDIAN?
AN ORPHAN?
YES, HOW DOES AN ORPHAN GET TO THE LIBRARY?
IF AN ORPHAN CAN GET THIS BOOK, THEY KNOW HOW TO GET OTHER BOOKS TOO.
SOUNDS LIKE A RESOURCEFUL ORPHAN.
OUR FIRST CHALLENGE IS TO GET TO THE LIBRARY.
CHALLENGE
"I NEED A RIDE"
HAZ LEVEL 3
HERE'S WHAT TO SAY:
DEAR, PARENT OR GUARDIAN--
OR EVIL ORPHANAGE OWNER!
TAKE ME TO THE LIBRARY. I WISH TO SPEND AN HOUR RESEARCHING THE HISTORY OF THIS FASCINATING NATION.
IF THAT DOESN'T WORK, TRY THIS:
MUMMY, I WANT TO READ!

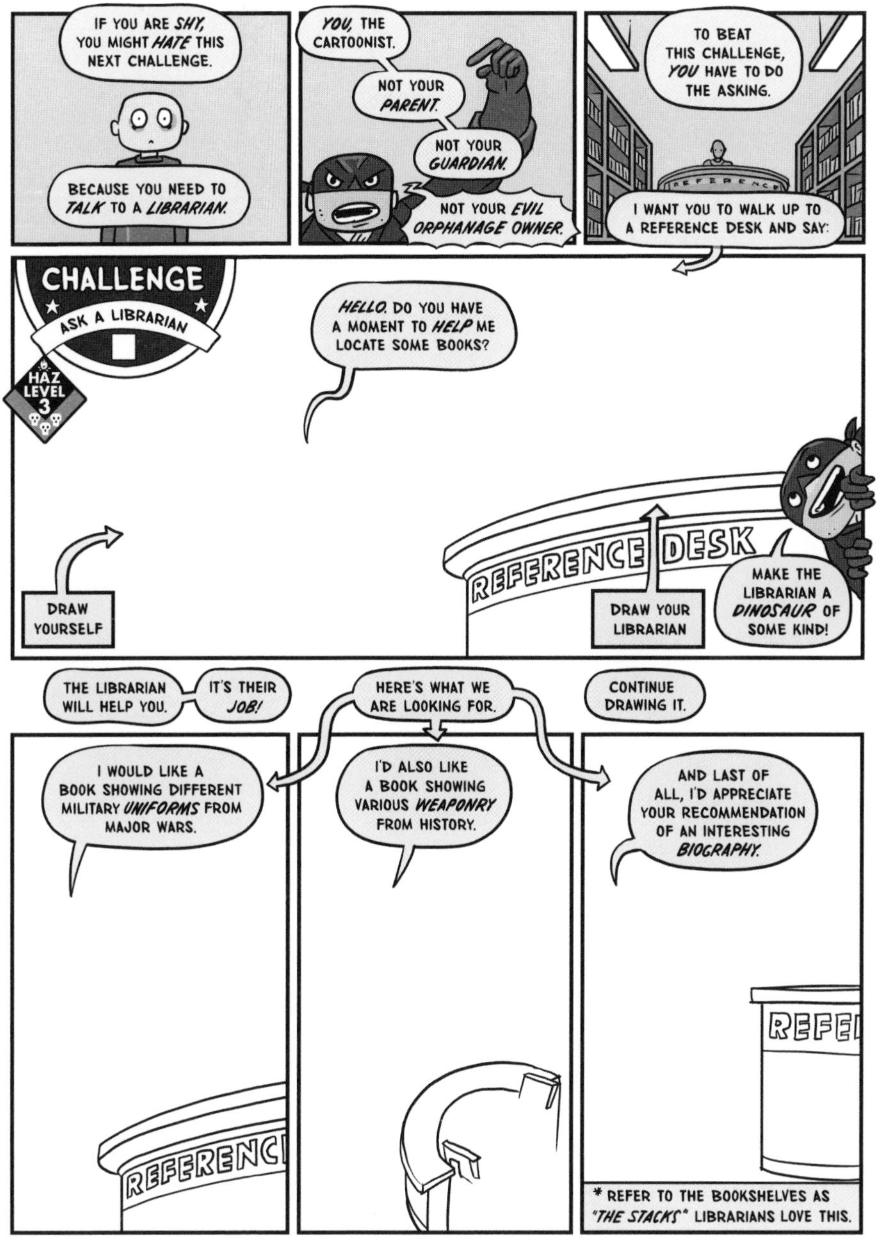
IF YOU ARE SHY, YOU MIGHT HATE THIS NEXT CHALLENGE.
BECAUSE YOU NEED TO TALK TO A LIBRARIAN.
YOU, THE CARTOONIST.
NOT YOUR PARENT.
NOT YOUR GUARDIAN.
NOT YOUR EVIL ORPHANAGE OWNER.
TO BEAT THIS CHALLENGE, YOU HAVE TO DO THE ASKING.
I WANT YOU TO WALK UP TO A REFERENCE DESK AND SAY:
CHALLENGE
ASK A LIBRARIAN
HAZ LEVEL 3
HELLO. DO YOU HAVE A MOMENT TO HELP ME LOCATE SOME BOOKS?
DRAW YOURSELF
REFERENCE DESK
DRAW YOUR LIBRARIAN
MAKE THE LIBRARIAN A DINOSAUR OF SOME KIND!
THE LIBRARIAN WILL HELP YOU.
IT'S THEIR JOB!
HERE'S WHAT WE ARE LOOKING FOR.
CONTINUE DRAWING IT.
I WOULD LIKE A BOOK SHOWING DIFFERENT MILITARY UNIFORMS FROM MAJOR WARS.
I'D ALSO LIKE A BOOK SHOWING VARIOUS WEAPONRY FROM HISTORY.
AND LAST OF ALL, I'D APPRECIATE YOUR RECOMMENDATION OF AN INTERESTING BIOGRAPHY.
REFERENC
REFE
* REFER TO THE BOOKSHELVES AS "THE STACKS" LIBRARIANS LOVE THIS.

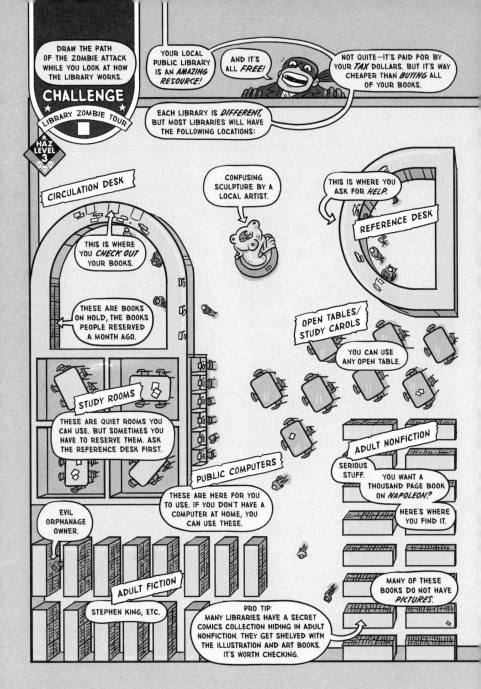

CHALLENGE
DRAW THE PATH OF THE ZOMBIE ATTACK WHILE YOU LOOK AT HOW THE LIBRARY WORKS.

LIBRARY ZOMBIE TOUR

HAZ LEVEL 3

YOUR LOCAL PUBLIC LIBRARY IS AN *AMAZING* RESOURCE!

AND IT'S ALL *FREE!*

NOT QUITE—IT'S PAID FOR BY YOUR *TAX* DOLLARS. BUT IT'S WAY CHEAPER THAN *BUYING* ALL OF YOUR BOOKS.

EACH LIBRARY IS *DIFFERENT*, BUT MOST LIBRARIES WILL HAVE THE FOLLOWING LOCATIONS:

CIRCULATION DESK

CONFUSING SCULPTURE BY A LOCAL ARTIST.

THIS IS WHERE YOU ASK FOR *HELP*.

REFERENCE DESK

THIS IS WHERE YOU *CHECK OUT* YOUR BOOKS.

THESE ARE BOOKS ON HOLD, THE BOOKS PEOPLE RESERVED A MONTH AGO.

OPEN TABLES/ STUDY CAROLS

YOU CAN USE ANY OPEN TABLE.

STUDY ROOMS

THESE ARE QUIET ROOMS YOU CAN USE. BUT SOMETIMES YOU HAVE TO RESERVE THEM. ASK THE REFERENCE DESK FIRST.

PUBLIC COMPUTERS

ADULT NONFICTION

SERIOUS STUFF.

YOU WANT A THOUSAND PAGE BOOK ON *NAPOLEON?*

HERE'S WHERE YOU FIND IT.

THESE ARE HERE FOR YOU TO USE. IF YOU DON'T HAVE A COMPUTER AT HOME, YOU CAN USE THESE.

EVIL ORPHANAGE OWNER.

MANY OF THESE BOOKS DO NOT HAVE *PICTURES*.

ADULT FICTION

STEPHEN KING, ETC.

PRO TIP:
MANY LIBRARIES HAVE A SECRET COMICS COLLECTION HIDING IN ADULT NONFICTION. THEY GET SHELVED WITH THE ILLUSTRATION AND ART BOOKS. IT'S WORTH CHECKING.

82

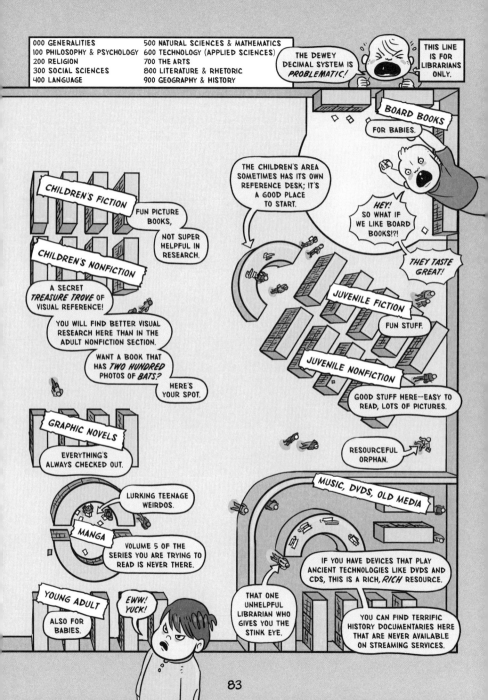

000 GENERALITIES
100 PHILOSOPHY & PSYCHOLOGY
200 RELIGION
300 SOCIAL SCIENCES
400 LANGUAGE

500 NATURAL SCIENCES & MATHEMATICS
600 TECHNOLOGY (APPLIED SCIENCES)
700 THE ARTS
800 LITERATURE & RHETORIC
900 GEOGRAPHY & HISTORY

THE DEWEY DECIMAL SYSTEM IS *PROBLEMATIC!*

THIS LINE IS FOR LIBRARIANS ONLY.

BOARD BOOKS

FOR BABIES.

HEY! SO WHAT IF WE LIKE BOARD BOOKS!?!

THEY TASTE GREAT!

THE CHILDREN'S AREA SOMETIMES HAS ITS OWN REFERENCE DESK; IT'S A GOOD PLACE TO START.

CHILDREN'S FICTION

FUN PICTURE BOOKS,

NOT SUPER HELPFUL IN RESEARCH.

CHILDREN'S NONFICTION

A SECRET *TREASURE TROVE* OF VISUAL REFERENCE!

YOU WILL FIND BETTER VISUAL RESEARCH HERE THAN IN THE ADULT NONFICTION SECTION.

WANT A BOOK THAT HAS *TWO HUNDRED* PHOTOS OF *BATS?*

HERE'S YOUR SPOT.

JUVENILE FICTION

FUN STUFF.

JUVENILE NONFICTION

GOOD STUFF HERE—EASY TO READ, LOTS OF PICTURES.

GRAPHIC NOVELS

EVERYTHING'S ALWAYS CHECKED OUT.

RESOURCEFUL ORPHAN.

MUSIC, DVDS, OLD MEDIA

LURKING TEENAGE WEIRDOS.

MANGA

VOLUME 5 OF THE SERIES YOU ARE TRYING TO READ IS NEVER THERE.

IF YOU HAVE DEVICES THAT PLAY ANCIENT TECHNOLOGIES LIKE DVDS AND CDS, THIS IS A RICH, *RICH* RESOURCE.

THAT ONE UNHELPFUL LIBRARIAN WHO GIVES YOU THE STINK EYE.

YOUNG ADULT

EWW! YUCK!

ALSO FOR BABIES.

YOU CAN FIND TERRIFIC HISTORY DOCUMENTARIES HERE THAT ARE NEVER AVAILABLE ON STREAMING SERVICES.

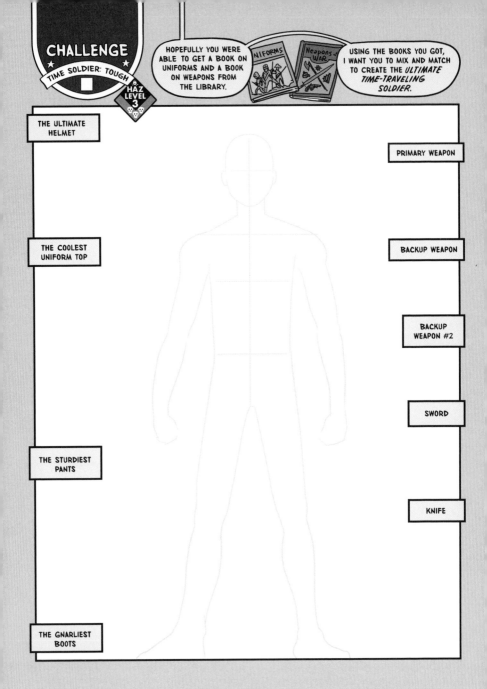

CHALLENGE

★ TIME SOLDIER: TOUGH ★

HAZ LEVEL 3

HOPEFULLY YOU WERE ABLE TO GET A BOOK ON UNIFORMS AND A BOOK ON WEAPONS FROM THE LIBRARY.

UNIFORMS

Weapons of WAR

USING THE BOOKS YOU GOT, I WANT YOU TO MIX AND MATCH TO CREATE THE *ULTIMATE TIME-TRAVELING SOLDIER.*

THE ULTIMATE HELMET

THE COOLEST UNIFORM TOP

THE STURDIEST PANTS

THE GNARLIEST BOOTS

PRIMARY WEAPON

BACKUP WEAPON

BACKUP WEAPON #2

SWORD

KNIFE

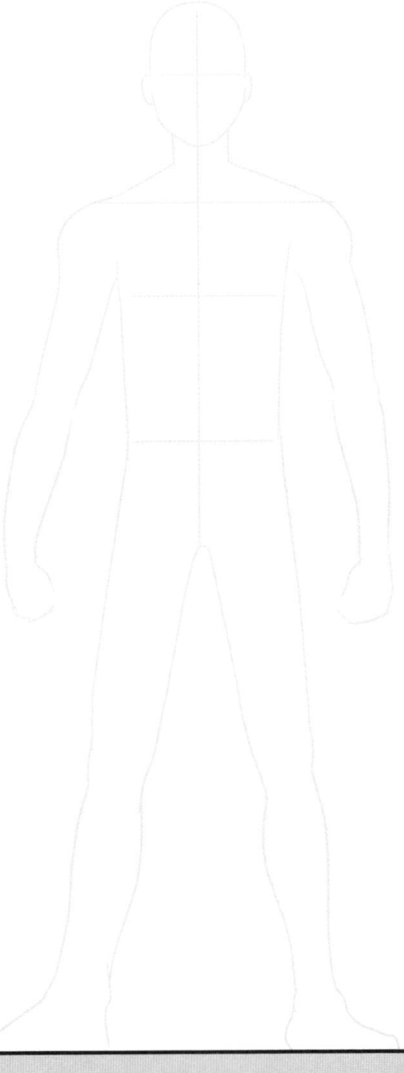

CHALLENGE

TIME SOLDIER: DOOFUS

HAZ LEVEL 3

NOW USE THOSE BOOKS TO DRAW THE *GOOFIEST POSSIBLE SOLDIER.*

OH, THIS WILL BE GOOD!

THE SILLIEST HELMET

PRIMARY WEAPON

THE MOST RIDICULOUS UNIFORM TOP

BACKUP WEAPON

BACKUP WEAPON #2

SILLY SWORD

THE WACKIEST PANTS

USELESS KNIFE

THE DUMBEST FOOTWEAR

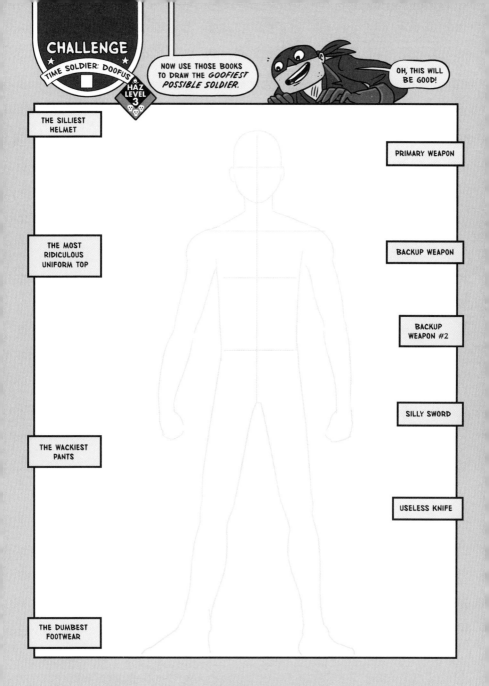

CHALLENGE

BIOGRAPHY BLITZ!

DID YOUR LIBRARIAN FIND YOU AN INTERESTING BIOGRAPHY?

IT'S TIME TO TURN THIS HISTORICAL PERSON INTO A COMIC!

HAZ LEVEL 4

FRONT

BACK

NAME: ______________________________

WHAT DOES IT *LOVE:* ______________________________

WHAT IS IT *AFRAID OF:* ______________________________

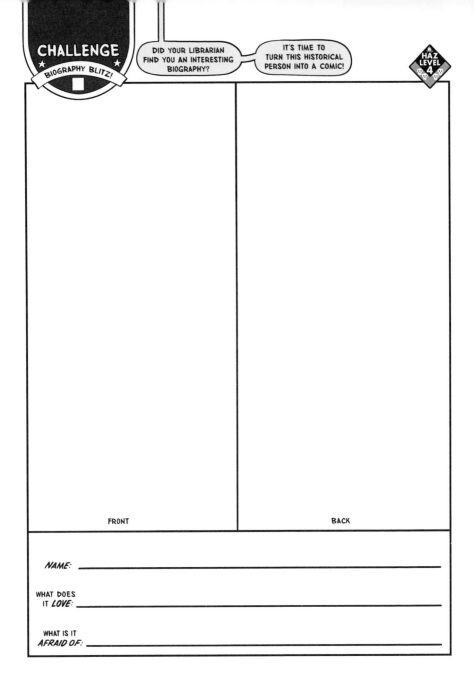

CHALLENGE

WHAT DID THEY DO?

USING THE BOOK AND YOUR CHARACTER SHEET, CREATE A ONE-PAGE COMIC ABOUT SOMETHING THAT HAPPENED TO THEM.

HAZ LEVEL 4

NAME AND TITLE

THE END

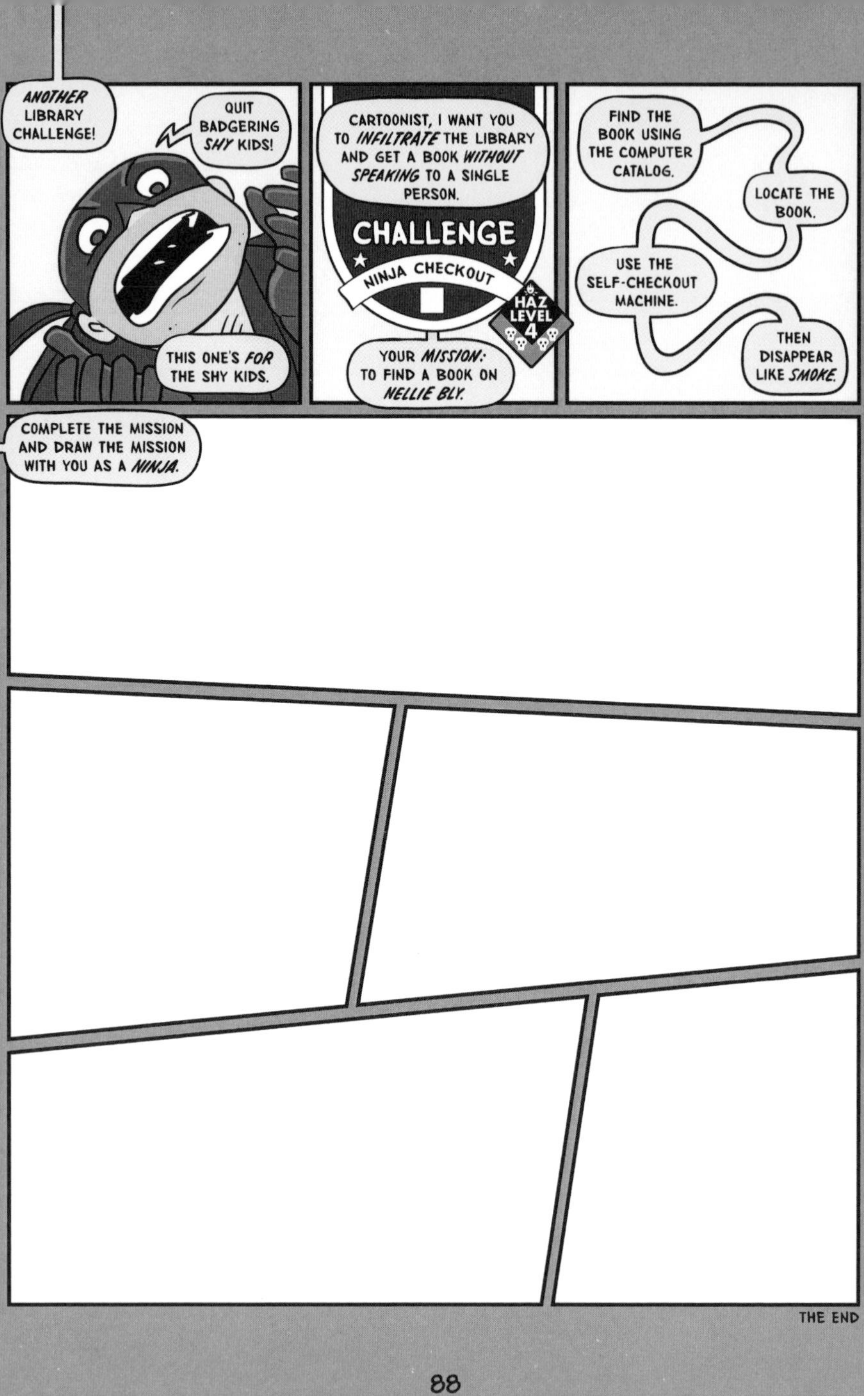
ANOTHER LIBRARY CHALLENGE!
QUIT BADGERING SHY KIDS!
THIS ONE'S FOR THE SHY KIDS.
CARTOONIST, I WANT YOU TO INFILTRATE THE LIBRARY AND GET A BOOK WITHOUT SPEAKING TO A SINGLE PERSON.
CHALLENGE
NINJA CHECKOUT
HAZ LEVEL 4
YOUR MISSION: TO FIND A BOOK ON NELLIE BLY.
FIND THE BOOK USING THE COMPUTER CATALOG.
LOCATE THE BOOK.
USE THE SELF-CHECKOUT MACHINE.
THEN DISAPPEAR LIKE SMOKE.
COMPLETE THE MISSION AND DRAW THE MISSION WITH YOU AS A NINJA.
THE END

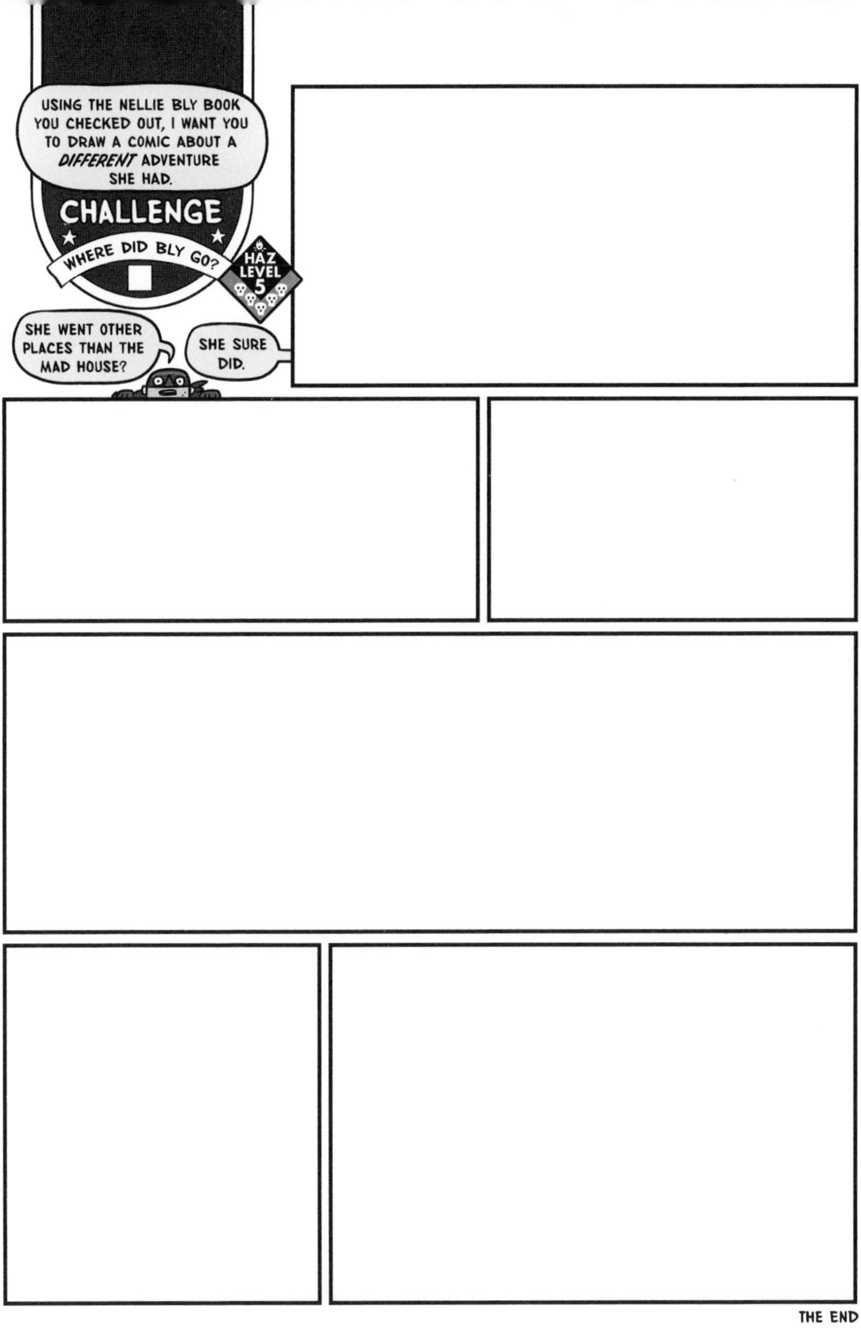
USING THE NELLIE BLY BOOK YOU CHECKED OUT, I WANT YOU TO DRAW A COMIC ABOUT A *DIFFERENT* ADVENTURE SHE HAD.
CHALLENGE
WHERE DID BLY GO?
HAZ LEVEL 5
SHE WENT OTHER PLACES THAN THE MAD HOUSE?
SHE SURE DID.
THE END

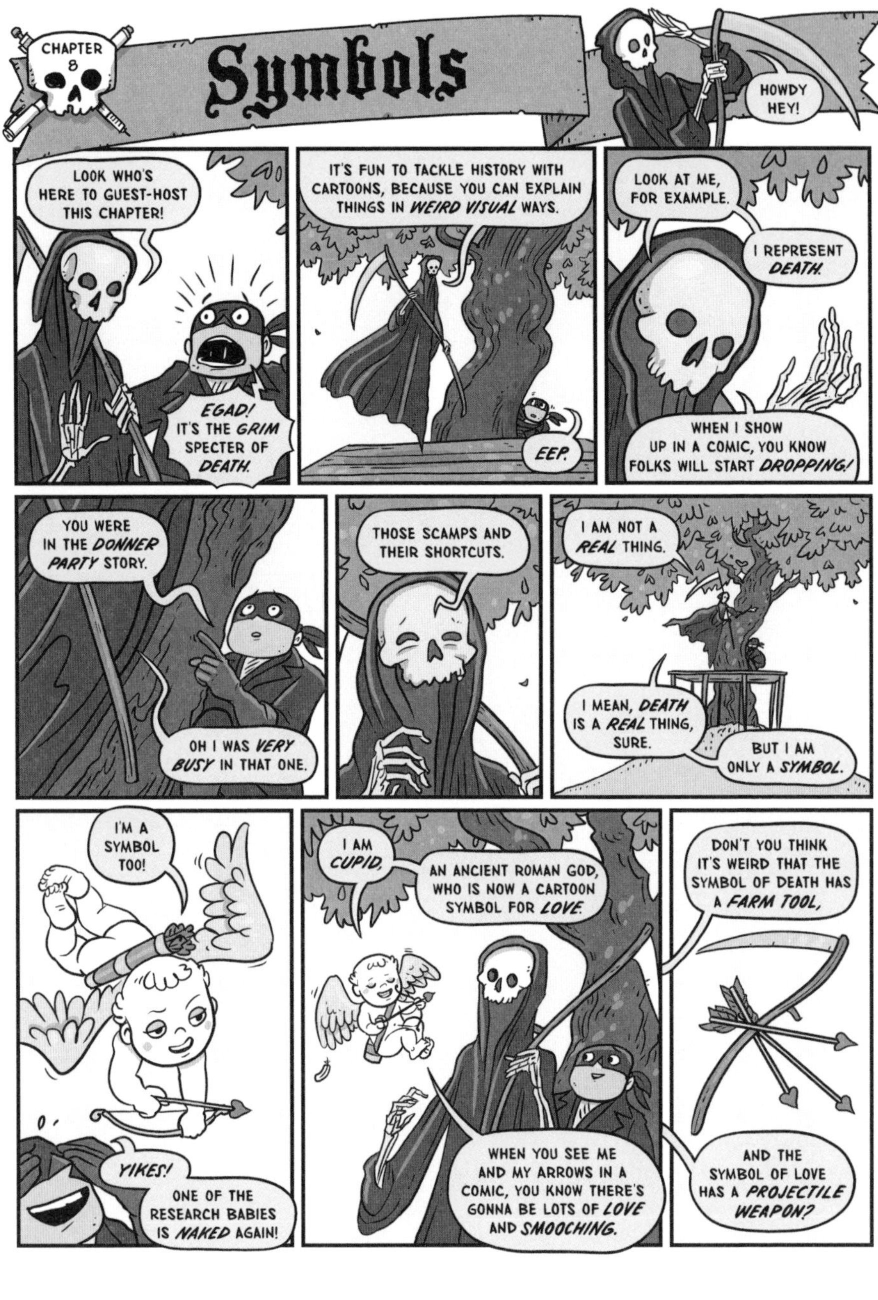
CHAPTER 8
Symbols
HOWDY HEY!
LOOK WHO'S HERE TO GUEST-HOST THIS CHAPTER!
EGAD! IT'S THE GRIM SPECTER OF DEATH.
IT'S FUN TO TACKLE HISTORY WITH CARTOONS, BECAUSE YOU CAN EXPLAIN THINGS IN WEIRD VISUAL WAYS.
EEP.
LOOK AT ME, FOR EXAMPLE.
I REPRESENT DEATH.
WHEN I SHOW UP IN A COMIC, YOU KNOW FOLKS WILL START DROPPING!
YOU WERE IN THE DONNER PARTY STORY.
OH I WAS VERY BUSY IN THAT ONE.
THOSE SCAMPS AND THEIR SHORTCUTS.
I AM NOT A REAL THING.
I MEAN, DEATH IS A REAL THING, SURE.
BUT I AM ONLY A SYMBOL.
I'M A SYMBOL TOO!
YIKES!
ONE OF THE RESEARCH BABIES IS NAKED AGAIN!
I AM CUPID,
AN ANCIENT ROMAN GOD, WHO IS NOW A CARTOON SYMBOL FOR LOVE.
WHEN YOU SEE ME AND MY ARROWS IN A COMIC, YOU KNOW THERE'S GONNA BE LOTS OF LOVE AND SMOOCHING.
DON'T YOU THINK IT'S WEIRD THAT THE SYMBOL OF DEATH HAS A FARM TOOL,
AND THE SYMBOL OF LOVE HAS A PROJECTILE WEAPON?

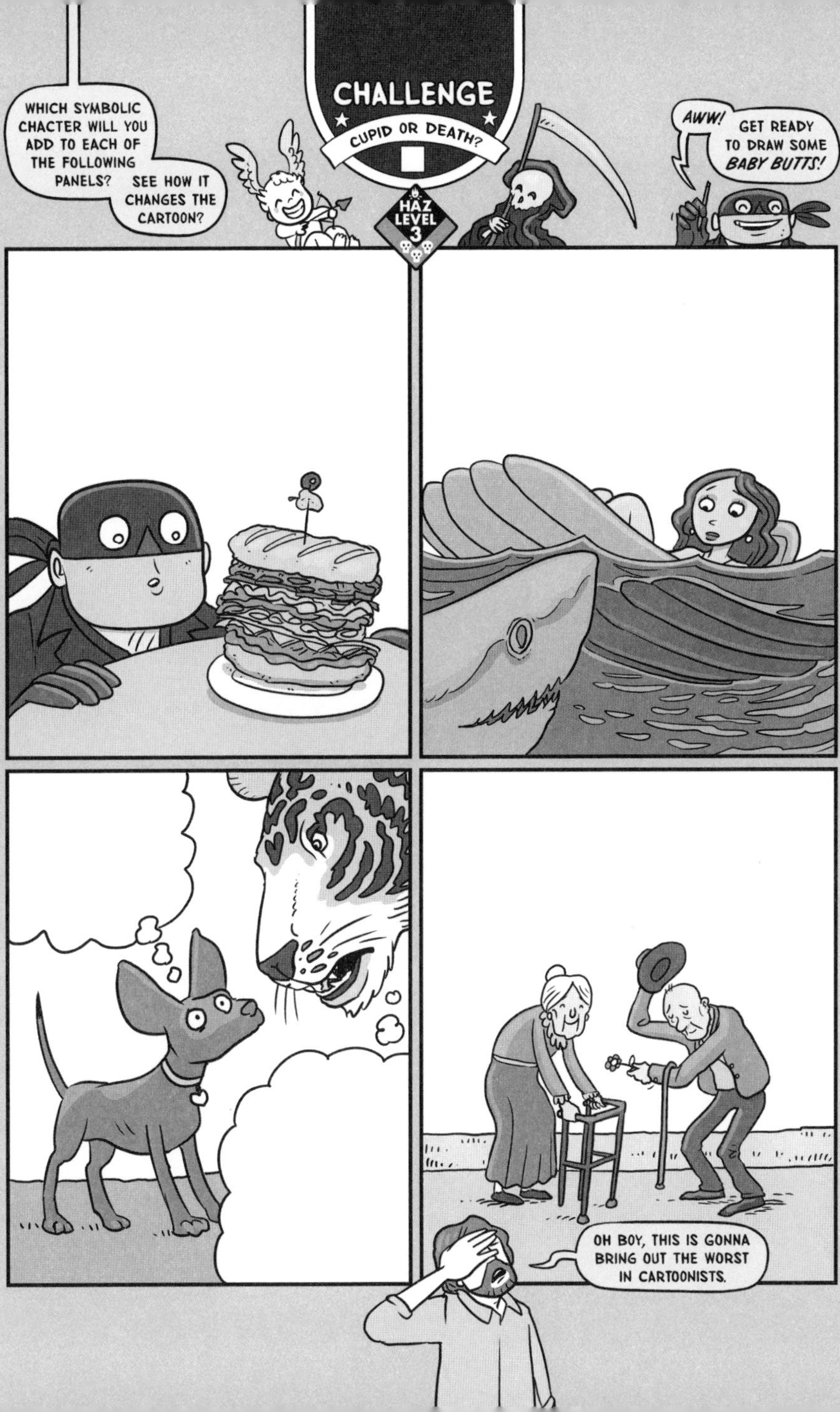

CHALLENGE
CUPID OR DEATH?
WHICH SYMBOLIC CHACTER WILL YOU ADD TO EACH OF THE FOLLOWING PANELS?
SEE HOW IT CHANGES THE CARTOON?
HAZ LEVEL 3
AWW!
GET READY TO DRAW SOME *BABY BUTTS!*
OH BOY, THIS IS GONNA BRING OUT THE WORST IN CARTOONISTS.

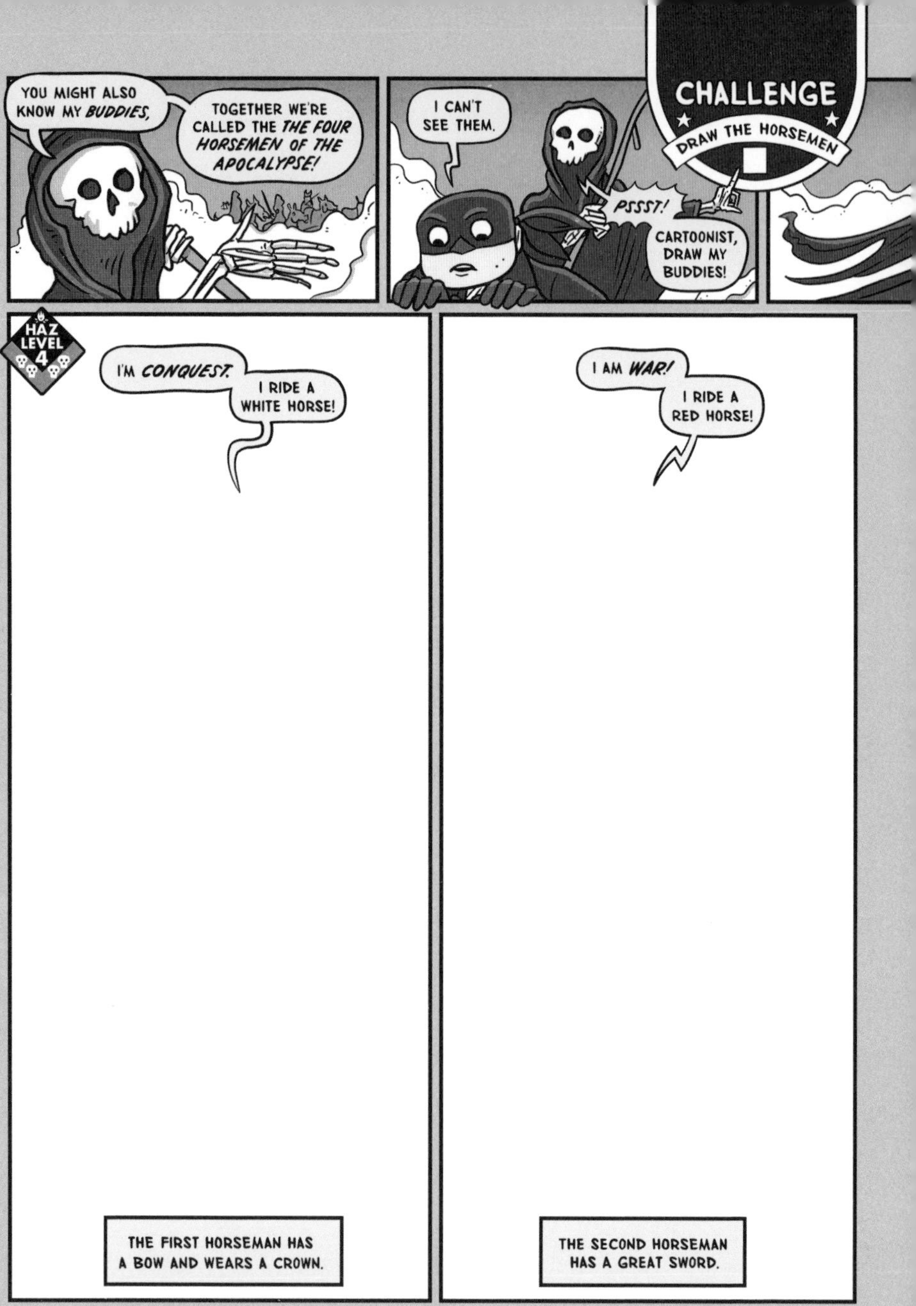
YOU MIGHT ALSO KNOW MY *BUDDIES*,
TOGETHER WE'RE CALLED THE *THE FOUR HORSEMEN OF THE APOCALYPSE!*
I CAN'T SEE THEM.
CHALLENGE
DRAW THE HORSEMEN
PSSST!
CARTOONIST, DRAW MY BUDDIES!
HAZ LEVEL 4
I'M *CONQUEST.*
I RIDE A WHITE HORSE!
THE FIRST HORSEMAN HAS A BOW AND WEARS A CROWN.
I AM *WAR!*
I RIDE A RED HORSE!
THE SECOND HORSEMAN HAS A GREAT SWORD.

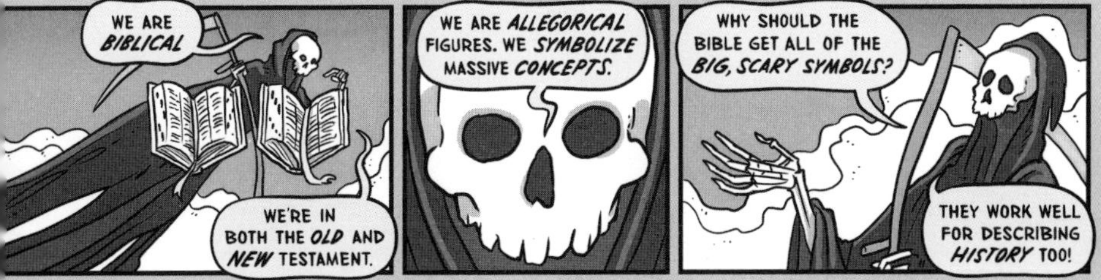
WE ARE BIBLICAL
WE'RE IN BOTH THE OLD AND NEW TESTAMENT.
WE ARE ALLEGORICAL FIGURES. WE SYMBOLIZE MASSIVE CONCEPTS.
WHY SHOULD THE BIBLE GET ALL OF THE BIG, SCARY SYMBOLS?
THEY WORK WELL FOR DESCRIBING HISTORY TOO!

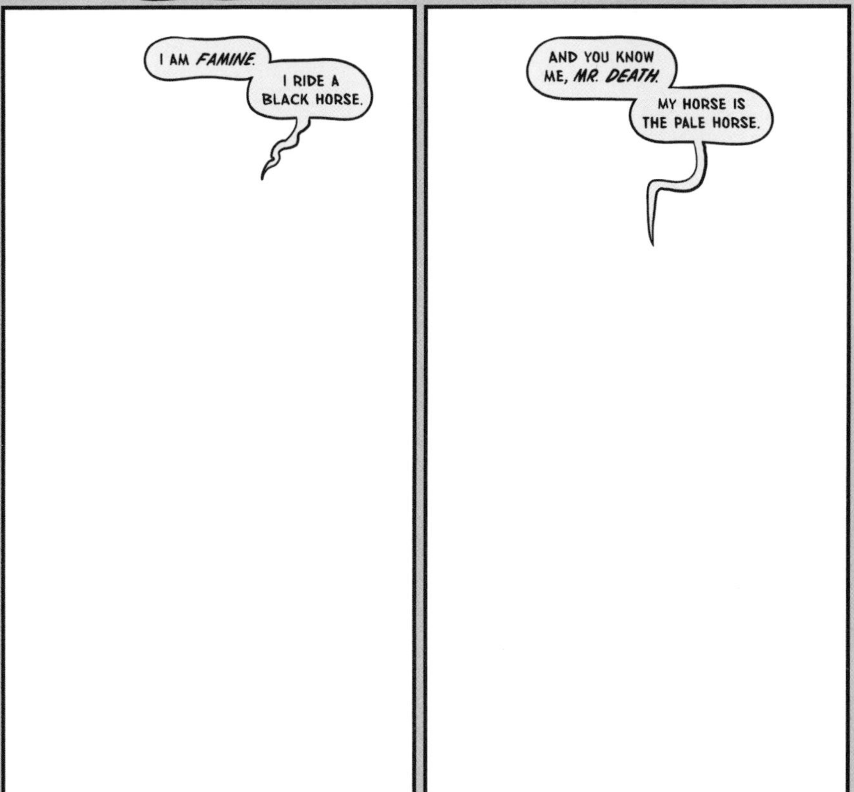
I AM FAMINE.
I RIDE A BLACK HORSE.
THE THIRD HORSEMAN CARRIES A BALANCING SCALE.
AND YOU KNOW ME, MR. DEATH.
MY HORSE IS THE PALE HORSE.
I'M JUST GONNA SAY IT, YOU GUYS ARE HUGE JERKS.

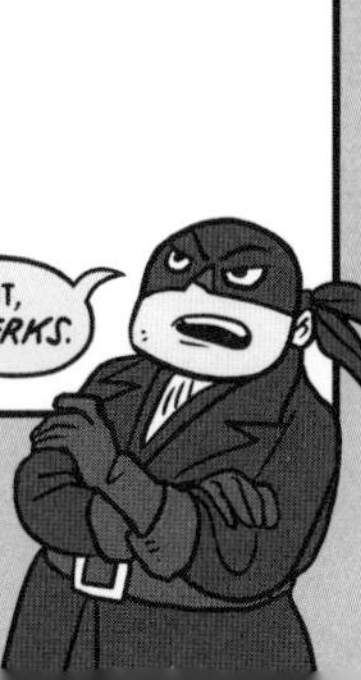

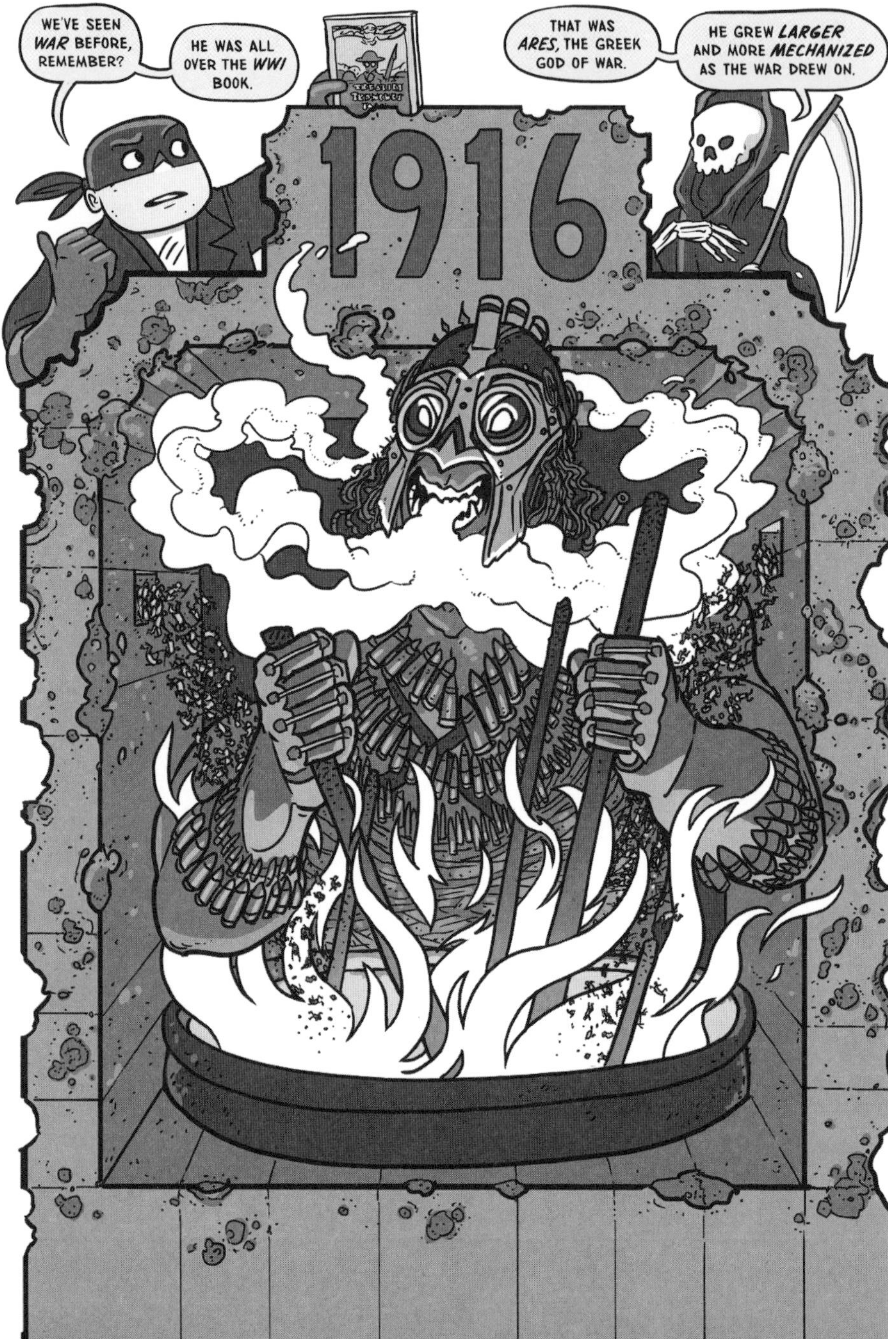
WE'VE SEEN WAR BEFORE, REMEMBER?
HE WAS ALL OVER THE WWI BOOK.
THAT WAS ARES, THE GREEK GOD OF WAR.
HE GREW LARGER AND MORE MECHANIZED AS THE WAR DREW ON.
1916

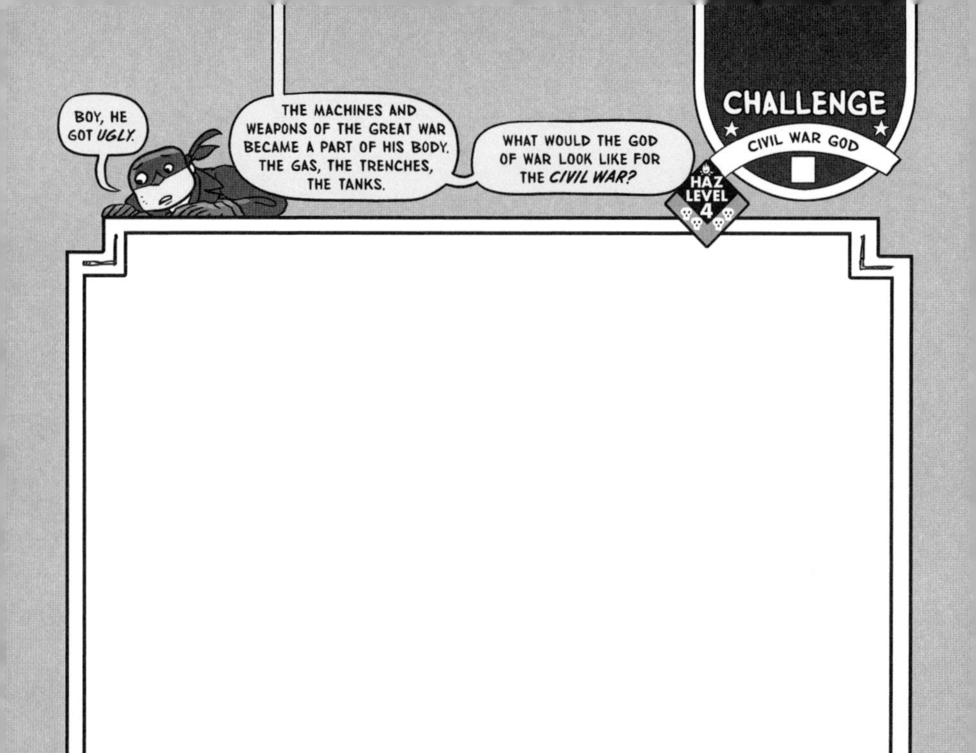
BOY, HE GOT *UGLY.*
THE MACHINES AND WEAPONS OF THE GREAT WAR BECAME A PART OF HIS BODY. THE GAS, THE TRENCHES, THE TANKS.
WHAT WOULD THE GOD OF WAR LOOK LIKE FOR THE *CIVIL WAR?*
CHALLENGE
CIVIL WAR GOD
HAZ LEVEL 4

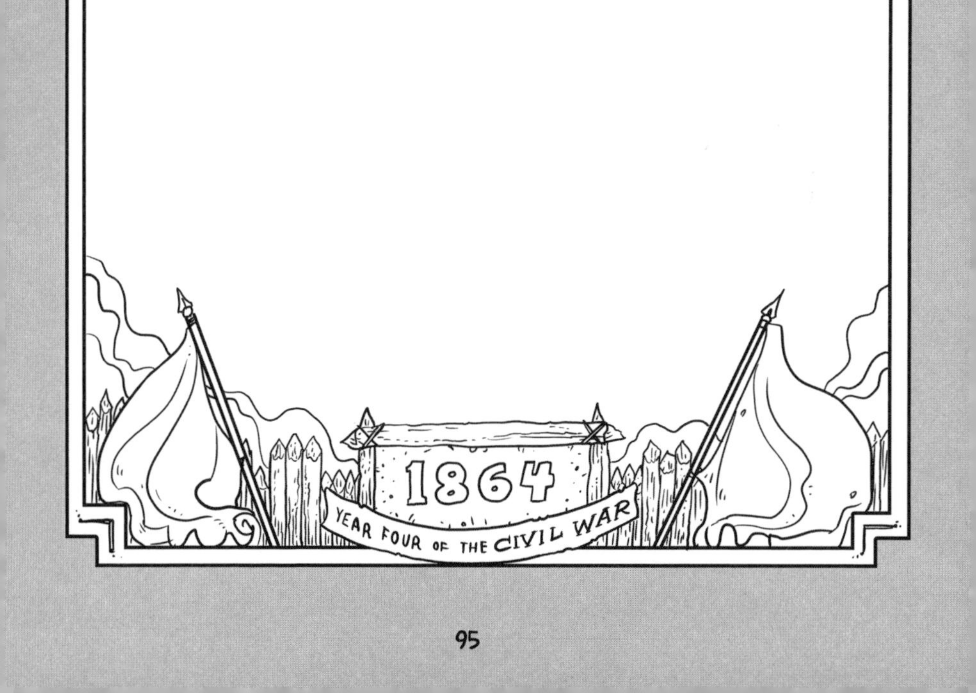
1864
YEAR FOUR OF THE CIVIL WAR

WHAT WOULD THE GOD OF WAR LOOK LIKE DURING ***WORLD WAR II?***

CHALLENGE

WORLD WAR II GOD

HAZ LEVEL 4

1944

FOR OUR LAST GOD OF WAR, DRAW YOUR VISION OF WHAT ARES WOULD LIKE LIKE DURING THE ***VIETNAM WAR.***

CHALLENGE

ARES IN VIETNAM

HAZ LEVEL 4

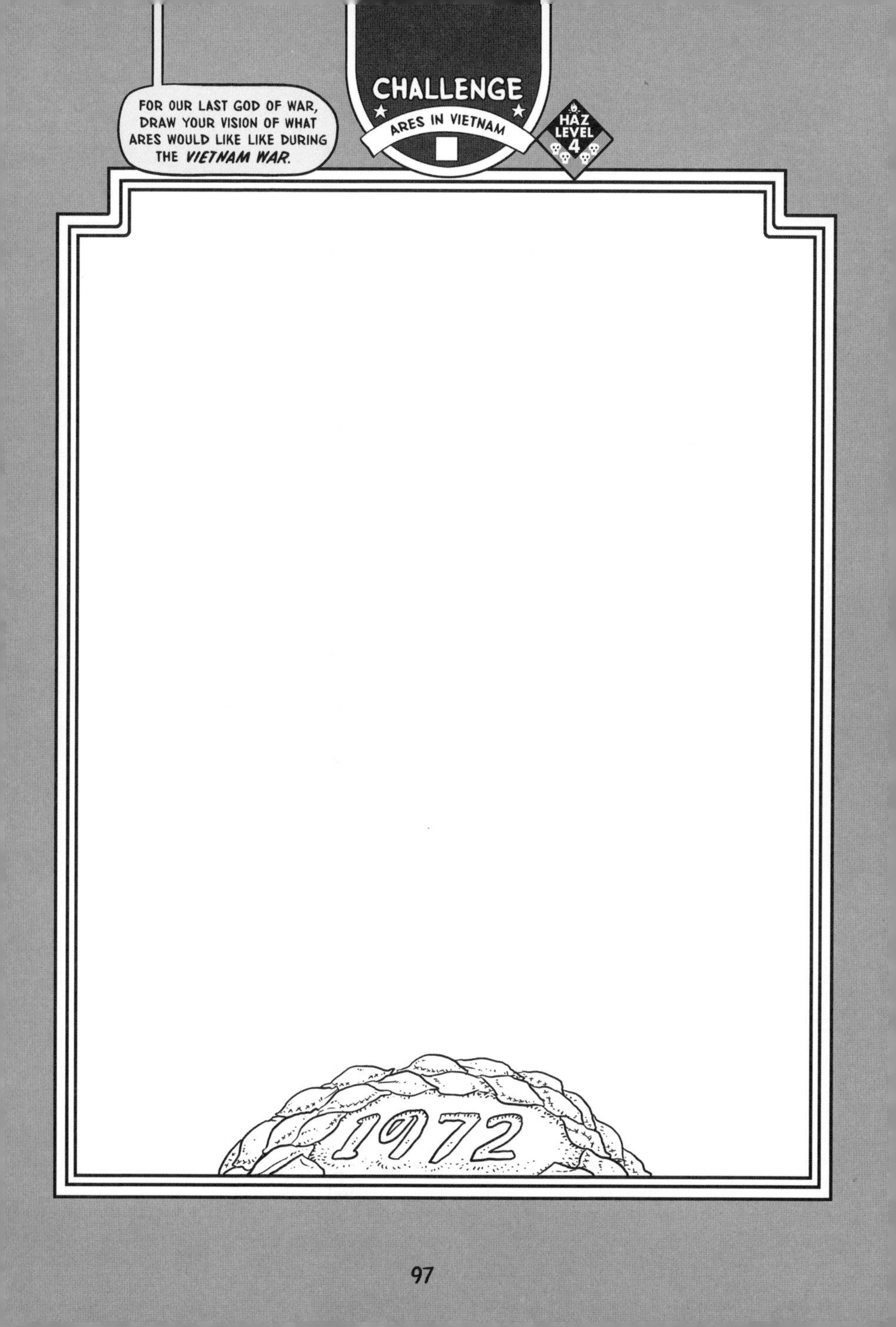
1972

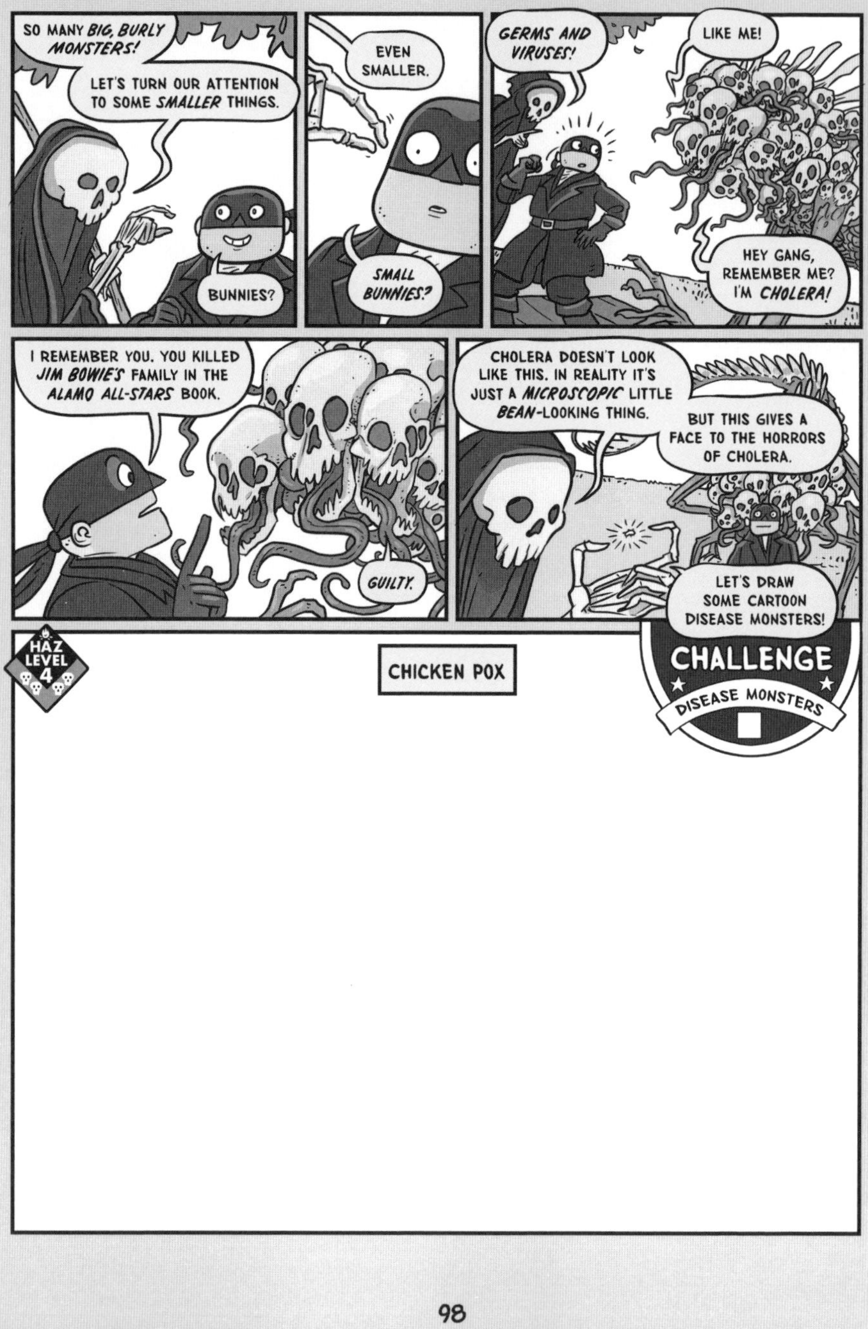
SO MANY *BIG, BURLY MONSTERS!*
LET'S TURN OUR ATTENTION TO SOME *SMALLER* THINGS.
BUNNIES?
EVEN SMALLER.
SMALL BUNNIES?
GERMS AND VIRUSES!
LIKE ME!
HEY GANG, REMEMBER ME? I'M *CHOLERA!*
I REMEMBER YOU. YOU KILLED *JIM BOWIE'S* FAMILY IN THE *ALAMO ALL-STARS* BOOK.
GUILTY.
CHOLERA DOESN'T LOOK LIKE THIS. IN REALITY IT'S JUST A *MICROSCOPIC* LITTLE *BEAN*-LOOKING THING.
BUT THIS GIVES A FACE TO THE HORRORS OF CHOLERA.
LET'S DRAW SOME CARTOON DISEASE MONSTERS!

HAZ LEVEL 4

CHALLENGE

DISEASE MONSTERS

CHICKEN POX

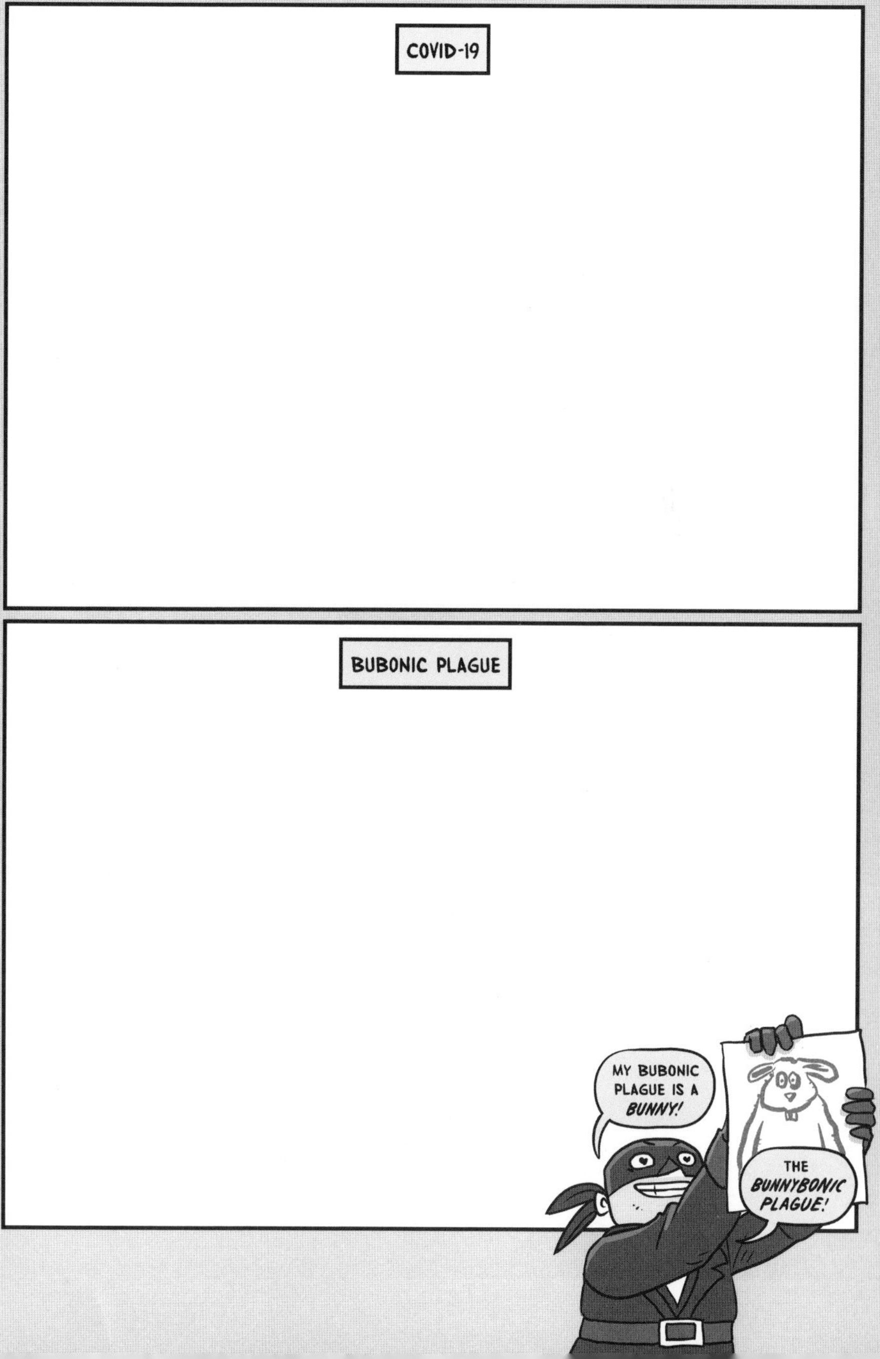
COVID-19
BUBONIC PLAGUE
MY BUBONIC PLAGUE IS A BUNNY!
THE BUNNYBONIC PLAGUE!

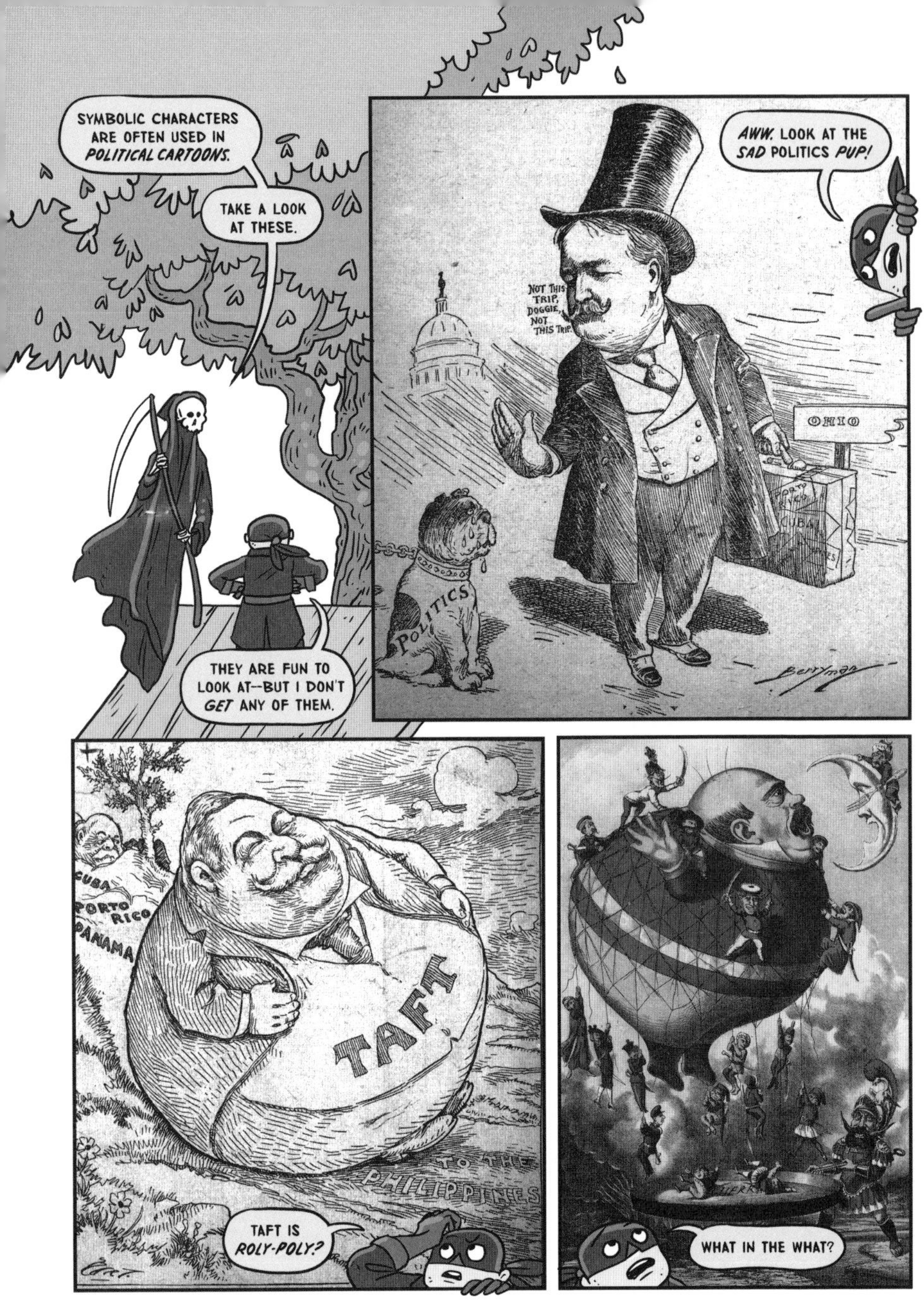
SYMBOLIC CHARACTERS ARE OFTEN USED IN *POLITICAL CARTOONS.*
TAKE A LOOK AT THESE.
THEY ARE FUN TO LOOK AT--BUT I DON'T *GET* ANY OF THEM.
NOT THIS TRIP, DOGGIE, NOT THIS TRIP.
OHIO
CUBA
POLITICS
Berryman
AWW. LOOK AT THE *SAD* POLITICS *PUP!*
CUBA
PORTO RICO
PANAMA
TAFT
TO THE PHILIPPINES
TAFT IS *ROLY-POLY?*
WHAT IN THE WHAT?

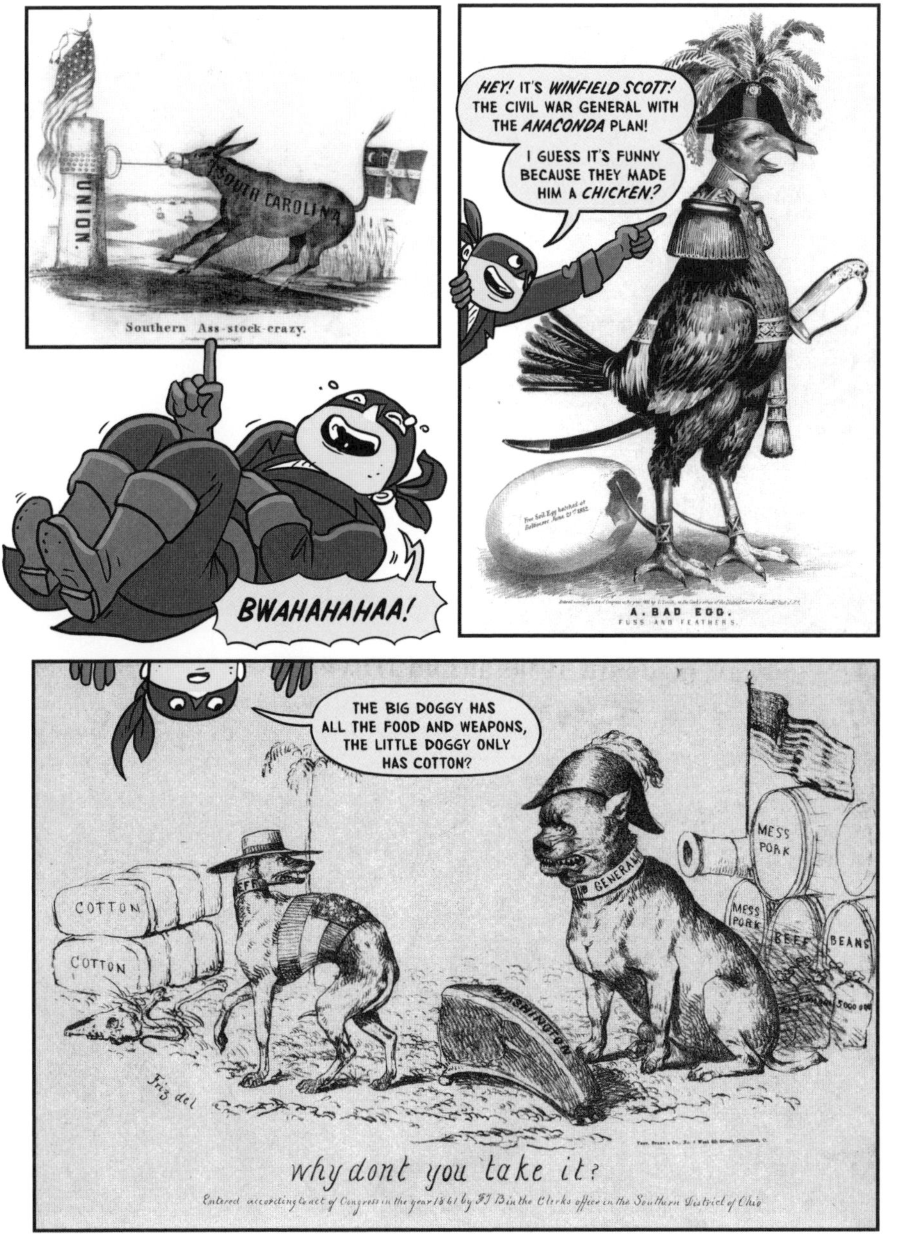
UNION
SOUTH CAROLINA
Southern Ass-stock-crazy.
HEY! IT'S WINFIELD SCOTT! THE CIVIL WAR GENERAL WITH THE ANACONDA PLAN!
I GUESS IT'S FUNNY BECAUSE THEY MADE HIM A CHICKEN?
BWAHAHAHAA!
A. BAD EGG.
FUSS AND FEATHERS.
THE BIG DOGGY HAS ALL THE FOOD AND WEAPONS, THE LITTLE DOGGY ONLY HAS COTTON?
COTTON
COTTON
GENERAL
WASHINGTON
MESS PORK
MESS PORK
BEEF
BEANS
Frig del
why dont you take it?
Entered according to act of Congress in the year 1861 by F J B in the Clerks office in the Southern District of Ohio

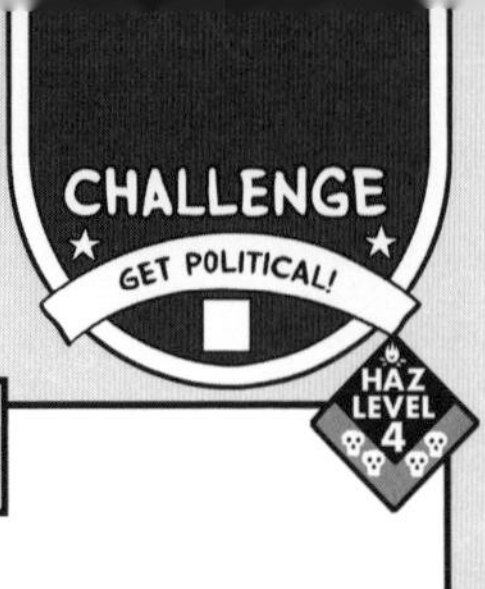
CHALLENGE
GET POLITICAL!
HAZ LEVEL 4

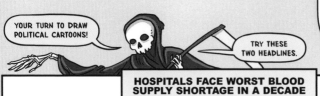

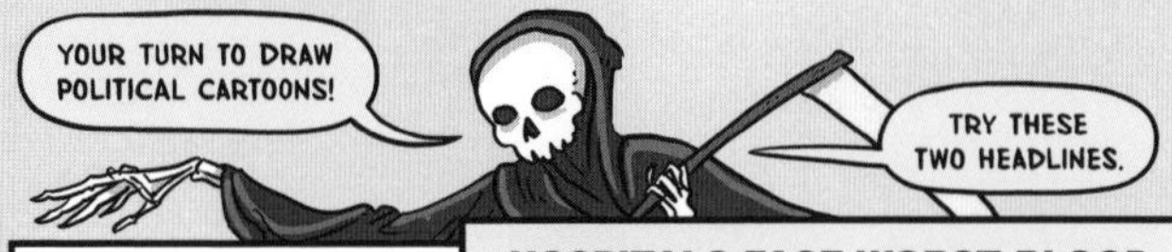
YOUR TURN TO DRAW POLITICAL CARTOONS!
TRY THESE TWO HEADLINES.

HOSPITALS FACE WORST BLOOD SUPPLY SHORTAGE IN A DECADE

PRESIDENT TRUMAN WIPES OUT SEGREGATION IN ARMED FORCES

CHALLENGE

DAILY SYMBOL STRIP

HAZ LEVEL 4

TIME FOR ANOTHER DAILY STRIP!

TAKE TWO CHARACTERS FROM THE SYMBOLS CHAPTER--

A DISEASE, A WAR, A HORSEMAN--AND SEE WHAT THEY HAVE TO SAY TO EACH OTHER.

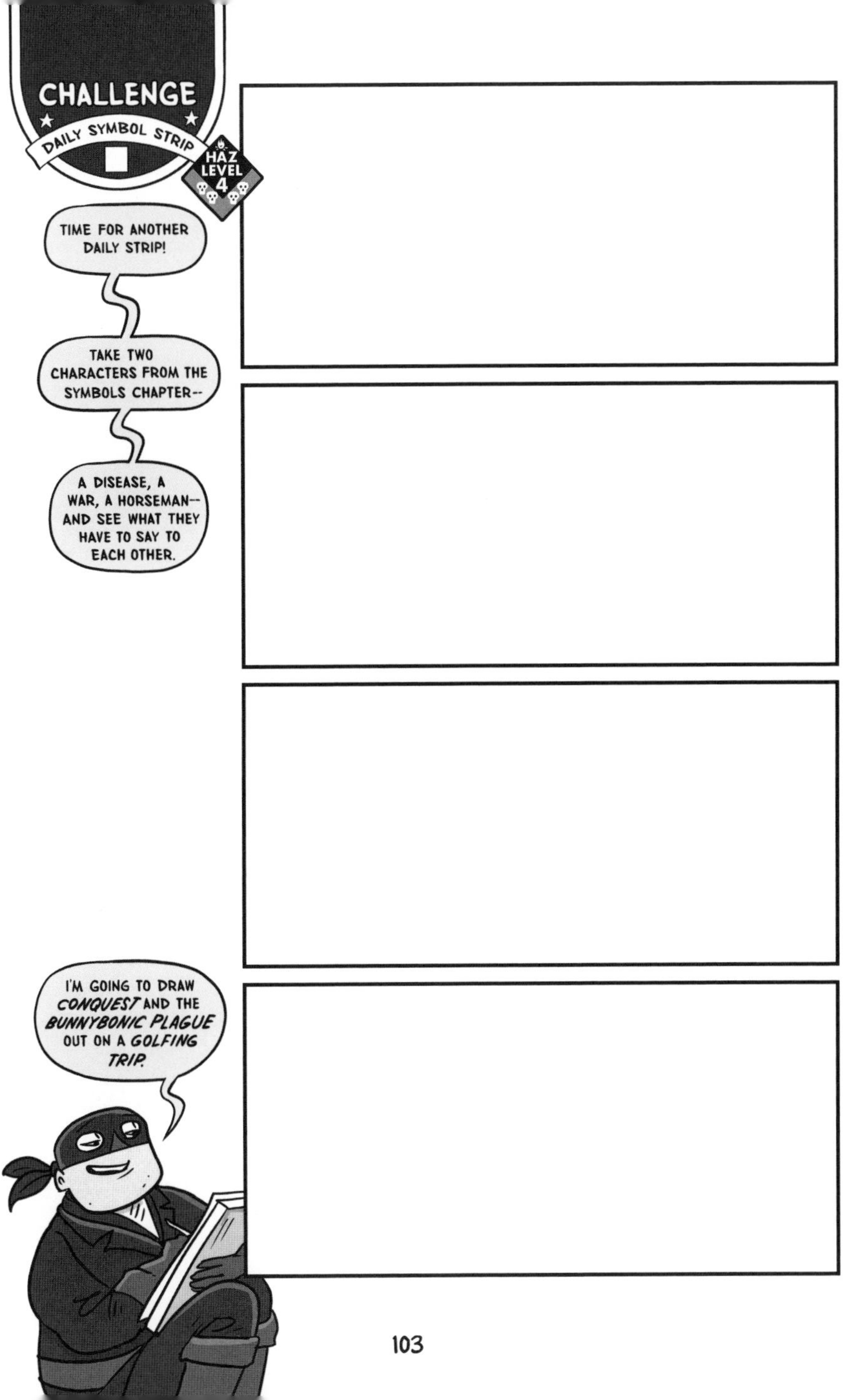
I'M GOING TO DRAW *CONQUEST* AND THE *BUNNYBONIC PLAGUE* OUT ON A *GOLFING TRIP.*

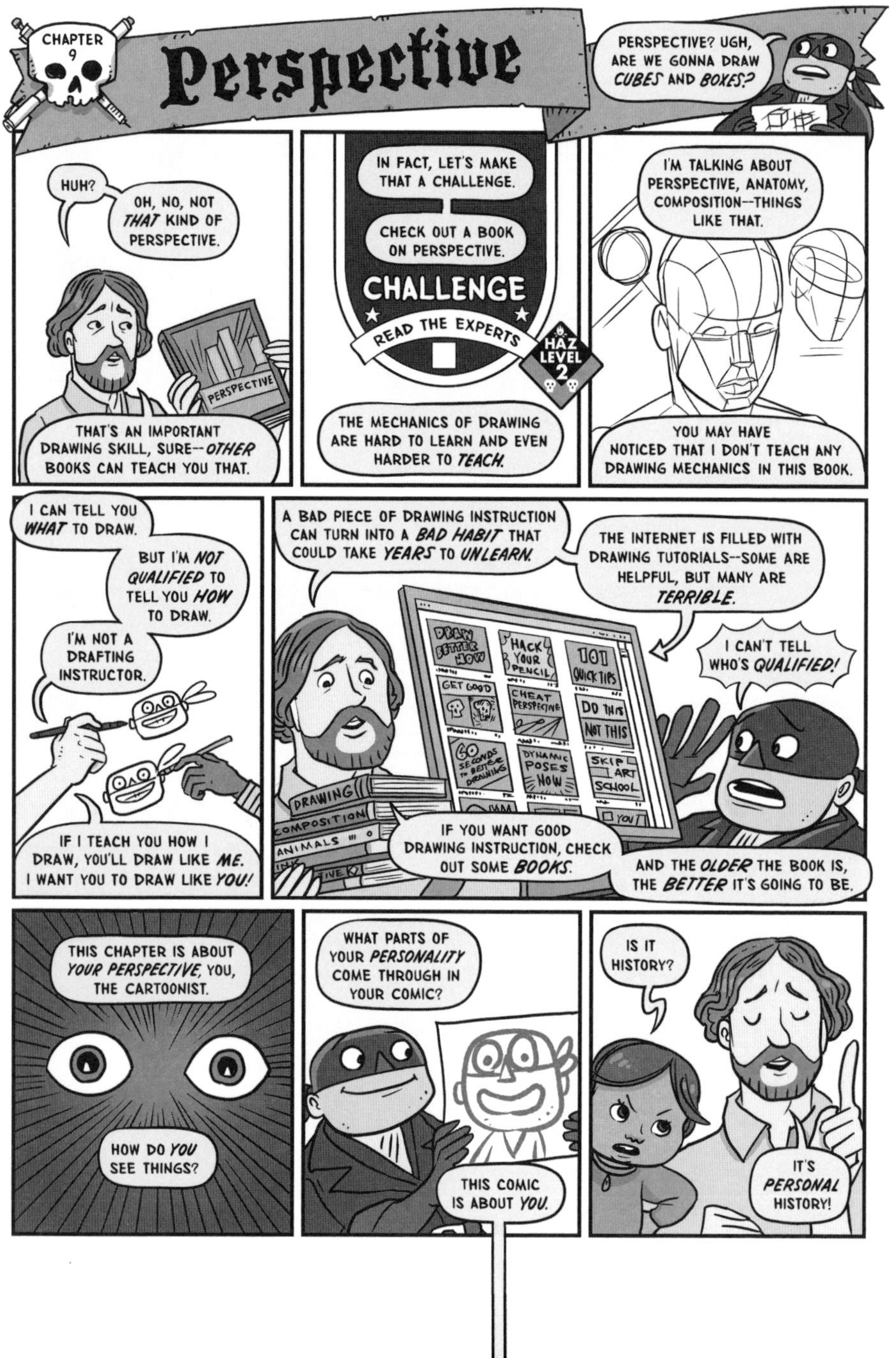
CHAPTER 9
Perspective
PERSPECTIVE? UGH, ARE WE GONNA DRAW CUBES AND BOXES?
HUH?
OH, NO, NOT THAT KIND OF PERSPECTIVE.
PERSPECTIVE
THAT'S AN IMPORTANT DRAWING SKILL, SURE--OTHER BOOKS CAN TEACH YOU THAT.
IN FACT, LET'S MAKE THAT A CHALLENGE.
CHECK OUT A BOOK ON PERSPECTIVE.
CHALLENGE
READ THE EXPERTS
HAZ LEVEL 2
THE MECHANICS OF DRAWING ARE HARD TO LEARN AND EVEN HARDER TO TEACH.
I'M TALKING ABOUT PERSPECTIVE, ANATOMY, COMPOSITION--THINGS LIKE THAT.
YOU MAY HAVE NOTICED THAT I DON'T TEACH ANY DRAWING MECHANICS IN THIS BOOK.
I CAN TELL YOU WHAT TO DRAW.
BUT I'M NOT QUALIFIED TO TELL YOU HOW TO DRAW.
I'M NOT A DRAFTING INSTRUCTOR.
IF I TEACH YOU HOW I DRAW, YOU'LL DRAW LIKE ME. I WANT YOU TO DRAW LIKE YOU!
A BAD PIECE OF DRAWING INSTRUCTION CAN TURN INTO A BAD HABIT THAT COULD TAKE YEARS TO UNLEARN.
THE INTERNET IS FILLED WITH DRAWING TUTORIALS--SOME ARE HELPFUL, BUT MANY ARE TERRIBLE.
DRAW BETTER NOW
HACK YOUR PENCIL
101 QUICK TIPS
GET GOOD
CHEAT PERSPECTIVE
DO THIS NOT THIS
60 SECONDS TO BETTER DRAWING
DYNAMIC POSES NOW
SKIP ART SCHOOL
I CAN'T TELL WHO'S QUALIFIED!
DRAWING
COMPOSITION
ANIMALS
IF YOU WANT GOOD DRAWING INSTRUCTION, CHECK OUT SOME BOOKS.
AND THE OLDER THE BOOK IS, THE BETTER IT'S GOING TO BE.
THIS CHAPTER IS ABOUT YOUR PERSPECTIVE, YOU, THE CARTOONIST.
HOW DO YOU SEE THINGS?
WHAT PARTS OF YOUR PERSONALITY COME THROUGH IN YOUR COMIC?
THIS COMIC IS ABOUT YOU.
IS IT HISTORY?
IT'S PERSONAL HISTORY!

CHALLENGE

IT'S ALL ABOUT YOU

HAZ LEVEL 3

YOU ARE THE MAIN CHARACTER NOW. WHAT DOES *CARTOON YOU* LOOK LIKE? ARE YOU A HUMAN, AN ANIMAL, WHAT?

FRONT

BACK

YOUR *NAME*: ____________________

WHAT DO YOU *LOVE*: ____________________

WHAT ARE YOU *AFRAID OF*: ____________________

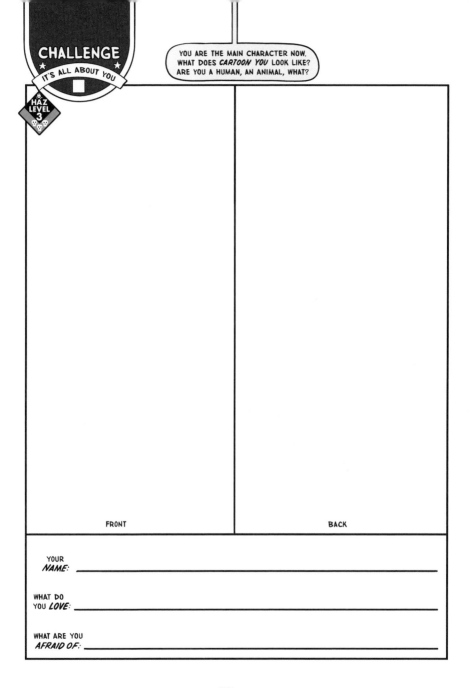

CHALLENGE

★ WRITE ABOUT PAIN ★

THIS IS YOUR TOPIC

"***MY WORST INJURY***"

OR

"***THE MOST TROUBLE I WAS EVER IN***"

I WANT YOU TO ***WRITE*** THIS STORY ***BEFORE*** YOU DO ***ANY*** DRAWING.

AWW! I LIKE TO WRITE THE STORY *AS I GO!*

THAT'S ONE WAY TO DO IT. BUT THERE ARE MANY WAYS TO CREATE A COMIC.

ON HAZARDOUS TALES, I DON'T START DRAWING UNTIL THE STORY IS COMPLETELY WRITTEN, EDITED, AND FACT-CHECKED.

TRY DOING ALL OF YOUR WRITING ***FIRST*** AND SEE IF IT MAKES DRAWING THE COMIC ***EASIER***.

WRITE DOWN YOUR EXPERIENCE.

HOW DID IT HAPPEN?

WHAT DID IT ***FEEL*** LIKE?

HAZ LEVEL 5

THESE ARE CARTOON LETTERING LINES. PRACTICE YOUR LETTERING AS YOU WRITE!

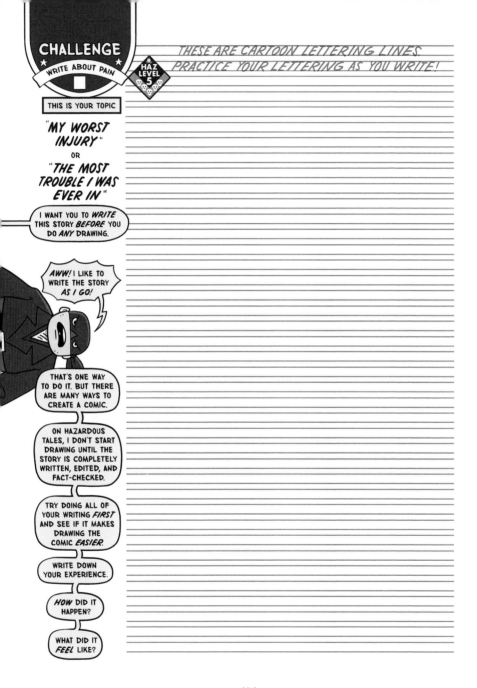

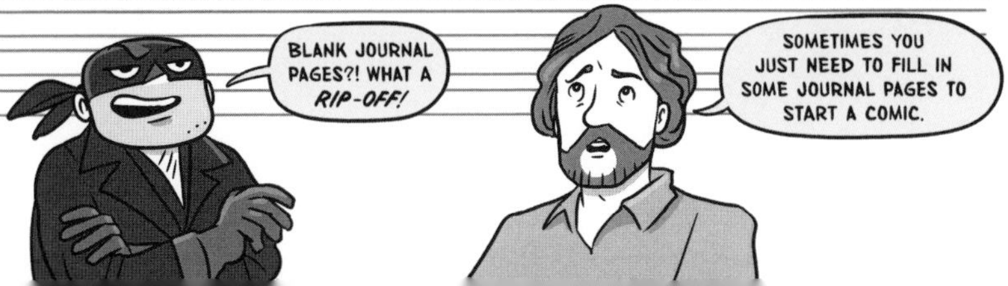
BLANK JOURNAL PAGES?! WHAT A RIP-OFF!
SOMETIMES YOU JUST NEED TO FILL IN SOME JOURNAL PAGES TO START A COMIC.

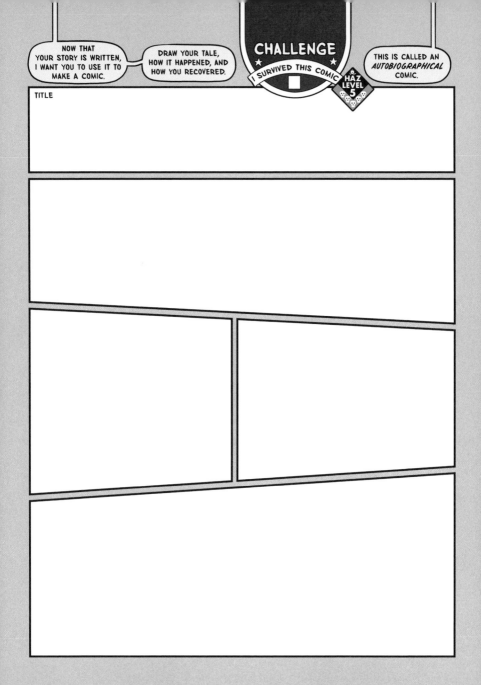

NOW THAT YOUR STORY IS WRITTEN, I WANT YOU TO USE IT TO MAKE A COMIC.

DRAW YOUR TALE, HOW IT HAPPENED, AND HOW YOU RECOVERED.

CHALLENGE

I SURVIVED THIS COMIC

HAZ LEVEL 5

THIS IS CALLED AN *AUTOBIOGRAPHICAL* COMIC.

TITLE

THE END

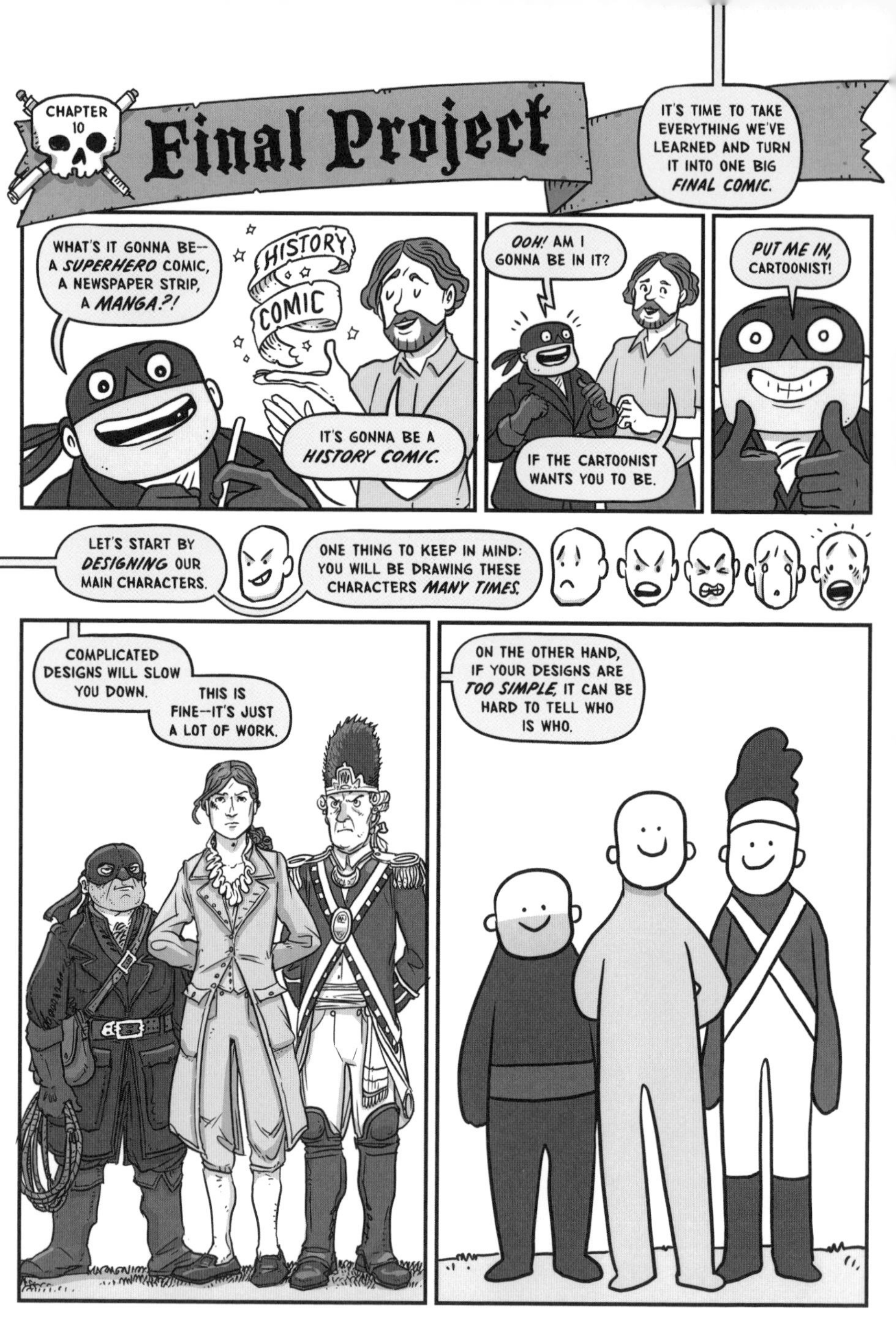
CHAPTER 10
Final Project
IT'S TIME TO TAKE EVERYTHING WE'VE LEARNED AND TURN IT INTO ONE BIG FINAL COMIC.
WHAT'S IT GONNA BE-- A SUPERHERO COMIC, A NEWSPAPER STRIP, A MANGA?!
HISTORY COMIC
IT'S GONNA BE A HISTORY COMIC.
OOH! AM I GONNA BE IN IT?
IF THE CARTOONIST WANTS YOU TO BE.
PUT ME IN, CARTOONIST!
LET'S START BY DESIGNING OUR MAIN CHARACTERS.
ONE THING TO KEEP IN MIND: YOU WILL BE DRAWING THESE CHARACTERS MANY TIMES.
COMPLICATED DESIGNS WILL SLOW YOU DOWN.
THIS IS FINE--IT'S JUST A LOT OF WORK.
ON THE OTHER HAND, IF YOUR DESIGNS ARE TOO SIMPLE, IT CAN BE HARD TO TELL WHO IS WHO.

CHALLENGE

THE THIRD PRESIDENT

THE FIRST CHARACTER WE ARE DESIGNING IS THE THIRD PRESIDENT OF THE UNITED STATES,

HERE IS A PORTRAIT.

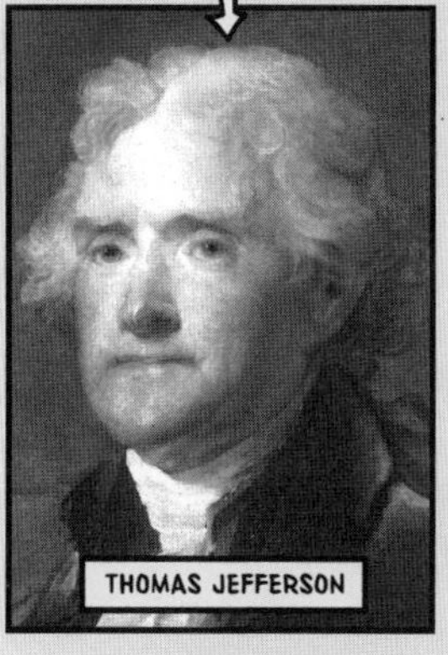
THOMAS JEFFERSON

YOU DON'T HAVE TO MAKE HIM LOOK REALISTIC IF YOU DON'T WANT TO.

THIS IS A COMIC.

YOU CAN DRAW HIM AS A *TALKING DONUT* IF YOU WANT.

HAZ LEVEL 2

THIS IS A LEWIS AND CLARK STORY

WILLIAM CLARK AND MERIWETHER LEWIS WERE EXPLORERS. THEY WERE SENT INTO THE NEWLY ACQUIRED LOUISIANA TERRITORY IN 1803. THEIR MISSION: TO TRACK THE RIVERS ALL THE WAY TO THE PACIFIC OCEAN. THEY WERE TO MAKE PEACEFUL CONTACT WITH ANY NATIVE AMERICAN COMMUNITIES, AND KEEP JOURNALS ABOUT EVERYTHING THEY SAW.

THEY BROUGHT FANCY UNIFORMS, LIKE THE ONES YOU SEE IN THE STATUE BELOW. THEY WOULD HAVE WORN THESE IMPRESSIVE SUITS WHEN MEETING NATIVE AMERICAN LEADERSHIP. MOST DAYS THEY WOULD HAVE WORN BUCKSKIN FRONTIER CLOTHING LIKE YOU SEE IN THE NORTHERN PACIFIC POSTER.

MERIWEATHER LEWIS WAS THOMAS JEFFERSON'S SECRETARY. THE PRESIDENT DESCRIBED HIM THIS WAY:

"IT WAS IMPOSSIBLE TO FIND A CHARACTER WHO TO A COMPLEAT SCIENCE IN BOTANY, NATURAL HISTORY, MINERALOGY & ASTRONOMY, JOINED THE FIRMNESS OF CONSTITUTION & CHARACTER, PRUDENCE, HABITS ADAPTED TO THE WOODS, & A FAMILIARITY WITH THE INDIAN MANNERS & CHARACTER, REQUISITE FOR THIS UNDERTAKING."

HE ALSO SAID LEWIS HAD "SENSIBLE DEPRESSIONS OF MIND."

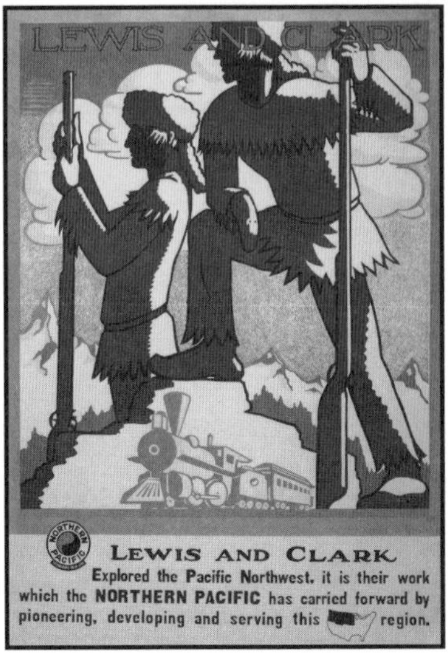
LEWIS AND CLARK
NORTHERN PACIFIC
LEWIS AND CLARK
Explored the Pacific Northwest. it is their work which the NORTHERN PACIFIC has carried forward by pioneering, developing and serving this region.

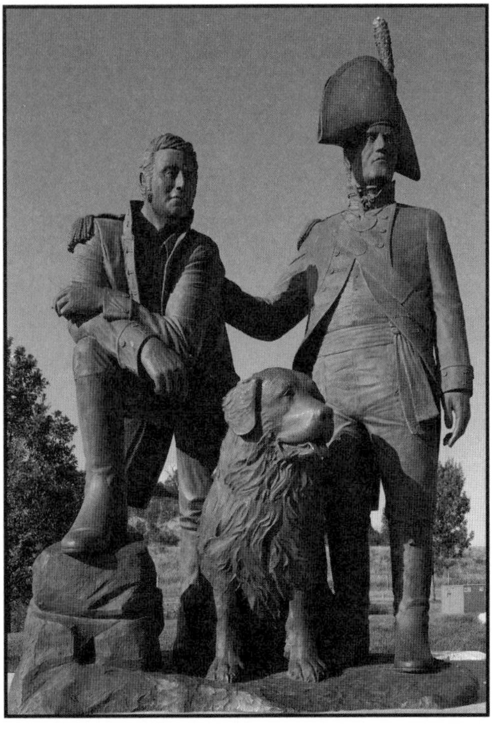

WILLIAM CLARK WAS A TALL, STRONG REDHEAD. HE HAD BEEN A COMPANY COMMANDER IN THE ARMY. HE DREW THE MAPS AND KEPT A JOURNAL FILLED WITH SOME OF THE WEIRDEST SPELLING IN AMERICAN HISTORY.

THE BIG DOG IS MERIWETHER'S NEWFOUNDLAND. HE IS NAMED SEAMAN, BECAUSE DOGS OF THIS BREED CAN SWIM AND ARE KEPT ON SAILING SHIPS. LEWIS PAID TWENTY DOLLARS FOR HIM--A VERY EXPENSIVE DOG FOR THE TIME.

DRAW YOUR DESIGNS FOR LEWIS, CLARK, AND SEAMAN. YOU CAN USE THE IMAGES I'VE PROVIDED, OR THE INTERNET, OR--BEST OF ALL--THE LIBRARY.

I GUARANTEE YOUR LIBRARY IS ABSOLUTELY PACKED WITH BOOKS ON LEWIS AND CLARK.

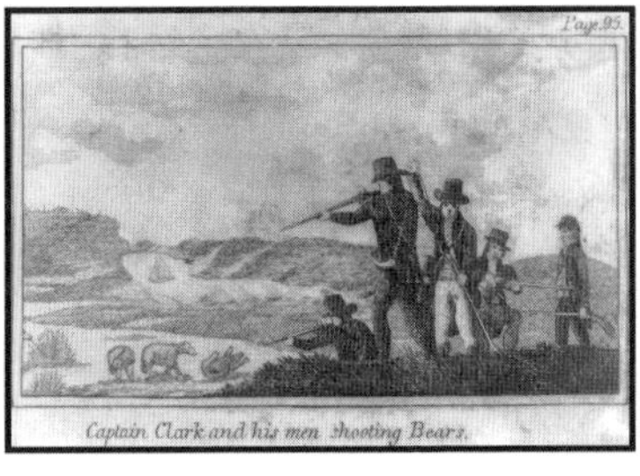
Page 95.
Captain Clark and his men shooting Bears.

CHALLENGE

TWO CAPTAINS

HAZ LEVEL 3

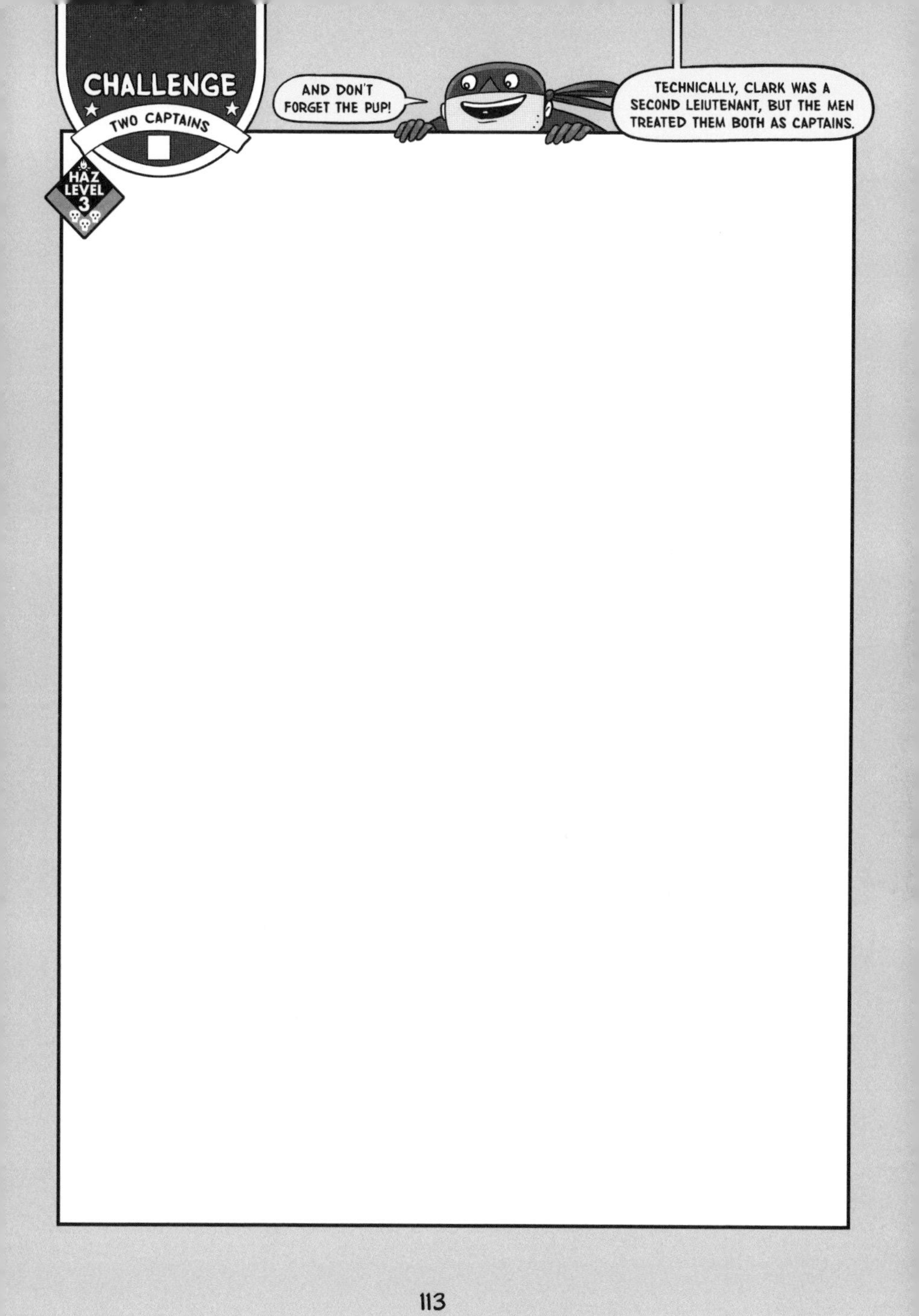
AND DON'T FORGET THE PUP!
TECHNICALLY, CLARK WAS A SECOND LEIUTENANT, BUT THE MEN TREATED THEM BOTH AS CAPTAINS.

LEWIS TOLD WILLIAM CLARK TO:

"FIND AND ENGAGE SOME GOOD HUNTERS, STOUT, HEALTHY, UNMARRIED MEN, ACCOSTUMED TO THE WOODS, AND CAPABLE OF BEARING BODILY FATIGUE."

THESE RECRUITS WERE KNOWN AS THE *CORPS OF DISCOVERY.* IT WAS A MILITARY EXPEDITION. THEY WERE SOLDIERS IN THE UNITED STATES *ARMY.*

THEY SET OUT FROM ST. LOUIS IN MAY OF 1803. THEY REACHED THE PACIFIC COAST AND RETURNED IN SEPTEMBER OF 1806.

YOUR COMIC WILL NOT COVER THE ENTIRE JOURNEY. WE ARE GOING TO FOCUS ON ONE *SMALL* ADVENTURE.

DOES IT INVOLVE ANY SMALL CUDDLY *ANIMALS?*

IT DOES.

BUT LET'S GET A FEW MORE CHARACTERS DESIGNED.

 HAZ LEVEL 5

YORK

THE ONLY AFRICAN AMERICAN MEMBER OF THE CORPS. YORK WAS *ENSLAVED* TO CLARK. HE IS DESCRIBED AS THE *LARGEST* AND *STRONGEST* MEMBER OF THE GROUP. HE CARRIED A LARGE RIFLE AND WAS AN EXCELLENT HUNTER.

CHALLENGE
FOUR IN THE CORPS

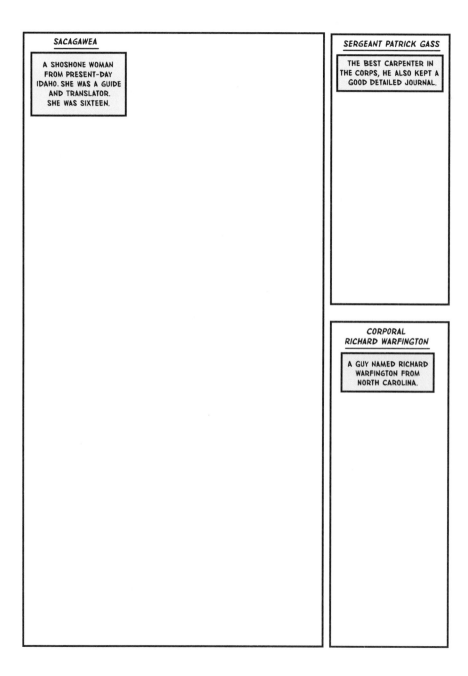

SACAGAWEA

A SHOSHONE WOMAN FROM PRESENT-DAY IDAHO. SHE WAS A GUIDE AND TRANSLATOR. SHE WAS SIXTEEN.

SERGEANT PATRICK GASS

THE BEST CARPENTER IN THE CORPS, HE ALSO KEPT A GOOD DETAILED JOURNAL.

CORPORAL RICHARD WARFINGTON

A GUY NAMED RICHARD WARFINGTON FROM NORTH CAROLINA.

THE LAST TWO DESIGNS ARE FOR *ANIMALS*.

YESSSS!

CHALLENGE
★ ★
CUTE AND CUDDLY?

HAZ LEVEL 3

WE NEED TO DESIGN A WOOLLY MAMMOTH AND A PRAIRIE DOG.

WOOLLY MAMMOTH

PRAIRIE DOG

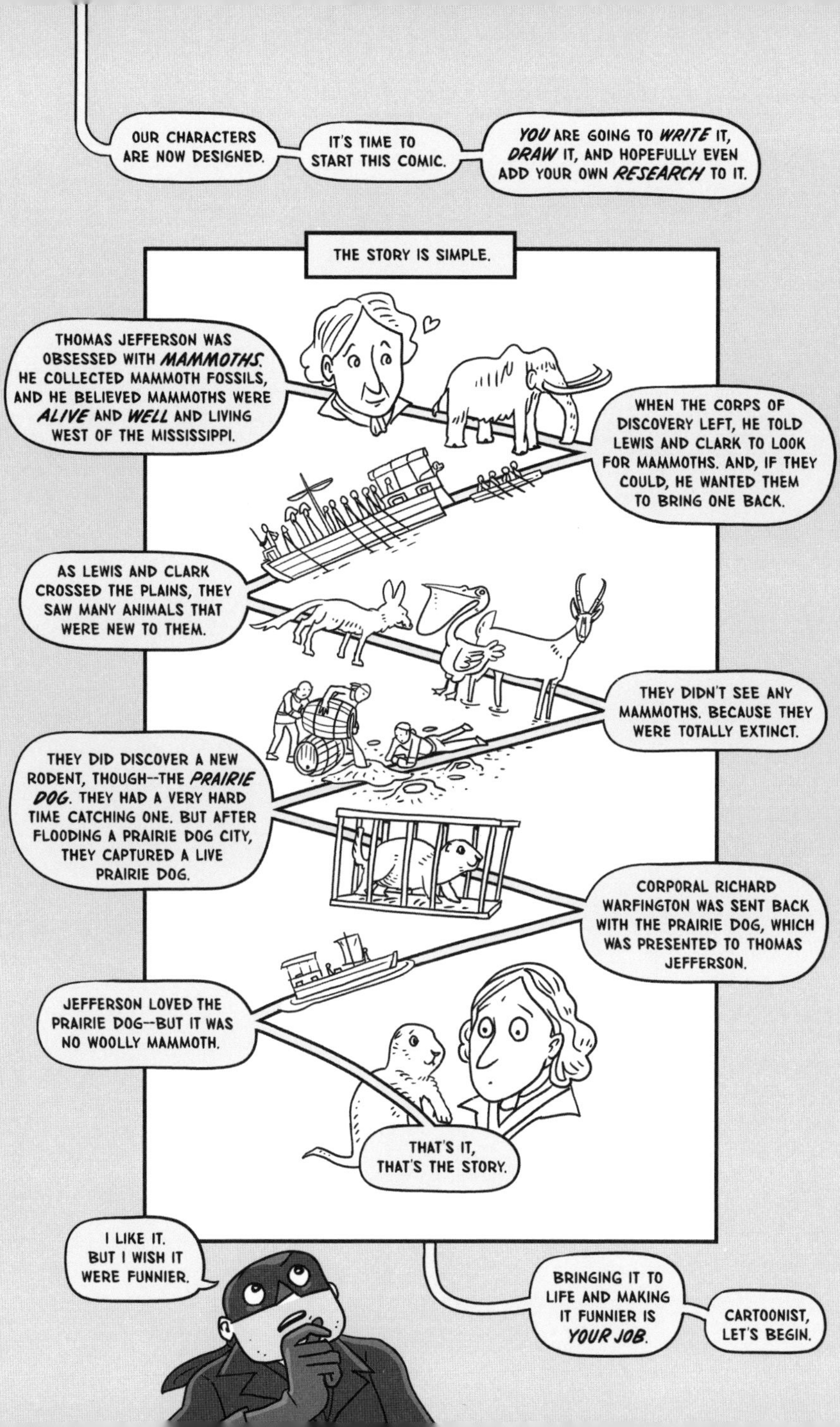
OUR CHARACTERS ARE NOW DESIGNED.
IT'S TIME TO START THIS COMIC.
YOU ARE GOING TO *WRITE* IT, *DRAW* IT, AND HOPEFULLY EVEN ADD YOUR OWN *RESEARCH* TO IT.
THE STORY IS SIMPLE.
THOMAS JEFFERSON WAS OBSESSED WITH *MAMMOTHS*. HE COLLECTED MAMMOTH FOSSILS, AND HE BELIEVED MAMMOTHS WERE *ALIVE* AND *WELL* AND LIVING WEST OF THE MISSISSIPPI.
WHEN THE CORPS OF DISCOVERY LEFT, HE TOLD LEWIS AND CLARK TO LOOK FOR MAMMOTHS. AND, IF THEY COULD, HE WANTED THEM TO BRING ONE BACK.
AS LEWIS AND CLARK CROSSED THE PLAINS, THEY SAW MANY ANIMALS THAT WERE NEW TO THEM.
THEY DIDN'T SEE ANY MAMMOTHS. BECAUSE THEY WERE TOTALLY EXTINCT.
THEY DID DISCOVER A NEW RODENT, THOUGH--THE *PRAIRIE DOG*. THEY HAD A VERY HARD TIME CATCHING ONE. BUT AFTER FLOODING A PRAIRIE DOG CITY, THEY CAPTURED A LIVE PRAIRIE DOG.
CORPORAL RICHARD WARFINGTON WAS SENT BACK WITH THE PRAIRIE DOG, WHICH WAS PRESENTED TO THOMAS JEFFERSON.
JEFFERSON LOVED THE PRAIRIE DOG--BUT IT WAS NO WOOLLY MAMMOTH.
THAT'S IT, THAT'S THE STORY.
I LIKE IT. BUT I WISH IT WERE FUNNIER.
BRINGING IT TO LIFE AND MAKING IT FUNNIER IS *YOUR JOB*.
CARTOONIST, LET'S BEGIN.

FIRST, GIVE YOUR COMIC A TITLE. AND PUT YOUR NAME IN THE BOX TOO. THIS WILL BE A HISTORY COMIC BY YOU. THE OPENING SCENE IS MERIWETHER LEWIS MEETING WITH THOMAS JEFFERSON. THE PRESIDENT IS EXPLAINING ALL OF THE THINGS HE WANTS THE CORPS OF DISCOVERY TO DO. JEFFERSON MENTIONS WANTING A MAMMOTH.

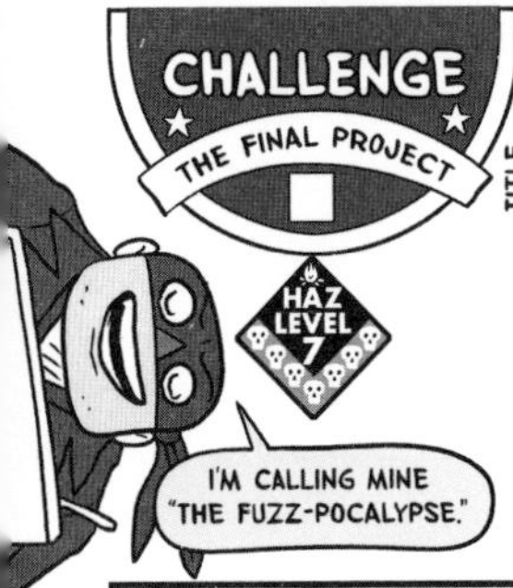
CHALLENGE
THE FINAL PROJECT
HAZ LEVEL 7
I'M CALLING MINE "THE FUZZ-POCALYPSE."

TITLE

LEWIS ASKS JEFFERSON WHY HE WANTS A MAMMOTH. JEFFERSON SHOWS HIM HIS COLLECTION OF MAMMOTH BONES. HAVE SOME FUN SHOWING JUST HOW EXCITED JEFFERSON IS ABOUT MAMMOTHS. WHAT DO YOU THINK THE PRESIDENT MIGHT DO WITH A MAMMOTH? DRAW JEFFERSON'S IMAGINATION OF THE FUN HE AND HIS PET MAMMOTH WOULD HAVE.

THE CORPS SETS OUT FROM ST. LOUIS. THEY HAVE A LARGE KEELBOAT (RESEARCH!) WE MEET WILLIAM CLARK AND YORK. THE CORPS OF DISCOVERY IS FIFTY MEN AND A DOG (SEAMAN.) THEY ARE TRAVELING UPSTREAM, AGAINST THE RIVER'S CURRENT. IT IS HARD WORK. MOSQUITOS BOTHER EVERYONE. CLARK BEGINS MAPPING. LEWIS WRITES IN HIS JOURNAL.

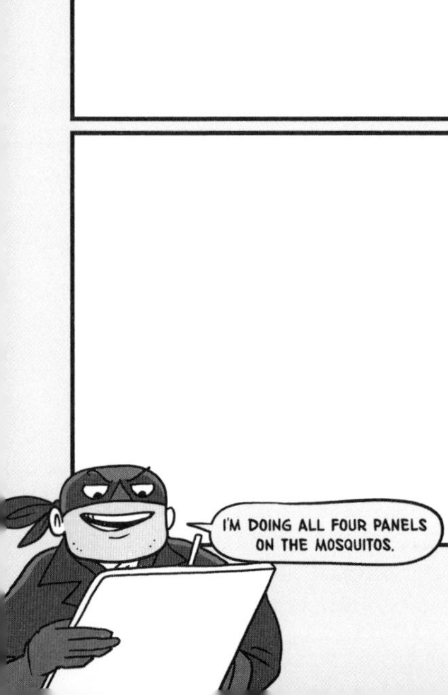
I'M DOING ALL FOUR PANELS ON THE MOSQUITOS.

ONE MORNING, THE CORPS SEES THE RIVER IS MYSTERIOUSLY WHITE. AS THEY GET CLOSER, THEY REALIZE THE ENTIRE RIVER IS COVERED IN FEATHERS. AHEAD IS AN ISLAND COVERED WITH MOLTING PELICANS. THEY HAVE JUST DISCOVERED A NEW SPECIES. LEWIS WRITES ABOUT THEM IN HIS JOURNAL. THEY SEE A COYOTE AND CALL IT A PRAIRIE WOLF. THE LAND IS OVERFLOWING WITH WILDLIFE. HOW DOES THE CORPS REACT? ARE THEY SCARED? EXCITED?

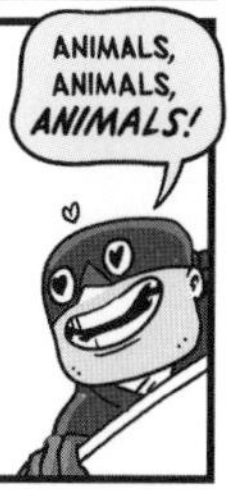
ANIMALS, ANIMALS, *ANIMALS!*

THE CORPS FINDS A PRAIRIE DOG VILLAGE—A FIELD COVERED WITH HILLS AND HOLES DUG BY PRAIRIE DOGS. THEY TRY TO CATCH ONE, BUT CAN'T DO IT. THEY CHASE THEM AND DIG SIX FEET DOWN FOR THEM, BUT THE PRAIRIE DOGS ESCAPE. FINALLY, THEY DECIDE TO FLOOD THE BURROW WITH FIVE BARRELS OF RIVER WATER. THIS FLUSHES OUT A PRAIRIE DOG, WHICH THEY CAPTURE AND PUT IN A CAGE. IT TOOK AN ENTIRE DAY TO CATCH ONE. A NEW ANIMAL HAS BEEN DISCOVERED.

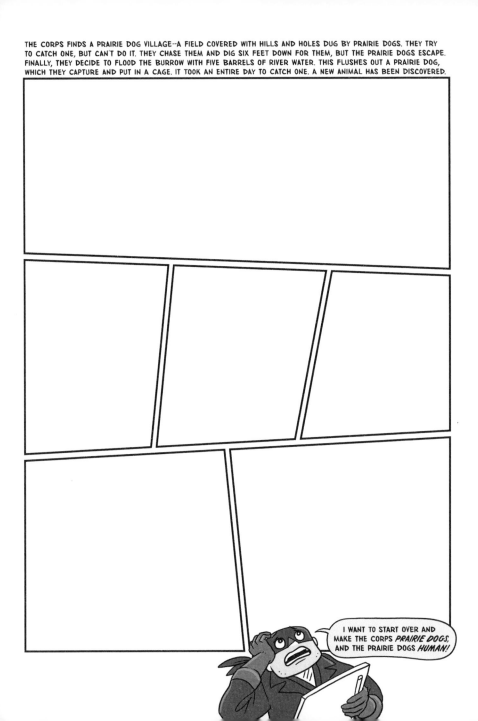

I WANT TO START OVER AND MAKE THE CORPS *PRAIRIE DOGS,* AND THE PRAIRIE DOGS *HUMAN!*

IT IS WINTER NOW. THE CORPS IS BUILDING A FORT. IT IS NAMED FORT MANDAN, AFTER THE NEARBY MANDAN VILLAGES. RESEARCH WHAT FORT MANDAN LOOKS LIKE. THE PRAIRIE DOG IS STILL WITH THEM. HOW DO THEY TREAT IT? IS IT A PET? SACAGAWEA ARRIVES AT THE FORT WITH HER HUSBAND, A FRENCH TRAPPER NAMED CHARBONNEAU. SHE IS PREGNANT. THEY JOIN THE CORPS AND MOVE INTO THE FORT.

IN FEBRUARY, SACAGAWEA GIVES BIRTH TO A BABY BOY. HE IS NAMED JEAN BAPTISTE CHARBONNEAU, BUT EVERYONE CALLS HIM POMP. DOES POMP MEET THE PRAIRIE DOG? ARE THEY FRIENDS? HOW DOES SEAMAN FEEL ABOUT POMP? SPRING COMES AND THE CORPS PLANS TO MOVE ON FROM FORT MANDAN. IT'S STILL A LONG JOURNEY TO THE PACIFIC.

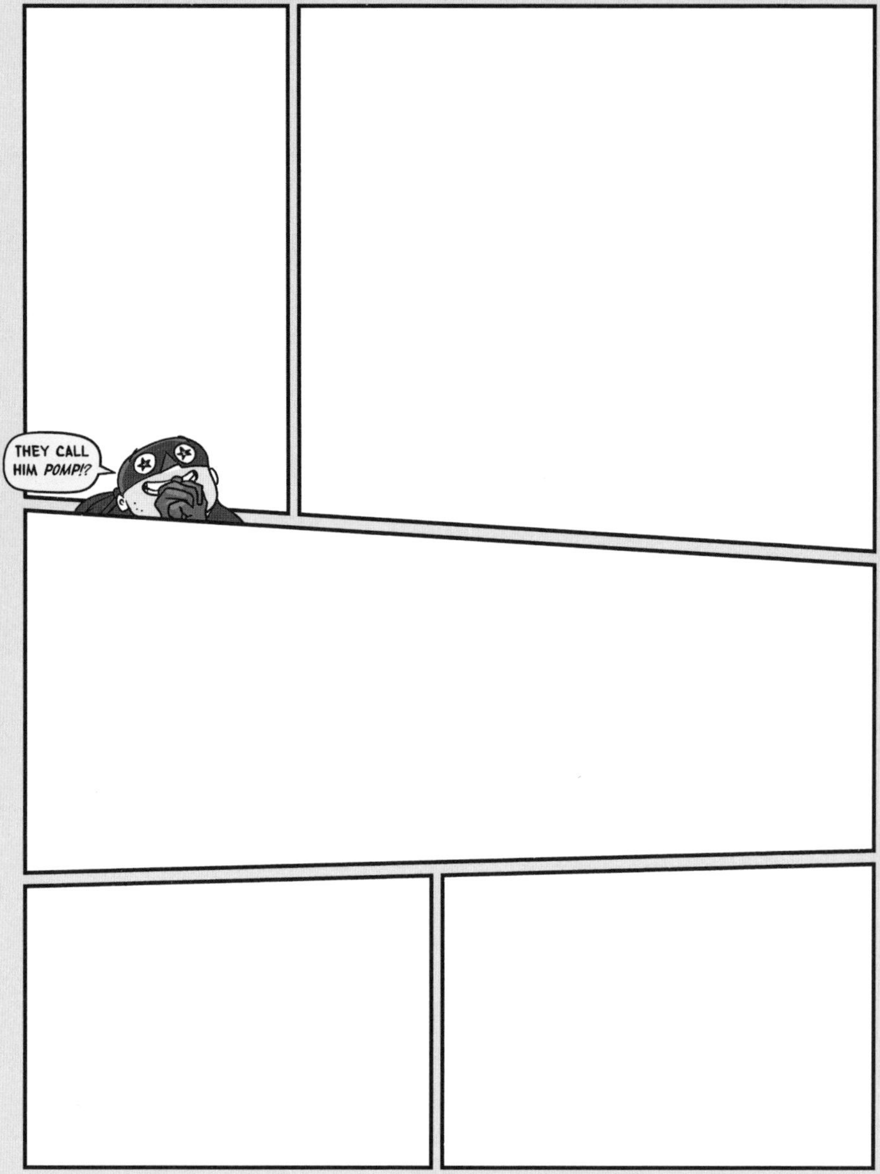
THEY CALL HIM *POMP!?*

THE KEELBOAT WILL NOT BE GOING ON. IT IS GOING TO BE SENT BACK DOWN THE MISSOURI RIVER. CORPORAL RICHARD WARFINGTON WILL TAKE IT BACK. IN THE BOAT, SEVERAL SPECIMEN'S—INCLUDING THE PRAIRIE DOG—ARE BEING SENT TO THOMAS JEFFERSON. DOES EVERYONE SAY GOODBYE TO IT? WARFINGTON WAVES TO THE CORPS AS THEY HEAD WEST.

THE KEELBOAT TRAVELS 1,600 MILES BACK TO ST. LOUIS. THE PRAIRIE DOG IS PUT ON A BIG BARGE TRAVELING DOWN THE MISSISSIPPI TO NEW ORLEANS. THE PRAIRIE DOG SEES THE CITY. FROM NEW ORLEANS, IT IS PUT ON A SAILING SHIP CALLED *THE COMET* WHICH SAILS ALL THE WAY UP TO BALTIMORE. THE PRAIRIE DOG HAS TRAVELED 4,000 MILES. RESEARCH THE ROUTE AND DRAW A MAP, IF YOU'D LIKE.

THOMAS JEFFERSON MEETS THE PRAIRIE DOG.
WHAT DOES HE THINK OF IT? WHAT DOES THE PRAIRIE
DOG THINK? HOW DO YOU END YOUR COMIC?

YOU'RE ABOUT TO COMPLETE
A TEN PAGE STORY!

THE END

CHALLENGE

BRAG ABOUT YOURSELF

HAZ LEVEL 3

WRITE YOUR *AUTHOR BIOGRAPHY.*

WHO ARE YOU? WHERE ARE YOU FROM? WHAT JOBS HAVE YOU HAD? HOW MANY PETS DO YOU HAVE?

WHAT MAKES YOU COOL?

WHAT OTHER BOOKS HAVE YOU DONE?

LIST YOUR FUTURE PROJECTS HERE.

GIVE YOURSELF FAKE REVIEWS FROM FAMOUS AUTHORS. (THIS IS CALLED A *"BLURB".*)

About the Author

DRAW YOUR SELF PORTRAIT HERE.

Tally Your Score
COMPLETED CHALLENGES:

1-20 — TENDERFOOT SCRIBBLER

21-40 — APPRENTICE GAGSTER

41-60 — DEXTEROUS DRAFTER

61-70 — HAZARDOUS CARTOONIST

71 — IMPOSSIBLE TO ACHIEVE FOR AT LEAST FIFTY YEARS

IF YOU COMPLETE "THE SCHULZ" YOU ARE AMERICA'S NEXT GREAT CARTOONIST.

THANKS FOR CARTOONING!

NOW GET OUT THERE AND CREATE SOME *COMICS!*